Praise for SKY GIRLS

"This is not just an excellent story of female pilots at the beginning of the twentieth century, but a stirring history of the early years of aviation."

—*Booklist*

"A fascinating history."

—*Publishers Weekly*

"Jessen's story of the 1929 Powder Puff Derby exposes so very convincingly the grit and determination of those remarkable women to gain their rightful foothold in yet another bastion of male domination."

—Scott Crossfield, legendary X-15 rocket test pilot

"A beautiful and inspiring book...fascinatingly told."

—Donna Shirley, former head of the U.S. Mars program, NASA

SKY GIRLS

Sky GIRLS

THE TRUE STORY OF THE FIRST
WOMEN'S CROSS-COUNTRY AIR RACE

GENE NORA JESSEN

sourcebooks

Published by Sourcebooks, Inc.
P.O. Box 4410, Naperville, Illinois 60567-4410
(630) 961-3900
Fax: (630) 961-2168
sourcebooks.com

Originally published as *The Powder Puff Derby of 1929* in 2002 by Sourcebooks, Inc.

Library of Congress Cataloging-in-Publication Data

Names: Jessen, Gene Nora, author.
Title: Sky girls : the true story of the first women's cross-country air race / Gene Nora Jessen.
Other titles: Powder Puff Derby of 1929
Description: Naperville, Illinois : Sourcebooks, [2018] | "Originally published as The Powder Puff Derby of 1929 in 2002 by Sourcebooks, Inc." | Includes bibliographical references and index.
Identifiers: LCCN 2017052013 | (pbk. : alk. paper)
Subjects: LCSH: Powder Puff Derby. | Women air pilots--United States--History.
Classification: LCC GV759.2.P74 J47 2018 | DDC 797.5--dc23 LC record available at https://lccn.loc.gov/2017052013

Printed and bound in the United States of America.
VP 10 9 8 7 6 5 4 3 2 1

For Page Shamburger,
who insisted that I tell this story.

DEDICATED TO

Florence L. Barnes	1901–1975
Marvel Crosson	1900–1929
Amelia Earhart	1897–1937
Ruth Elder	1903–1977
Claire Fahy	Unknown–1930
Edith Foltz	1905–1956
Mary Haizlip	1910–1997
Opal Kunz	1896–1967
Jessie Keith-Miller	1901–1972
Ruth Nichols	1901–1960
Blanche Noyes	1900–1981
Gladys O'Donnell	1904–1973
Phoebe Omlie	1903–1975
Neva Paris	Unknown–1930
Margaret Perry	Unknown–1951
Thea Rasche	1899–1971
Louise Thaden	1905–1979
Bobbi Trout	1906–2003
Mary Von Mach	1896–1980
Vera Walker	1897–1978

CONTENTS

"I, for one, hope for the day when women will know no restrictions because of sex but will be individuals free to live their lives as men are free. Women must try to do things as men have tried. When they fail, their failure must be but a challenge to others."

—AMELIA EARHART

FOREWORD

by Eileen Collins

Amelia Earhart, Louise Thaden, Bobbi Trout, and many more: These women are my heroes! They had three things in common: a connection to aviation, a fearless spirit, and a thirst for adventure. I am not sure they understood how their apparently glamorous lives would inspire so many other people, both men and women, to pursue the adventure of flight. In fact, they inspired me to learn to fly.

My connection to aviation began when I was about eight years old, in Elmira, New York. I attended summer camp at Harris Hill, the location of today's National Soaring Museum. During camp activities, I watched tow planes carry gliders to a high altitude and release them, allowing the gliders to turn and "dance" through the warm afternoon thermals. Flying lessons were out of the question for me, as my family skimped by on a tight budget. Fortunately, my Irish American parents had a sense of adventure. My dad would take us to the local airport, where we would sit on the hood of our car and watch the occasional aircraft take off. My mother would take me and my three siblings to the local library, where I discovered books on flying. In these simple ways, I connected to a desire to fly. And as I read more about aircraft and the daring pilots who flew them, I wanted not only to fly, but to go farther, faster, and higher than anyone ever had before!

I met Gene Nora Jessen in 1994 in Oklahoma City at the first reunion of the Mercury 13 women. I was fascinated to learn their story. In the early 1960s, many outstanding young women pilots were asked to participate in the Mercury Astronaut medical testing, and thirteen of them did so well they were called back for further testing. Gene Nora was one of these women. Although NASA never gave them an opportunity to fly in space, they all contributed greatly to the spaceflight program. NASA knew that women would have the physical endurance and aptitude to perform as astronauts due to the performance of the Mercury 13 and formally invited them to apply as astronauts at the beginning of the Space Shuttle program. Later, when I was selected as the first woman Space Shuttle pilot in 1990, it was due partly to the work the Mercury 13 completed three decades earlier. I am thankful for their participation, patience, and sacrifice, as I stand on their shoulders.

As I learned about the Powder Puff Derby of 1929, I thought about my own family and what they would have been doing in that time. My grandmother and grandfather were thirty-five years old. They had a toddler at home—my dad, who was only three years old. They lived a simple life—no washing machine, no television, meat was stored in salt vats in the cellar—and ran an Irish pub in a small town in upstate New York. The world was so different in 1929, but it was still less than one hundred years ago. My mother was only two years old, the daughter of an Irishman who worked on the railroads. I am sure they read about the air races in the newspaper. Nineteen women had the guts to enter into a new world of competitive air races, while also facing the dangers of aircraft emergencies, hazardous weather, and potential disapproval from family and friends. Oh, how I wonder what my grandparents were thinking!

Likewise, what would those pilots of 1929 think about our world today? I am sure they would be pleased by the advancement in commercial aviation, the "comfortable" seats, the warm air, the low noise, and the ease of travel that we routinely complain about. And what would they think of the space program? Although today's space programs are still in their early years, there are similarities to the aviation programs of the 1920s. In fact, many of them were alive to see Neil Armstrong walk on the moon only forty years later. However, an interesting difference is the amount of risk pilots were willing to assume in the 1920s versus almost a century later.

Early aviation progressed so very quickly compared to today's spacecraft mainly because of the overall freedom in the system. Because of the low number of regulations in the 1920s, aircraft designers had the freedom to experiment, and pilots had the freedom to expand the envelope of the aircraft. The price of this freedom was the high accident rate and high death rate, but it allowed aviation to rapidly advance from the Wright Brothers' first flight to the first operational jet aircraft of the 1940s and 1950s. These early, seemingly fearless pilots were willing to test the corners of the envelope, so to speak, while refusing to be slowed down by rules and regulations. After the Challenger and Columbia space shuttle accidents, space flight was determined to be so risky that it took almost two and a half years to get the next shuttle off the launch pad. Many pilots lost their lives over the years in aviation accidents, so was this the right price to pay for more rapid advancement in aviation? That appeared to be so in my grandmother's world, and had we used a conservative risk management strategy in the 1920s, we most certainly would have slowed down the progress of aviation.

Of course, the women racers had much more than just a simple connection to aviation and a sense of fearlessness: a passion for flight! They had an attraction to the sky. Was it the clouds? Was it the sunsets? Was it the desire to look down at the tiny dots of people going about their everyday business? Or did they desire fame and fortune, power or competition? Most certainly, they loved the sense of freedom. Perhaps some of them loved the exactness of hitting flight parameters and navigation milestones. Maybe it was a desire to travel to faraway place, the thrill of loading up the turns and pulling g's. Maybe it was a desire for solitude, up and away from the stresses of life. Or maybe it was all of these.

These pilots of the 1929 Powder Puff Derby were living in a very different time—the Wild West of aviation! But I grew up in a much more conventional era. Today, we would never accept the mechanical malfunctions, the physical discomfort, and certainly not the death rate. I am fascinated not only by their bravery in the face of physical danger and their willingness to operate in such a cramped, cold, noisy environment, but also by the fact that these women chose to do this although it was perceived as a male-only activity and profession.

I can't help but wonder what it would have been like to work and fly with these amazing pilots. I realize how difficult it must have been for those women to enter an unconventional field. And I can only imagine the bravery it took to learn to fly in the first place! I remember how much courage it took for me, at twenty years old, to go to my local airport and ask them to teach me to fly. I was afraid they would tell me no simply because I was a girl. I ruminated about this for many, many months, until my calling got the best of me, and I made the trip to the local fixed-base operator. I immediately discovered the friendliness and professionalism of the local pilots, and they were thrilled to have another student in their school.

Without a doubt, the Powder Puff Derby pilots truly loved what they did. They are an inspiration, not only to those in aviation careers, but to all of us, men and women alike. The pilots that followed them built on their experiences and lessons learned. During World War II, the Women Airforce Service Pilots (WASP) ferried and flight-tested aircraft here in the United States, so men could fly combat missions overseas. Women were allowed to train as naval pilots for the first time in 1974, and air force women were allowed to train in 1976. I was thrilled when I was selected for air force pilot training in 1978, but I could not fly my dream aircraft, as women were prohibited from combat aircraft until the restriction was lifted in 1993.

I see these generations of women pilots as a unified team. Each of these incredible women built upon the work that was successfully completed prior. They are my role models. As an astronaut, flight instructor, and mother, I know that role models provide an important impetus as we try to develop wisdom, courage, and strength: wisdom to make the right decisions, courage to take the first steps, and strength to carry it through. I hope many people, young and old, men and women, pilots or not, learn this story. They will most certainly draw inspiration from a generation of women who had aviation in their heart, who were fearless adventure-seekers with a competitive spirit, and a passion for flight.

—*Eileen Collins, first female space shuttle commander*

INTRODUCTION
BEGINNINGS

aturally, participants in the first Women's Air Derby of 1929 were not the first pioneering aviators of the fairer sex. They rode on the wings of predecessors who had braved even less reliable aircraft.

In 1784, before America had even elected its first president, Madame Thible ascended as a balloon passenger in Lyons, France. A century later, in 1880, American aeronautical engineer and inventor Carl E. Myers called upon his wife, Mary, to be his test pilot, choosing the more exotic Carlotta as her stage name. She probably made more than five hundred balloon ascents testing her husband's theories, and she became quite an experienced aeronaut in her own right.

By 1909, the vivacious French Baroness Raymonde de Laroche had driven racing cars and made flights in balloons. She didn't hesitate to fly a Voisin biplane a short six years after the Wright brothers initially flew. She learned to manipulate the unstable and unpredictable machine and became the first woman licensed to fly by the Fédération Aéronautique Internationale. To questions about engine failures and even structural collapse, she spoke of fate and fear.

"Most of us spread the perils of a lifetime over a number of years," the daring de Laroche said. "Others may pack them into a matter of only a few hours. In any case, whatever is to happen will happen—it may well be that I shall tempt Fate once too often. Who knows? But it is to the air that I have dedicated myself, and I fly always without the slightest fear."

Fate did catch up with the intrepid French baroness, as it overtook so many early fliers. She was killed in an airplane crash in 1919 at the age of twenty-three.

In 1909, across the Channel, Lilian Bland of Belfast, Ireland, was a successful writer and press photographer for London newspapers. Bland constructed a model biplane that she flew as a kite, then, encouraged with that success, she built a full-size glider of spruce. She designed wings like those of seagulls, and she coated the fabric surfaces with a photographic solution to make them waterproof.

Ready to fly her glider under power, Bland ordered a two-cylinder engine that developed twenty horsepower at one thousand revolutions per minute. Starting it up, the plane's wooden propeller spun off, miraculously missing nearby spectators. Her next try resulted in vibrations that snapped most of the wires between the struts. Soon, the repaired airplane flew thirty feet, hopping short distances like a rabbit, a rocky type of flight that was all too typical of aeronautical advancements of the day.

Hélène Dutrieu was already famous as a trick bicyclist when she took up flying in 1910, becoming Belgium's first licensed female pilot. She gained fame by flying the inconceivable nonstop distance of twenty-eight miles. People gathered in the streets and church bells pealed as she climbed to the extreme height of thirteen hundred feet. Dutrieu's feats brought her France's coveted Legion of Honor award in 1913.

The first solo female pilot could have been **Aida de Acosta**, a young Cuban American visiting Paris with her mother in 1903. Intrigued with Brazilian inventor Alberto Santos-Dumont's dirigibles, the young girl was soon taking flight instruction. After three lessons, de Acosta flew the dirigible alone for two hours, and said, "I stopped the petrol motor and came down like a feather. I've never had so much fun in my life." That was five months before the Wright brothers' flight, which made de Acosta the first woman of powered flight.

The event was nearly lost to history, because de Acosta's angry father extracted a promise from Santos-Dumont to never mention Aida de Acosta by name in recounting her flight. Señor de Acosta reminded his wife and daughter that "a proper woman should only be mentioned in the newspaper twice—to announce her marriage and her death."

There are many shades of "first." Who was America's first female pilot? Resourceful **Bessica Raiche** built her own airplane in her drawing room, then she flew it on September 16, 1910. The intrepid lady, who later became a physician, exemplified the unquenchable enthusiasm of the early dreamers. Her entire instruction had been how to move the wheel to make the airplane go up and down. Since there was no throttle control, volunteers held on to the wings while the engine engaged. When the restraints were released, the air machine flew.

Blanche Stuart Scott, an unabashed tomboy, reveled in firsts. She became a trick bicycle rider, then drove an automobile across the United States—a sixty-nine-day journey at a time when there were only 216 miles of paved road in the entire country. She became a member of the famous Glenn Curtiss exhibition team, and Curtiss himself declared her America's first aviatrix on September 6, 1910, though she never did obtain a pilot's license.

Petite **Harriet Quimby**, called the "Dresden Doll," became America's first licensed woman pilot at the Moisant School in 1911, the year before her death at age twenty-eight. Quimby traveled to France to fly a Bleriot monoplane across the English Channel. She sat outside in the open, before there was such a thing as a cockpit, enveloped by mist and chilling cold. Only three months later, she died in the unstable Bleriot over Boston Harbor. Fellow student **Mathilde Moisant**, after a grand total of thirty-two minutes of flight instruction, became licensed pilot number two, and she soon established an altitude record of fifteen hundred feet.

Ruth Law and **Katherine Stinson** both learned to fly in 1912, Law touring with her own Ruth Law Flying Circus, the first woman to perform a loop. Law became famous for her death-defying wing-walking stunts. Stinson, along with her mother, formed the Stinson Aviation Company in Chicago, Illinois, to manufacture and sell airplanes. In 1913, she was purported to be the first woman to carry the mail. Both Law and Stinson petitioned the government to allow them to fly for their country during World War I, but they were denied.

The flying circuses (or air shows) faded at about the time of the

1929 air derby, as the government put restrictions on the barnstorm-ers' wild antics. The barnstormers were airborne gypsies, prone to buzzing a town to lure the populace out to a nearby farmer's field. They'd show off a few loops and spins, then sell rides. **Jessie and Jimmie Woods** produced one of the last and most successful opera-tions with their Flying Aces Air Circus, with Jessie riding the top of the upper wing throughout a variety of aerobatic maneuvers. After having been retired from aviation for some sixty years, Jessie stood on the upper wing of a modern open-cockpit airplane to fly at an air show in 1991 at the age of eighty-two.

Against staggering odds, **Bessie Coleman** gained renown in aviation. One of thirteen children, Coleman had picked cotton to earn money for school. Inevitably, as an African American and as a woman, she found the door locked at flying schools. Undaunted, in 1920 Coleman studied French and sailed for Paris where prejudice didn't bar her from learning to fly. She returned to the States in 1921 as the world's first licensed black pilot. "Brave Bessie," as she became known, became a popular attraction on the air-show circuit.

Prior to a 1926 air show, Bessie rode as a passenger without fastening her parachute so she could rise up high enough in her seat to take a look at the terrain for a planned parachute jump the next day. A loose wrench jammed the controls throwing the airplane into a spin and Bessie out to her death.

There were many such tragedies. The early years exacted a horren-dous toll on aviation's pioneers. During 1910 alone, thirty-seven professional flyers were killed performing at air exhibitions. Today, we can hardly comprehend the rudimentary nature of machines they called airplanes and the often-flimsy construction that too often sent people to their deaths.

Among the courageous firsts, each aviator could conceivably be called foolhardy, and certainly all were daredevils. Their bravery, however ill-advised, became our bounty. And because they breached the unknown, safer machines evolved as more eager aviators followed. The air knew no boundaries nor gender distinctions. If men could achieve benchmarks and set records, so too could women. And that, in 1929, became irrefutable.

SKY GIRLS

Flight is abiding peace.

Absolute serenity.

It is faith and compassion.

Purest joy.

It is a spirit totally free.

Flight is yesterday's yearning.

The fulfillment of today's dreams.

Tomorrow's promises.

—LOUISE THADEN

DECEMBER 7, 1928
OAKLAND, CALIFORNIA

Ψhe tall, slender pilot outfitted in a fur-lined flying suit looked a little incongruous on the warm January afternoon at Oakland International Airport. Louise Thaden's bright blue eyes betrayed a modicum of apprehension as she looked over her brand-new open-cockpit biwing Travel Air 3000 carefully before flight. Her test flights in preceding days had not been encouraging. She'd suffered three engine failures, calling for dead stick (or powerless) landings. Successful ones, fortunately, but that experience didn't build confidence in her engine, a high-compression 180 horsepower Hispano-Suiza. The villain the first two times was a clogged fuel vent, the third time, shavings in the fuel tank stopped the flow of gasoline to the engine.

Thaden was attempting to break the women's altitude record, and the airplane had been modified, stripped of any unnecessary equipment whose weight would inhibit a maximum climb. Thaden would be reaching an altitude with insufficient oxygen for the pilot to remain functional. She had found a small oxygen cylinder at a local machine shop, then got an ether mask from a hospital. A rubber hose and a pair of pliers to turn the control valves on the tank completed her oxygen equipment for high-altitude flight. She inquired how to use oxygen, and she was told by an intern at the hospital that if she used too much she'd pass out, and if she didn't use enough she'd pass out. So much for high-altitude orientation.

Climbing through fifteen thousand feet on the historic flight, Thaden donned her makeshift oxygen mask and opened the valve of her tank a fraction of an inch with the pliers. She climbed for an hour, carefully hoarding airspeed, and at twenty thousand feet, she gave the control valve another quarter turn. Her ether mask was collecting moisture which dripped down her chin, and her breathing made a strange bubbling sound. Still mushing upward, she last remembered seeing one altimeter read twenty-seven thousand feet above sea level, and the other twenty-nine thousand. The temperature was twenty-four below.

Too soon, her oxygen tank was empty. With her ears ringing and her brain oxygen-deprived, Thaden's consciousness had faded, and certainly her judgment was impaired. The airplane spiraled down of its own accord. As the fog slowly lifted from Thaden's brain at around sixteen thousand feet, she thankfully pulled off her frozen mask to breathe real air again. Thaden took back control of the pilotless aircraft and landed safely, to the relief and pride of her factory support team. After calibration, the official barograph reading showed a disappointing 20,260 feet above the earth. Nevertheless, it was higher than any woman had ever flown.

No one would pick quiet and thoughtful Louise Thaden out of a crowd for an aviator. She wasn't the flamboyant type like colorful

Roscoe Turner, complete with waxed mustache, snappy uniform, and jodhpurs, who flew with his live lion, Gilmore. Nor was she like Wiley Post, who exuded glamour and mystery behind a black eye patch, proclaiming his macho roustabout credentials from the Oklahoma oil fields. Gentle Louise sported none of the outlandish, attention-grabbing glitz of many aviators of the day. She was just a pretty, unassuming young woman who simply adored flying airplanes. She had enough competitive spirit to go after flying records, but she did so without undue flash.

Only a couple years before, young Thaden's introduction to flying came serendipitously. She landed a job in Wichita, Kansas, selling coal for the J. H. Turner Coal Company. That her boss, Mr. Turner, also happened to be a large stockholder in and director of Walter Beech's Travel Air Company tantalized her. Thaden revived her long-secret yearning to fly, while simultaneously learning a thing or two about the airplane business.

The day she heard that the Travel Air cabin monoplane was set for its first flight, the coal salesgirl was compelled to sneak off to watch. Though she was embarrassed to run into her boss there, he appreci-ated her fascination with the airplanes and promised to speak to the boss, Walter Beech, on her behalf. The two men arranged a sales job with their Pacific Coast distributor for Thaden. It was a life-changing opportunity; she would get to learn to fly…and in the same way other pilots of the epoch did—by defying the odds.

Engine failures, lost bearings, cross-country fatigue, and heart-stopping aerobatics—it all added up to experience. Though the pilots could trade their whoppers, share exaggerated flying tales called "hangar flying," and boast their macho understated responses to real danger, Thaden succinctly summarized the largely self-schooled process of learning to fly: "A pilot who says he has never been frightened in an airplane is, I'm afraid, lying."

After five hours and fifteen minutes in the air, in February 1928, Thaden earned Fédération Aéronautique Internationale Private Pilot Certificate #6850, signed by Orville Wright. Her twenty-minute check-ride by E. E. Mouton was flown in a Travel Air with an OX-5 engine. Though flown in February, by the time the paperwork was completed, Thaden's pilot certificate read May 16. No matter. When the eager pilot's log book totaled two hundred hours in the air, she was eligible for a transport pilot's license. At the time, she was told there were only three transport pilots who had come before her. She passed the lengthy written exam and prepared for a flight test. The flight examiner, like so many others, intensified the ordeal so he wouldn't be accused of going easy on "the girls." In April 1929, twenty-three-year-old Louise Thaden became a certificated transport pilot.

In the meantime, Herb Thaden, her reserved young engineer beau, had proposed marriage. They eloped to Reno, Nevada. Instead of a honeymoon, Louise hurried east with a stop in Wichita, Kansas, to persuade Walter Beech to build her a racing airplane for the first women's transcontinental air race.

In 1929, for the very first time, the National Exchange Club, a men's service club, had elected to sponsor an all-women's air derby from Santa Monica, California, to Cleveland, Ohio, a distance of about twenty-seven hundred miles, as their national publicity project

for the year. Air race promoter Cliff Henderson organized the first
Women's Air Derby, patterning it after the men's transcontinental air
races. Elizabeth L. McQueen, founder of the Women's International
Association of Aeronautics, recruited the contestants from across the
nation, and, indeed, word even spread to Europe. Never a pilot herself,
McQueen always supported any women pilots' activities. The small
group of women licensed to fly airplanes in 1929 received the plan
with huge excitement. It was a toss-up whether the Exchange Club or
the women pilots were more determined to make a good showing. It
was a momentous occasion—for women and for aeronautics.

Race officials anticipated enormous crowds at the Cleveland
Air Races, the derby's finish line. People would come from all over
the country, and some even from abroad, expecting state-of-the-art
entertainment—roaring airplanes racing around pylons, a breathtaking air show, military demonstrations, and the chance to look over the
newest airplane models. And in 1929, for the first time, women would
be racing airplanes from the far western edge of the country, adding
to the excitement in Ohio where the cross-country race would end.

Just before the festivities commenced in Cleveland, transcontinental air races would start from both ends of the country—the
women from the west and two men's races from west and east, culmi-
nating in front of Cleveland's huge throngs. Timers organized to
clock each racer in and out of the designated stops. Though there
would be great glory for arriving at the finish line first, the shortest
total elapsed time would win. At stake was $8,000 in prize monies,
plus generous prizes for each leg of the trip.

The women competitors certainly wanted the prize money, but

they were ecstatic simply to be competing. Most were able to find aircraft company sponsorships to help shoulder expenses. Either Thaden was a super salesgirl or Walter Beech knew a champion pilot when he saw one. Soon after her own request, five new Travel Airs were coming down the production line for women racers, one with the name "Thaden" on it. All were built specifically for the Derby with speed wings (a thinner cross section) and Wright engines, though some older Travel Airs already out in the field were entered also. Thaden's airplane came off the assembly line last, she supposed because she wasn't buying hers. The factory would be her sponsor. The Travel Air was the racing airplane of choice, mostly because Walter Beech himself was committed to racing activities at the terminus in Cleveland, and he thought interest generated by the ladies' racing would sell airplanes.

Walter Beech and Louise Thaden

Though Beech would one day manufacture airplanes flown world-wide under his own name, the Travel Air Manufacturing Company, located on the east side of Wichita, Kansas, was already making a name for strong, fast, and reliable airplanes. It had been building and selling an astonishing one airplane per day the previous year. Travel Air's location was, in part, responsible for Wichita's legitimate claim to its immodest title, "Aviation Capital of the World," though the town's location in the middle of tornado alley, with its springtime thunderstorms and hail, did not engender a sense of comfort.

Travel Air had a close affiliation with the Curtiss-Wright Corporation through the Wright interests, and it kept a winning record due to constant modifications to its products. In fact, the rumor was out that the Travel Air factory had a new "mystery ship," which Beech would introduce in Cleveland. Thaden would have given her right arm to fly this as-yet-unseen aircraft in the women's race. The Mystery Ship Model R was radically new—low wing with lots of power and rumored to be up to a hundred miles per hour faster than the earlier design. One wag remarked that "it was so fast it takes three men lined up to see it!" Walter Beech had covered the windows in the area of the factory where the Model R was being developed, whether on purpose or by happenstance, creating great interest in and conversation about the mystery airplane. As a result, the Model R was forever known as the Mystery Ship because of its mysterious birth.

The Travel Airs flown by the women were a well-proven and popular current design: biwing (one wing above the other), open cockpit, and a choice of engines of varying horsepowers. It was not a small airplane, though derby participant Marvel Crosson's racing model was more diminutive, and it took either a running leap, a small stepladder, or an agile pilot to climb up into the high cockpit. As office space, the Travel Air cockpit left a lot to be desired. It was noisy, dirty, too cold or hot, and not comfortable. On the other hand, it was the magic carpet right out of *One Thousand and One Nights*. The airplane provided a view of the earth—the neat farms and geometric row crops; herds of exquisite wild horses running in total freedom; deep, dark canyons swallowing meandering rivers looking for the ocean; and miniature people burdened with their daily lives and troubles.

Thaden's arrival at the factory invariably lent a happy tone to the place. The combination of her modest air and taking the time to speak to each of the workmen who put together her airplane made them want to make a special effort for the girl with the slight southern cadence. Dark curls slipping out of her cloth flying helmet framed a rather square face, which was dominated by her light blue luminous eyes. A subtle sense of humor complemented her barely contained wonder that God had seen fit to give her the gift of flight. Her unusually calm demeanor distinguished her among the sometimes-volatile women who chose to fly airplanes in 1929. The guys on the assembly line approved of the boss's unexpected decision to follow Thaden as far as Fort Worth, Texas, to make sure everything was working perfectly on his "baby," the Travel Air. As it turned out, this decision made all the difference for Thaden and for the race.

Thaden had said goodbye to her parents and her sister Alice, who came over from Arkansas on a hot mid-August day in 1929 to see her off from the Travel Air factory in Wichita. Thaden prepared to trail the others already on the way to the race start in Santa Monica. She still had sufficient time to get there. However, she didn't want to dillydally. The two airplanes landed in Tulsa, Oklahoma, for fuel en route to Fort Worth, navigating in reverse the course she'd be flying in just a few days. Walter Beech's enthusiasm was high, and as they prepared to depart southbound, the great aviation legend saluted Thaden, "Good luck, fella." Then, looking at her with concern, he added, "Do you feel all right?"

On that late summer day, Walter Beech's warmth was an unbiased acknowledgement of a fellow aviator. And her faint reply, "Sure, swell," spoke volumes about the persistence and enthusiasm that led Louise Thaden and nineteen other daring women to broach a new aviation frontier for women and for pilots.

When Thaden had said she felt "swell" to Beech in Tulsa, it was a lie. Thaden felt awful. She was dizzy and nauseated. *Must be the heat and excitement of the race*, she reflected. She had thought a cold drink would settle her down as the airplane was being refueled during the quick Oklahoma stop, but it had not. *Oh, for some cool rain*, she hoped. She was distracted, and she laughed just thinking about it. Student pilots learning about weather never seemed to forget Thaden's explanation of rain: "Fill a heavy paper bag half full of water, hold it suspended, and watch while the bottom slowly sags, gradually giving way until finally a hole appears and water flows in a steady stream, and you will have seen a rain storm as it looks from the air."

Pulling herself up into the high cockpit, leg over the edge, then dropping down on the low seat, Thaden departed Tulsa, as did Beech, in their separate airplanes. Beech pulled ahead in an enclosed cabin

Model 6000 as Thaden throttled back to a cruise setting, breaking in her new engine. She leaned her head out of the open cockpit into the slipstream, hoping to feel better by finding some fresh air and clearing her head. But the only air rushing by was scorching hot and not refreshing at all.

In March, just a few months before the derby, a "Hisso" Travel Air (Hisso engine), which incorporated the newly designed speed wing airfoil, had been trucked to Oakland, California, for an endurance trial. A letter was attached to the wing that read, "We believe the wings to be sufficiently strong, but since they are a new development, we do not want you to take any unnecessary risks or chances." It was signed by Walter Beech. Sure, Thaden had thought, nothing "unnecessary." "Okay, I'll be a test pilot," she decided. Thaden knew that flying airplanes carried some risk, but she was a cautious risk taker. The risk had to be worth taking, with positive odds for success.

First, Thaden set an endurance record of more than twenty-two hours aloft in the Travel Air. She described the challenge of staying awake as "torture." Then in April, diving for speed across the course, she had drawn on all the speed the airplane had, and set the new 156-miles-per-hour record. (Speeds were usually noted in statute miles per hour rather than nautical miles per hour, simply so the airplane would seem faster in advertising. Since a knot, or nautical mile, equals 1.15 statute miles, Thaden's record of 156 miles per hour was really only 136 nautical miles.) No one woman had ever held three flight records simultaneously. That made Louise Thaden the pilot of the hour. This quiet, unassuming, and talented pilot was deeply embarrassed to read about herself in the press: "Louise

Thaden with her classic features and slim, light-footed figure might be a sister to Icarus, god of flight."

Repeatedly, Thaden leaned her head out the side of the open cockpit into the slipstream. Her cloth flying helmet kept her hair contained from the wind, but sweat dripped onto her once-starched shirt collar. She wore goggles to protect her eyes, and her face had a farmer's suntan. Instead of a white forehead though, Thaden, like other racers, sported owl eyes—white circles around her protected eyes, with sun- and wind-burned cheeks and forehead. Later, when they were on display at social events en route, the racers' tanned V-necks presented a startling contrast in their party dresses.

Thaden and Beech departed Kansas to the south, having opted for the lower route to California. Kansas and Oklahoma were then, as they are now, laid out in one-mile section lines, county roads and farmers' fence lines defining the points of the compass. In fact, a pilot could cut across the section lines at a consistent angle, hardly needing a wet (swimming in alcohol) compass. Once across the Red River into Texas, the section lines curved and disappeared as if the designer had run out of paint. The swaying wheat and tall grasses, along with laundry hanging out on the lines and little whitecaps on farm ponds served as a wind indicator for direction and velocity.

Thaden could then turn west after Fort Worth, taking the southern route to the coast. Seventy-five hundred feet in altitude would just about clear every terrestrial obstacle. It was certainly lower than crossing mountainous Colorado. This would also give her a chance to experience some of the airports they'd be landing on in the actual race. They could not fly after sunset, for there were no lights with which to read the instruments. Thaden and Beech would run out of daylight at Fort Worth, a good place for their remaining overnight (RON) stop.

Thaden flew with her head down below the rim of the open cockpit, pulling up periodically to check her position against her road map. "Dead reckoning" it was called, kind of an unfortunate term. She called on all the grit and experience she could muster to overcome her strange lightheadedness. But good judgment was slipping away as if it were used-up fuel, irretrievable.

Louise resorted to murmuring aloud, "One hundred-eighty degrees, 180 degrees, hold a heading of 180 degrees." Holding a heading turned into a difficult chore. Maintaining altitude was worse. She commanded her eyes to stay open, against their willful desire to close. A piercing headache hammered, while the roar of the engine grew faint in her ears. Thaden cherished the freedom and beauty of flight. She couldn't remember ever wishing a flight to hasten to its conclusion, but that was her desperate wish this day.

The terrain and the map didn't jibe as she tried to concentrate on matching the roads and towns she saw below to the highway map clutched in her left hand. Fort Worth simply had to be near. Her thoughts ran hot and cold, from "I'm just about on it" to "I must be hopelessly lost." She knew she had passed the Oklahoma Arbuckle Mountains. She'd seen the place out the right side where a "giant foot" had stomped the earth millions of years ago, causing layers of subsurface rock to rise at a forty-five-degree angle. Thaden always got a chuckle that the flatlanders called those little bumps mountains. But the Arbuckles meant she was on course. The higher

Ouachita Mountains were off to the left, and they led to home, Arkansas.

Pilots consistently swore they were never lost, simply "momentarily disoriented." Thaden knew not to wander looking for an identifiable landmark. Holding the course would bring her within a reasonable proximity to her destination. Well, it always had, she thought. But she'd never been so befuddled, and crossing the Red River to the south had taken away her backup compass, the section lines. She had only limited time to find herself, for fuel was the defining factor for distance. There were plenty of good farmers' fields if she ran it dry, but Beech was waiting for her in Fort Worth.

Louise Thaden with her plane.

Miraculously, the suffering pilot soon spotted the Fort Worth airport twenty degrees off the nose. Suddenly, it didn't matter what

direction the wind was or how many airplanes were in the traffic
pattern. Louise Thaden desperately seized the conviction that she
was going to get this brand-new airplane on the ground in one piece.
The well-known "pilot's ego" snapped into place. No matter how sick,
Thaden knew she could land the airplane. She headed straight in to
the airport with no thought of the good manners of complying with
traffic. She simply aimed the nose downward for a powered descent.

Walter Beech had been worriedly scanning for Thaden when
someone yelled, "There she is, against traffic." Walter immediately
rejected what he was seeing. Louise Thaden was too good a pilot to
ignore traffic pattern rules. Another airplane on track to meet her
head-on swerved out of her way. Her approach was sloppy. She was
much too fast. "FLARE, FLARE!" Beech yelled, as if she could hear
him. Something was very wrong.

Once a safe height above the ground, she pulled the power and
bounced the plane on in. As the airplane hopped down the field,
witnesses presumed they were watching the antics of an inexperienced student pilot who would probably lose directional control
next and make a sharp turn into a ground loop. The pilot didn't seem
to be doing anything to salvage the shabby landing.

Not pretty, but both Thaden and the airplane were through flying.
She finally seemed to wake up and pull the stick back, killing off the
remaining flying speed, making the bucking bronco settle. She didn't
even clear the landing area, but shut the engine down while finally
fanning the rudder pedals to forestall a ground loop as the airplane
slowed. Too dazed to fathom how or where to taxi the plane and
park, Thaden immediately climbed out of the cockpit and folded

over the side. Standing up was too difficult. Her legs wouldn't work any better than her head. A curtain of darkness closed in as the Travel Air's lower wing broke her fall.

Walter Beech and others made a dash for the blue and gold Travel Air and Thaden, who was collapsed on the ground. She came around pretty quickly, but her sponsor was badly scared.

"I shouldn't have let you leave Tulsa," Beech berated himself. "I thought you didn't look good."

"I don't feel very well," Louise responded.

The men pulled the airplane over to a corner of the field, but found nothing wrong with the engine or the controls. Thaden's physical condition, a strong headache and near unconsciousness, made it obvious that she had succumbed to carbon monoxide poisoning. Despite the open-cockpit airplane and her tall stature, Thaden was getting exhaust fumes from the engine while sitting down low behind the Wright J5 engine.

Walter Beech hastened to jerry-rig a solution so Thaden could continue and race. He ran a four-inch pipe back from the leading edge of the cowling into the cockpit for a source of fresh air. Louise judged the solution as satisfactory.

The racer's predawn arrival at her airplane the next morning found Thaden in an optimistic state of mind. Her first-day troubles were simply break-in glitches, and she was confident of the coming day's promising flight. As the morning sun first hinted of its approach in the eastern sky, Louise said goodbye to Walter Beech and was airborne, actually singing in her happiness, despite what was sure to be a long, hot day ahead.

Thaden was flying the reverse of the race route, taking a look at the airports, the terrain, the checkpoints, the challenges ahead. West Texas was huge country—no wonder those Texans bragged on it. The early morning shadows turned the barren ground into rainbows of brilliant reds and yellows. Whenever she stopped for fuel, the people fell all over themselves being kind and helpful. They let her know they were rooting for her, even those who had no idea who she was, and they would watch for her going back the other direction.

Finally, after exiting Texas, Thaden flew the U.S.–Mexican border, crossing the very bottom of New Mexico. The day heated up, and the puffy white marshmallow clouds dug potholes in the airway. Summertime wind jolts rocked the airplane, but they were not unexpected. The oasis of Phoenix, Arizona, meant green trees, brilliant flowers, and prompt, professional service for the airplane. Several of the racers had reverse-flown the race route, and the fuelers were eager to meet these daring women.

Thaden had had enough desert and heat, and cut straight across from Phoenix toward San Bernardino, California, then Santa Monica. The airplane was running well, and she was getting anxious to meet the other racers. Thaden flew the trip to California, and the entire race, with her face up close to Walter Beech's four-inch fresh-air pipe, her make-do source of life-sustaining atmosphere. Oddly enough, the others racing Travel Airs didn't seem to have the same problem.

SATURDAY, AUGUST 17, 1929
SANTA MONICA, CLOVER FIELD

If your time is worth anything, travel by air. If not, you might just as well walk.

Yours, Will Rogers
Syndicated newspaper column

Jim and Clema Granger's aviation operation at Clover Field in Santa Monica, California, was a madhouse, and Clema declared herself the Mad Hatter. She was trying to keep up with the sponsors' ever-changing race rules, even as the racers had been arriving and checking in all day. Jim, a Swallow Airplane distributor, was sponsoring Ruth Elder in the race, since Clema didn't have enough flying hours to be eligible. Some other racers had fudged, making the decision that a little Parker Pen time padding their log books to meet the experience requirement wouldn't hurt.

With the motion-picture industry nearby, stunt flying was common, and the movie royalty hung around or kept their airplanes on the field with one of the nearly dozen fixed-base operators. Large wooden hangar buildings, derived from barns and even an old movie studio, lined the perimeter of Clover Field. The imposing Douglas Aircraft Company factory along the boulevard nearby was already a major factor in Santa Monica's prosperity.

Pilots claimed to believe that all city fathers had perversely pledged to place telephone lines and the tallest trees around airports to challenge pilot skills. Cemeteries were often sited next to airports, causing a plethora of facetious comments among the pilot population. However, Clover Field shared open space with the Santa Monica Municipal Golf Course, giving it an open feeling despite being situated just west of the city and right in the Los Angeles Basin.

Amid all this, the Grangers had a large new metal hangar for their flying school they used to host the air racers.

Aviation received a generous boost from a private source in the mid-twenties when the Daniel Guggenheim Fund for the Promotion of Aeronautics provided bequests totaling $2.5 million to support aeronautics. A national safe-airplane competition led to the Curtiss-Wright Corporation's successful design of an early STOL (short takeoff and landing) aircraft. The event that impacted aviation most dramatically was a single man's audacious act in 1927: Charles Lindbergh's solo flight across the Atlantic Ocean. Though the ocean had been crossed numerous times, Lindbergh was the first to do it alone. He galvanized the public to believe airplanes were viable transportation of the future.

The Grangers' hangar and ramp boasted the finest racing ships of the day, with the world's elite female pilots doting on them. The military promoted early air racing as a way to improve aircraft design and cultivate more pilots. The public supported the exciting and dangerous sport; their enthusiasm made successful pilots household names.

Manufacturers, eager for military patronage, took advantage of the ongoing rivalry between the U.S. Army and U.S. Navy civilian teams and, in turn, tried to beat out both military services.

The Curtiss racing airplanes dominated these national air races. Cross-country derby races had been added, terminating at the nationals in Cleveland. Now, in 1929, there was to be a new trophy event sponsored by manufacturer Charles E. Thompson. The Thompson, as the race was dubbed, would be a fifty-mile race open to all. Walter Beech had big plans for his secret new airplane to beat the government planes and to take the Thompson trophy home to Kansas.

Roscoe Turner was equally ready to claim the Thompson for his own, flying a Lockheed Vega. A flamboyant Southern gentleman, Colonel Roscoe Turner was the master promoter, equally as famous for his attire as for his exceptional flying ability. Turner's self-designed uniform was immaculate (forget greasy, white coveralls)—a soft, blue coat with Sam Browne belt, spiffy riding breeches, boots shined to a fare-thee-well, and, of course, a white silk scarf, an aviator's helmet, and goggles. Roscoe's waxed mustache and inspired mascot, a live lion, completed his costume. Fortunately, he was good enough in the saddle to carry off his splendiferous attire.

The Women's Air Derby had brought the women together. They were fierce competitors, but they were totally united in their effort to force open the door to the male pilots' world. As they became acquainted, the eastern racers regaled the western girls with their descriptions of life in the sophisticated East, especially the New York musical theater. George Gershwin's *Funny Face* and Kern and Hammerstein's *Show Boat* were enjoying long runs on Broadway. Babe Ruth had hit sixty home runs for the Yankees, and Maestro Toscanini was the new conductor of the New York Philharmonic.

The *New York Times* had installed an astonishing moving electric sign around One Times Square.

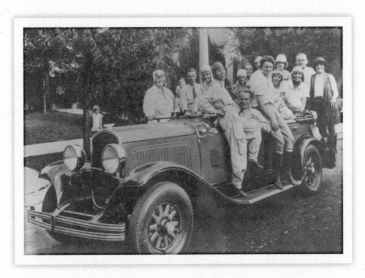

The air derby brought women pilots from different backgrounds together. Front: Vera Dawn Walker and Louise Thaden. Back: Thea Rasche, Margaret Perry, Neva Paris, Chubbie Keith-Miller, Ruth Elder, and Edith Foltz.

The western girls could brag on their more relaxed lifestyle and the nearby movie industry, the first talking movie *The Jazz Singer* with Al Jolson, and Disney's first Mickey Mouse cartoon film, *Steamboat Willie.* Everyone was singing "Bye Bye Blackbird," and the slow fox-trot was the fashionable dance. A sharp crystal ball of the immediate future would have shown Richard Byrd's flight over the South Pole coming up, Chicago's gang war and the St. Valentine's Day Massacre, astronomer Edward Hubble's measurements of extragalactic nebulae, and the Nazi party gaining 107 seats in the German elections. Within two months, the world would see Black Thursday collapse the New York Stock Exchange. Hard times were coming, even to the skies.

Clema had set up a table in the hangar where all the competitors were gathered to process papers and compare rumors and tips. Louise Thaden was frantic, and her co-competitor Marvel Crosson matched her pacing in the hangar. Thaden ranted, alluding to the worst possible cause of competitor Mary Haizlip's tardiness, "If Mary is alive, I'll kill her! Where is she? If she's down and safe somewhere, why doesn't she call?"

Crosson cast about for a soothing explanation. "Louise, Mary has simply put it down somewhere and can't get to a phone. Or she's seen the fog and turned back across the mountains."

Thaden looked at Crosson blankly. That comment was a mistake. They both knew Mary Haizlip wouldn't have enough fuel to get back east of the low stratus, and probably the whole basin was socked in by now. Whenever the low stratus clouds drifted off the ocean into the Los Angeles Basin, all airplanes had best find a safe harbor immediately or they'd be stuck "on top." It would be clear and beautiful above the undercast of low, flat clouds. A pilot would feel as if she were flying above an ocean of cotton. But that was on top.

Crosson's comment reminded them that below, hidden in that benign-looking layer of moist air, were buildings and trees and other "airplane catchers"—hard things. The pilots jokingly called mountains in clouds *cumulo granite*, or a cloud with a rock in it. In those days, there was no way to fly down through the clouds safely, and if stuck on top and out of fuel, a pilot could only "take to the silk," parachuting and abandoning the airplane. Los Angeles pilots knew that if low stratus filled the basin, the mountains to the east would often halt the clouds like a barricade. The only safety for a pilot on top of that cotton was on the desert side, and one needed fuel to get that far. Where was Mary? She should've been in by now.

Like Louise Thaden, Mary Haizlip was a favorite of those who had watched her flying skills evolve from timid to poised. Haizlip's flying could be laid at the door of oil prospecting, because her father had been drilling for oil in Oklahoma. In fact, the unlucky man had drilled nineteen dry holes. Out visiting her father, Mary heard about a handsome pilot, Jim Haizlip, recently returned from the Great War. He had learned to fly in France, and he was now running a flight school while taking an engineering course at the University of Oklahoma. Mary made it a point to meet the charming young man, and, ten days later, the teenager and the glamorous pilot were married. "It took me that long to lure him away from all the other girls," Mary explained. "He had to break a date with the campus queen to get married."

Jim had a slightly different version. "Her parents were horrified. We had to wait 'til they left town to elope." Of course, he taught Mary to fly. Their romance lasted for the rest of their lives. But for the moment, nineteen-year-old race pilot Mary Haizlip was missing.

A stir at the hangar door revealed Amelia Earhart trying to tell the crowd the news she had, while making her way to Thaden. "There's an airplane down in a field just outside the airport. It's a woman pilot, and she's being taken by the Feds to the sheriff's office. They think she's a dope smuggler."

It took Thaden a minute to take that in. Then she laughed. "Well, it must be Mary. She's overdue, and leave it to her to find the sheriff. She'll probably trade him an airplane ride for the keys to the jail."

Thaden was still uneasy, but Crosson assured her it was too logical to be anyone else. They started looking for a ride to wherever the sheriff was. Since Earhart had a car, she gathered up Thaden and Crosson to locate the airplane. A line boy described the airplane's location and how to get there, adding, "You can't miss it."

Mary Haizlip

"Argggh," said Crosson. "I hate 'you can't miss it' 'cause it jinxes so you do!"

They took the tight turn out of the airport in a skid, much too fast for the fog and growing darkness, and headed toward the field the line boy had described. No one wanted to talk about their fears that they would find a wrecked airplane and injured pilot. There were a couple of fence posts down and some airport types looking toward the dark outline of an airplane in the field. It was an enclosed cockpit airplane, high wing with two seats side-by-side—a Monocoupe. Thaden knew Haizlip would be flying a three-place open-cockpit American Eagle biplane. Phoebe Omlie was the only pilot entered in a Monocoupe. She had to be the "dope smuggler."

The women rushed to find Omlie, who was overwhelmed to see them. She was detained by the sheriff, who knew nothing about flying, much less women pilots. She needed some supporters.

"I've been flying around trying to locate the airport in the dark," she said, "but the lights were apparently off. Since I was low on fuel, I picked out a dark spot, hoping it was a hay field, and landed. What a blessing that the field was fairly smooth, with no potholes to fall into. I taxied up to the lights of a house, and a farmer and his boys helped me tie the airplane down for the night. About that time, the sheriff arrived. He's accusing me of running dope, but he's having a heck of a time finding any!"

Thaden had to giggle at Omlie's predicament. One of the most admired and experienced women pilots in the country had become the victim of mistaken identity and was in trouble with the law. By that time, the sheriff recognized Amelia Earhart, and fortunately her fame helped smooth the way for Omlie. Earhart told the skeptical officer that the women were in town for a transcontinental air race, "and this woman will most likely win it, 'cause she was the first female transport pilot licensed in this country and the most accomplished of us all." She went on, "The only reason she landed at this out-of-the-way pasture is because the lights aren't on at the airport, which is only six miles away. We all vouch for her good character, and insist that you release Mrs. Omlie and go look for your smuggler elsewhere." Aware of Omlie's political connections with the top level of the Democratic Party, Thaden, with a twinkle in her eye, suggested to the lawman that he could also check with Franklin D. Roosevelt for an additional character reference. With a harrumph, the sheriff washed his hands of the whole thing and faded into the night.

Phoebe Omlie actually started her aviation career as a parachute jumper in St. Paul, Minnesota, in 1921 at the age of eighteen. Her inauspicious inaugural jump left her hanging, unhurt, by her parachute shrouds from a tree. Three months later, she made it into the flying circus with a jump from 15,200 feet—almost three miles high and a world record. The teenage girl partnered with Glenn Messner, daredevil of the air. Together, they did any aerial stunt they could think up. Omlie wing-walked, stood on her head on the wing, hung by her teeth, changed planes in mid-air, swung on a trapeze, and perfected the double parachute jump. After the first chute opened, Omlie would cut it loose, free fall, then open the second chute.

By age twenty, Omlie had become the first woman to head up her own flying circus, a means to an end to save enough money for her own aviation business. Omlie learned to fly in 1922 and married her flight instructor the same year, not an unusual happenstance between a female student and her revered mentor. They settled in Memphis, established a commercial aviation business, and Phoebe, with an astonishing two thousand flying hours, became the first woman to hold a transport license. The year 1927 brought the great Mississippi River floods. Ground transportation was all but gone, and the Omlies gained both fame and gratitude for their aerial support for stranded citizens.

Two serious crashes failed to persuade Phoebe to quit flying. Once, when teaching someone how to fly, she was unable to get a "frozen" student off the controls. The two rode out a spin clear to the ground. Phoebe suffered fractures of the arms, legs, and skull, and she never quit. In 1928, a control problem led to a crash, and her legs were broken again. She walked with a cane during the 1929 air derby, but at least she was walking.

Phoebe Omlie

Phoebe's dilemma with the local sheriff left the elusive Mary Haizlip, the original object of the hunt, still missing. But within a few hours, word arrived that she was, in fact, in Los Angeles, but without an airplane. Like Thaden, she had left Tulsa for the race start, but flying a stock model American Eagle with the newly approved Wright model J-6-7 radial engine. She encountered strong winds at Tucson, then landed, dragging a wing and bending the propeller, not an unusual event in the early years of aviation. The promised delivery of a replacement airplane had not materialized, and she was frantically tracking it down. Mary Haizlip, another early female transport pilot, had received more than a modicum of attention from the press, though they mistakenly and consistently referred to her as Mae.

Though Mary Haizlip and Marvel Crosson had never met, Louise Thaden was friends with both, and Crosson was happy to accompany Thaden out in the foggy darkness to look for their sister pilot. Of Marvel Crosson, one usually heard "Marvel and Joe" or "Joe and Marvel." People described both Crosson and her pilot brother with "coal-black hair and flashing smiles."

The Crosson kids grew up on a Kansas farm. Joe was coming up on eleven and Marvel was fourteen when they saw their first airplane. They never got over it. When the family moved to San Diego, Joe and Marvel each worked and saved $150—an enormous amount of money in those days—with which they bought the motorless wreck of a Curtiss N-9 seaplane. The two hid it behind their house and scrounged junkyards for parts to replace the floats with wheels. Next, they bought an old OX-5 engine for it from a boat dealer. When they tested the engine in the backyard, they simultaneously tested their mother's love and patience by plastering her chickens up against the fence. Turned out of the yard, Marvel and Joe got help carting the airplane to the airfield where, surprisingly, it actually flew. Both Marvel and Joe soloed their hybrid craft, and they barnstormed together for several years before seeking their aviation fortune in Alaska.

In 1925, the Crossons actually got paid to fly. They were true pioneers in the brutal flying of the far north. Subsequently, just two months prior to the air derby, Marvel made the front page of the *New York Times Pictorial* magazine for setting a new women's altitude record four feet short of 24,000 feet. Soon, Marvel became the first woman to apply for entry in the transcontinental air race and made a practice run over the entire route. Familiarity with the route and her vast flying experience made her a formidable competitor in her Speedwing Travel Air. Marvel Crosson's plane had been the first of the racers' planes off the assembly line and flown at the factory, and her brother Joe came out to get it. She got the fastest of the lot, a clipped wing single seater with one of the new Wright J-6-7 engines, clocked at 168 miles per hour. It was an exciting time to be flying, since her plane was one of tremendous innovation in aeronautics.

Marvel Crosson

The years between the wars were the golden years of aviation. By the year of the Women's Air Derby, the old, war-weary Jennies were being deliberately destroyed. Airplanes had been dramatically improved, and prices fell below $1,000 for a trainer, so that ordinary people with flying fervor could own an airplane and learn to fly it. Ninety-six aircraft manufacturers delivered more than six thousand airplanes in 1929. The majority were open cockpit, but enclosed monoplanes were increasing in popularity. Production had increased 50 percent above the year before, and by the end of the year, more American plants were manufacturing airplanes than automobiles.

The armistice expressly forbade certain aviation activity in Germany, and as a result, the Germans were excluded from the development of powered aircraft. Instead, Germans were making extraordinary progress in innovative aerodynamics and glider flight.

American development of the dependable radial air-cooled Wright Whirlwind engine revolutionized aircraft propulsion. Ground-adjustable propellers led to more efficient flight regimes. Next, the controllable-pitch, constant-speed propeller was developed, which could be adjusted in flight by the pilot to climb or descend as required. (A malfunctioning constant-speed prop took some blame for Amelia Earhart's Lockheed accident in Hawaii on her first attempted flight around the world.)

More streamlined aircraft came next. Commercial cross-country travel had become a combination of flying, then transferring to a train at night, then back on an airplane the next morning. The first regularly scheduled carriage of passengers at night by air reduced their plane/train ride time by 75 percent. There were 27 major transport lines in 1929, and 80 big corporations were now so attuned to airplane travel that they approved employee expense accounts for business travel by air. The Department of Commerce issued 282 approved type certificates that year for aircraft designs meeting the government's engineering requirements.

Looking ahead, in October following the air race, Lieutenant James Doolittle took off, flew, and landed successfully flying "blind," with no reference to the ground. He utilized two-way radio communication and could follow a radio beacon to his destination. A Heinkel seaplane, catapulted from a ship, inaugurated the first ship-to-shore mail service. The General Electric Company was experimenting with an instrument called a radio altimeter that gave the exact height of the airplane above the ground. Westinghouse Electric produced a siren that turned on floodlights for a landing field through sound waves caught and amplified by a megaphone.

And it wasn't all "winged" aircraft. Back in Cleveland, the Navy dirigible *Los Angeles* was moored to a mobile mast for the duration of the National Air Races. Successful demonstrations of airplane hook-ons to a trapeze apparatus hanging under the dirigible stunned the crowd. The idea was that the airship could be a refueling base for airplanes at sea. Excited spectators at the air races were convinced there could be no more fruitful time for aviation than 1929. The women air racers now gathering in Clover Field agreed.

Will Rogers and his sidekick, Wiley Post, were wandering around kicking tires to the delight of the racers who considered the two their own. Will Rogers was a Cherokee Indian whose ancestors had made the forced march in 1838 called the Trail of Tears in which one-quarter of the Cherokee Nation perished en route to the Indian Territory. Rogers liked to say, "My ancestors didn't come on the Mayflower, but they met the boat." Rogers was born in 1879 in the Indian Territory, now Oklahoma (in Choctaw language, *okla homma* meant "red people").

Young Rogers's father put together a cattle ranch, eventually totaling sixty thousand acres, where Willie reveled in ranch life, especially wrangling horses and swinging the lariat. In fact, that hobby led to Rogers's expulsion from several boarding schools. Eventually, the U.S. government gave in to settlers pushing westward into the territory, and they bought out the Cherokee Strip. Each Indian got five annual payments of $367.50 in cash, and Rogers and his father together received just less than 150 acres of land. Their large ranch was now a small farm. Several blocks of land, on varying dates, were opened up to settlers who ran to make land claims upon a pistol shot signal. The "Boomers" ran at the shot. A few "Sooners" stole out early. This is the reason Oklahoma is called the Sooner State.

Rogers joined Texas Jack's Wild West Circus billed as "The Cherokee Kid, Fancy Lasso Artist, and Rough Rider," swinging the lariat for pay around the world. He eventually made the jump from Wild West shows to vaudeville with his novel act. The complexity of his rope tricks showed up later in his silent film, *The Ropin' Fool*, in which he completed fifty-three different tricks. Discovering that his audiences loved to hear him talk during his act with his drawl and self-depreciating humor, Will Rogers became a humorous talker who spun a rope.

During Rogers's gig with Ziegfeld's Midnight Frolic, the popular humorist decided to talk about what he read in the papers. It was a huge hit, and with evolving topics, he had a new act every day. He worked for Florenz Ziegfeld for ten years on a handshake oral contract. And then it was time for the movies, which is why Will Rogers lived down the road from Clover Field, where the 1929 air derby started. His comments on the political events of the day ("Well, all I know is just what I read in the papers.") had led to Rogers's newspaper column and eventual syndication.

Will Rogers

After World War I, Will Rogers developed a great interest in aviation and concern about the government's disinterest in commercial aviation. He began to fly constantly, one time even through a snowstorm with derby participant Blanche Noyes. He was fearless and determined to "see everything" from the air.

His friend Wiley Post had lived in Oklahoma working as a

roughneck in the oil fields. An oil field accident in which Post lost his left eye brought $1,700 in compensation, money with which he quickly bought an airplane. Wiley Post learned to fly without depth perception, and he flew for two Oklahoma oil men—one bought a new Lockheed Vega (like Amelia Earhart's) and named it the *Winnie Mae* after his daughter. The Wiley Post–flown *Winnie Mae* became one of the most famous airplanes in history, and today it hangs in the Smithsonian.

Post flew around the world in eight days for a world speed record, then he did it again. He also developed a pressure suit to be worn on high-altitude flights. Will Rogers saw to it that Claremore, Oklahoma, his hometown, built a landing field so that Rogers and Post could fly in and the town could pay allegiance to Oklahoma's famous flyer.

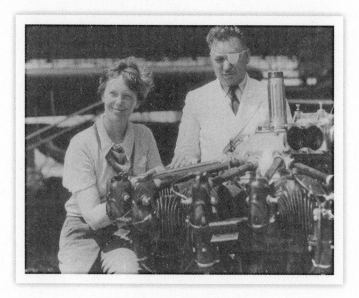

Amelia Earhart and Wiley Post

The two Oklahoma boys who loved airplanes wouldn't have missed the start of the women's race. They volunteered to fly the route, carrying officials and extra luggage for the racers. They were the chief cheerleaders.

As the host airport operator for the start of the race, Clema Granger held off her own racing ambitions until the next year. She would do anything for her fellow women pilots, she reflected, but this organized mayhem was almost over the line. Mary Haizlip hadn't made it in yet for the start of tomorrow's race; besides, the clouds were too low to expect to see her tonight, and the sun had already fallen into the sea. Two entrants, Marjorie Crawford and Patty Willis, had withdrawn, and Jim had just taken a call from Kansan Mabel Waters saying that she wasn't going to make it. The famous Irish pilot, Lady Mary Heath, had decided to enter some of the closed course competition at the terminus in Cleveland instead of flying the women's race, so she wouldn't be coming in either. The race sponsor, the National Exchange Club, was changing the route even at this late date, raising the volume of rumbles among the racers. Members of the press were underfoot everywhere. The takeoff banquet was late, there were airplanes to fuel, and somebody, as far as she knew, would have to get that dangerous "dope smuggler," Phoebe Omlie, out of jail. Other than that, things were running pretty smoothly.

SATURDAY, AUGUST 17, 1929

Banquet

Claremore, Oklahoma, is just waiting for a high-tension line so they can go ahead with locating an airport.

Yours, Will Rogers
Syndicated newspaper column

Get that goddamned midget ape outta here before I make a rug out of 'im." Pancho Barnes had spied an official's pet dog, and she was not impressed. Hosts and guests who gathered at the race headquarters' hotel evening gala were stunned in surprise. Little did they grasp that Pancho Barnes's singular flair was just unfolding.

In fact, to the jeweled and coifed National Exchange Club wives who came to fête the women air racers, the choice between gaping openly and impolitely at Barnes or simply letting a discreet glimpse suffice was a difficult one. Each of the racers was of an independent bent, but most conformed to a gentrified banquet dress code. However, Barnes was traveling light, with only her flying clothes, and she appeared at the banquet in jodhpurs and a beret, puffing as usual on her trademark black cigar. The fact that she was basically in her own hometown and had plenty of clothes in her closet was irrelevant.

"This is a solo pilot race, so ain't no bare-ass copilot dog gonna help any son-of-a-bitch pilot who can't keep the shiny side up and the pointy end headed east," exclaimed Barnes, unleashing a continuing string of colorful and creative insults.

Florence Leontine Lowe "Pancho" Barnes came by her aviation genes through her grandfather, Thaddeus Sobieski Constantine Lowe, called by some the founding father of the U.S. Air Force.

As a fifteen-year-old, Thaddeus had served a mundane apprentice-ship to a shoemaker in Boston, but his inherent curiosity and brilliant mind led to auspicious inventions. At a young age, Thad became entranced with hot air balloons, and his first effort in that direction was to send a cat up in a kite. The cat returned alive but enraged.

In 1857, Thaddeus constructed his first balloon and was soon taking passengers aloft for a tethered ride at a dollar each. Then he offered the thrill of free ballooning. He loved the quiet journey, the view of the earth below, and the dogs barking in confusion at the conversations coming from above.

**Pancho Barnes. This photo is inscribed to 1929
air derby competitor Opal Kunz.**

Thaddeus studied the upper air with its currents flowing like the sea, and he began preparation for a flight across the Atlantic Ocean, convinced that it could be done. He confidently petitioned the Smithsonian Institution, with backup evidence of charts and tables, to support his flight. Moving forward, a practice flight seemed in order, so Thaddeus shipped his balloon to Cincinnati, announcing a test flight to the East Coast to prove the feasibility of his planned ocean crossing.

The aeronaut had risen out of Cincinnati in his balloon named *Enterprise*, riding the air currents eastbound to twenty-two thousand feet. Nevertheless, unable to hold its altitude, the balloon barely made it over the Blue Ridge Mountains. When Thaddeus eventually spotted the Atlantic Ocean, he was satisfied that he had successfully completed his test flight and landed on what turned out to be Pea Ridge on the North Carolina–South Carolina border. He was in a lot more trouble than he could have imagined. While Thad was busy planning his test flight, six southern states led by South Carolina had seceded from the Union. On April 20, 1861, three days after Virginia seceded, northern-born Thaddeus Lowe dropped from the sky deep in the backwoods of Carolina.

A gathering mob, convinced that they had captured a Yankee spy, was persuaded by cooler heads to relinquish him to the authorities, and he was jailed in Columbia, South Carolina. He was eventually allowed to retrieve his balloon and go on his way, but his experience revealed further the seriousness of the South. Any ocean-crossing balloon flight at that time was off.

Early in June 1861, Thaddeus Lowe arrived in Washington, DC,

to find state militias on hand, having been called up by President
Lincoln for a three-month enlistment. Should there be any confron-
tation, it wasn't expected to last longer than that. There were some
troops in Union uniforms, but many served in their own colorful
state livery, carrying their personal weapons—some embarrassingly
obsolete. Thaddeus met with President Lincoln, who authorized him
to set up his balloon on the Smithsonian grounds tethered to twenty-
five hundred feet in order to take a practice look at the Federal forti-
fications. Pancho Barnes's grandfather telegraphed his observation
from aloft. His was the first message from air to earth.

On July 21, Barnes's grandfather flew free over the Battle of Bull
Run and inadvertently landed behind Confederate lines. Presumably,
the Rebels were so startled by their first view of a manned balloon
overhead that they didn't think to take a shot at him. Thaddeus's
landing site wasn't seen, and he was safe behind protective terrain.
However, he had no way to get out. He knew the Union Army, should
they search, would never find him. But his wife Leontine knew his
balloon, the air currents, and how he thought and planned. She came
after her husband. Disguised as an old country woman, Leontine
passed freely through the lines with her mule and cart to rescue her
husband. Lowe was stunned when she appeared. Leontine hid her
husband and his balloon basket and envelope on the cart and carried
him to safety.

President Lincoln considered a proposed Aeronautics Corps
invaluable, and finally his skeptical generals agreed. Fifty civilians were
assigned to the balloonist to transport, launch, and retrieve. Thaddeus
and his support troops were promised an army commission, though

none ever materialized. Thaddeus had envisioned himself as a spotter of enemy troop movements. However, the aeronaut metamorphosed into a much more proactive role. Using a white handkerchief to signal Union gunnery troops, he could direct the fire.

Needless to say, the Confederate troops could see what he was doing and, when in range, tried to shoot him down. Thaddeus lined his basket with sheet metal to deflect the gunfire and was recognized as the most targeted man in the war. Bullets never hit him, though malaria did.

Naturally, the South soon wanted their own spotting balloon, but they discovered on their first attempt that an envelope constructed with cotton was too heavy to lift. To Thaddeus's amazement, one day he saw a balloon of various bright, gay colors amid the enemy troops. The Confederate ladies had donated their vivid silk dresses to the cause.

The battle at Chancellorsville, Virginia, was Thaddeus's last effort for the army, but his creative mind didn't rest. After the war, the inventor developed an artificial ice machine, the beginning of commercial cold storage. In 1888, he moved his family to Pasadena, California, where he erected an astrological observatory and installed a cogwheel railroad to get to it. In 1890, the State of California named it Peak Lowe. Such was Pancho Barnes's genetic heritage.

Thaddeus and Leontine Lowe's seventh child, Thad Jr., married neighbor Florence Mae Dobbins, of old Philadelphia money. Thaddeus the elder had built a twenty-four-thousand square-foot, twenty-five room mansion on Pasadena's millionaire's row, but it was easily dwarfed by the Dobbins's palace. The widow of a successful architect, Caroline Dobbins soon built the young couple a thirty-five-room English manor-style home constructed with the bricks shipped west from the Dobbins's former Philadelphia mansion. Thad Jr. and Florence's firstborn was a sickly and fragile boy, worried over and protected by his mother. When daughter Florence Leontine arrived, she was raised as the son her father and grandfather had longed for. She was her grandfather's shadow until his death when she was twelve. His brilliant mind and individuality passed unaltered to Florence.

Pampered, Florence grew up with huge wealth, servants, horses, and an adolescence without limits. By the time her parents realized that she was incorrigible, it was too late. They unsuccessfully tried one private school after another to tame the wild child. The tomboy was already formed by her smart and adventuresome genes, cemented by her parents' lack of will or ability to control her. Grandmother Dobbins came to the rescue, arranging a marriage for young Florence with Rankin Barnes, the rector of fashionable St. James Episcopal Church in South Pasadena. No detail was overlooked during the extravagant wedding plans, with the exception of anyone bothering to supply the bride with any information about sex, wifely duties, and cooking. As related later by the bride, the wedding night was disaster. In fact, it was the only time the couple made any attempt to consummate their marriage. As it turned out, once was enough.

Florence made it known that as far as she was concerned, William Emmert Barnes, who came into the world exactly nine months after his parents' wedding day, was the product of a virgin birth. She named the baby after her brother who had by then died of leukemia. With nannies, housekeepers, and cooks, baby Billy really didn't interest his mother. She spent her time supplying horses from her stables to western movie makers.

Bored with her genteel lifestyle, Florence Barnes cut her black hair short, slipped into greasy, baggy clothes, and signed onto a banana boat to Mexico as a seaman, using the name Jacob Crane. On board, she smoked, drank, and cussed with such flourish that even the other sailors were awed at Jacob Crane's extensive and colorful vocabulary. Upon departure, the Panama flag was hoisted, and the crew, at least the unknowing ones, discovered that they were smuggling guns to revolutionaries, a dangerous business. At San Blas, Mexico, the ship was seized by port authorities and held for six weeks. Roger Chute, another crew member, was planning to jump ship, so Florence (as Jacob Crane) insisted on joining him. Along an old jungle trail, Chute rode a skinny white horse and Florence was astride a burro. She said he looked like Don Quixote, and his response was that she looked like Pancho. "No, no, you mean Sancho Panza." He didn't care. From that moment, for the rest of her life, Florence Leontine Lowe Barnes was known as "Pancho" Barnes.

When Pancho Barnes returned home in November 1927 to her life of privilege and domesticity, she found it suffocating. Her husband Rankin was busy with church business and was perfectly happy to have Barnes make her own life. Though their marriage went on for many years in separate directions, and the pair retained a certain fondness for each other from afar, she never lived with her husband again.

Movie folks hung out at Barnes's Laguna Beach house (bought for her by Grandmother Dobbins). Her parties, generosity, and outlandish exhibitionism became legendary. Shocking behavior put Barnes on center stage. Barnes loved the Hollywood crowd, and her equine passion expanded to include airplanes. She learned to fly, buying a used Travel Air and then the new Speedwing, in which she would fly the air race.

Pancho Barnes's Travel Air

When twenty-eight-year-old Barnes entered the 1929 air derby, she pre-flew the entire route to get a leg up on her competition, as did others competing. The first race publicity had announced that each woman pilot would be accompanied by a mechanic, since there was no question that mechanical problems would develop along the way. However, devious promoters pounced on that loophole immediately. Ravishing Hollywood starlets who had never been closer to an airplane than to watch one overhead suddenly were revealed to have become "pilots." They would pose prettily for the camera, while the male mechanics accompanying them would really do the flying. (Nobody gave a thought as to how long the starlets would last under the hardships of racing.) The women pilots were outraged and demanded that they be allowed to fly solo. So they did.

The media's growing ability to ignite national and even international enthusiasm was helping turn aviators into celebrities and celebrities into aviators. Public spirit was buoyed by those who dared to soar above earthly constraints. Aviators were heroic, and none more so than the brave women who overcame not only the considerable mechanical, financial, and technical obstacles, but also gender biases. Beautiful Ruth Elder made a grand entrance into the National Exchange Club banquet hall. She was a successful movie ingénue turned aviatrix, and the public was still spellbound by Elder's daring adventures two years earlier.

The frenzy to be first to fly the Atlantic solo had shifted from male to female after Charles Lindbergh captured the title. And as the pilots themselves vied, so too did the world that watched and waited. No other man could be first, but a woman could. Though the fall of 1927 hardly offered favorable weather for an Atlantic crossing, Ruth Elder had been afraid that another woman might beat her to the record. She pulled out all the stops to make the flight even though it was not to be solo. In fact, another female aviator, Frances Grayson, was just as determined to be the first woman pilot to cross the Atlantic, and she was hot on Ruth's heels.

Ruth Elder and her instructor, George Haldeman, had gathered sponsors and a Stinson Detroiter, which they christened *American Girl*. The disastrous Dole race to Hawaii, which had left ten dead at sea just two months prior, including female pilot Mildred Doran, dissuaded neither Elder nor Haldeman from attempting the Atlantic in the gathering winter weather. On October 11, 1927, *American Girl* took off for any land east of the Atlantic Ocean. They carried enough fuel for forty-eight hours of flying. October 13 brought no word of the flyers and the aircraft was obviously down.

On October 14, radio bulletins proclaimed that Elder and Haldeman were alive. An oil pressure drop had persuaded them to make a precautionary landing at sea alongside a Dutch freighter rather than go on with the excellent chance of engine failure. The aircraft was lost and Elder and Haldeman proceeded to Europe by freighter. The flyers were lauded for their survival, though the first female crossing title had eluded them.

Ruth Elder

Knowing that Ruth had not completed the crossing, Frances Grayson stepped up her efforts. She recruited pilot Wilmer Stultz, taking off October 17 in a Sikorsky Amphibian called *The Dawn*, only to return with fuel problems. They tried it again on October 23, to return once again with engine trouble. Stultz refused to give it a third try so late in the year. Furious, Grayson hired another pilot and navigator, and *The Dawn* took off from Roosevelt Field, New York, December 23, 1927. It was never seen again.

Wilmer Stultz lived to fly another day, and he was contacted by Mrs. Amy Phipps Guest of Pittsburgh to fly her across the Atlantic as a passenger. After her family persuaded her to abandon such a foolhardy scheme, Mrs. Guest asked her friend, publisher G. P. Putnam, to find a "suitable, aviation-minded young woman" to make the crossing under the Guests' sponsorship. Putnam located a social worker in Boston, a five-hundred-hour pilot named Amelia Earhart.

Earhart crossed the Atlantic as a passenger with pilots Wilmer Stultz and Louis Gordon in a Fokker Trimotor named *Friendship*. The trio departed Newfoundland June 17, 1928, and the rest, as they say, is history. Earhart was first. She was embarrassed at the adulation that came her way after the flight, giving credit to Stultz and Gordon at every opportunity, and pointing out that, "I was just a sack of potatoes in the back end." The public would have none of it. To Earhart's chagrin, "Lady Lindy" became her nickname. But she was infused with the passion to fly the Atlantic by herself one day.

Amelia Earhart

Barnstorming, record flights, stunting in Hollywood, and any kind of far-out publicity scheme seemed to be the primary avenue to flying jobs in 1929. Ruth Elder and Amelia Earhart had captured the public's hearts—Elder by her beauty and enthusiasm and Earhart by her modest demeanor in the face of acclaim. "I was only a passenger, you know," Amelia repeated again and again.

Most of the famous women pilots of the day were present in the room in Santa Monica. Their personalities, appearance, and flying experience ran the gamut. Even-tempered record holder Louise Thaden and Marvel Crosson with her striking black hair and lively eyes were other Walter Beech protégés flying the Travel Air.

Conversely, Blanche Noyes, a petite, budding actress whose large, innocent eyes rather demanded any nearby man's helping hand, had learned to fly only weeks before the race. As a result, Noyes was admitted on the basis of a rather exaggerated pilot history.

Reporters commented favorably on Bobbi Trout's boyish figure and buoyant demeanor. In January 1929, Bobbi Trout had flown an endurance record in a Golden Eagle and then surmounted her own milestone that same month. She was hired to demonstrate the Golden Eagle and was racing under her employer's sponsorship. Ruth Nichols was the first woman to fly in all forty-eight states. She was a saleswoman for the Fairchild Airplane and Engine Company, and they provided her a Rearwin, Ken-Royce model three-place open-cockpit biplane powered with a Curtiss Challenger engine. She was one of the so-called old-timers, having learned to fly in 1922, with a quiet, modest personality similar to Louise Thaden's. Nichols's startlingly bright blue eyes marked her unforgettably.

Flustered National Exchange Club officials shepherded the racers, club members, and guests to their banquet seats. Some of the hosts were clearly cowed by this gregarious group of astonishing ladies. Not one of them took orders. Each wanted to change the rules. And, adding to their insubordination, they possessed an unsettling, outdoorsy look. This was an extraordinary experience. Aside from the pilots, many present had never even ridden in an airplane, let alone helped direct an air race.

The women aviators dealt with the rising tension in various ways according to their personality types—from the demurring Earhart to the abrasive Barnes. The race committee grappled with their considerable challenge—control. Outside were the airplanes themselves, of uncertain reliability, though the manufacturers saw to it that the women had well-maintained ships. The National Exchange Club board had called the Santa Monica Club to duty, and the group desperately wanted to get the takeoff done tomorrow in an orderly manner. From the looks of things, they suspected they were alone in that wish.

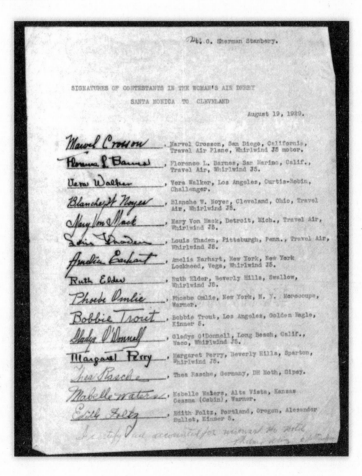

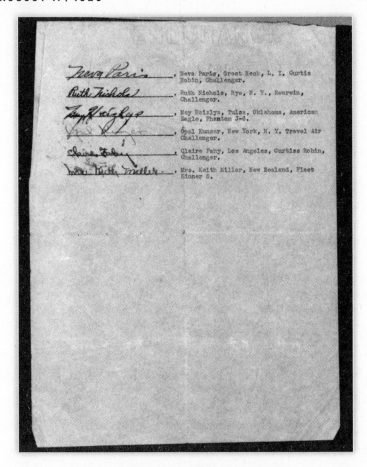

The official sign-in sheet for the derby.

One official quietly told his wife that he didn't really want to know what Mrs. Omlie was doing at the sheriff's office. He had been eager to meet Phoebe Omlie, a senior pilot of the group in terms of flying hours. She and her husband had done rescue work during the Mississippi River floods, and they were highly regarded flyers. That Pancho Barnes, well, she was almost too much to bear. He didn't know many men with such a zesty vocabulary.

A partial lineup at the start of the derby. From left: Louise Thaden,
Bobbi Trout, Patty Willis (who did not compete), Marvel Crosson,
Blanche Noyes, Vera Dawn Walker, Amelia Earhart, Marjorie
Crawford (did not compete), Ruth Elder, and Pancho Barnes.

The pilots were gathering papers, including their racing numbers,
at a table in the back of the room. Pretty Marvel Crosson was number
one, Pancho Barnes was number two, Blanche Noyes was number
three, Louise Thaden was number four, and then there were some
odd ball numbers such as Bobbi Trout's number one hundred and
Thea Rasche's number sixty-four for the twenty airplanes entered.
There was no number thirteen.

Even at this eleventh hour, the route still was being changed. It
seemed that any town with a National Exchange Club wanted the
racers to come through it, and stops were being added. Though
the sponsors had sought professional advice for the suitability
of the stops in terms of normal fuel range and adequate landing
fields, the racers found fault with some of the choices.

Will Rogers insightfully commented, "It was too bad Mexico City couldn't raise fifty dollars, or it too could have seen our women fliers." Folksy Will Rogers was known nationally as a favorite political commentator in both print and radio. Rogers's California home near the Santa Monica airport included a polo field where the horsy set gravitated. Rogers spent considerable hours riding with friends and perfecting his astounding rope tricks. The humorist's selection as the takeoff banquet speaker had met with unanimous favor.

Louise Thaden joined Thea Rasche to enjoy Will Rogers's speech, take a look at the just-circulated latest changes, and dine. Rasche, a stalwart, no-nonsense German pilot, had made a name for herself in the United States via her German aerobatic license. The Moth Aircraft Corporation asked Rasche to fly a de Havilland Gypsy-Moth for them, to which she agreed with pleasure. The promised airplane was not ready in time, but a substitute was available, and Thea had been scrambling around Los Angeles trying to locate it. She would take off tomorrow without even having test-flown her aircraft. It was no wonder she looked worried.

Thea Rasche handed a telegram to Louise Thaden asking in her thick German accent, "What do you think about this?" Her face became somber. Thaden, without comment, passed the yellow paper along to the other racers. It said, "Beware of sabotage." It was unsigned.

SUNDAY, AUGUST 18, 1929

Race Day 1

SANTA MONICA, CALIFORNIA

Just read the Smithsonian Institution's explanation about the Wright flying machine. They say
the trustees decided Langley's machine could
have flown first but didn't. I could have flown
first but didn't. I could have flown to France
ahead of Lindbergh, but I just neglected to do it.
I had a lot of other things on my mind at the time.

Yours, Will Rogers
Syndicated newspaper column

Although takeoff wasn't scheduled until 2:00 p.m., nineteen pilots and their entourage arrived at the airport near dawn after a full night's revelry and prerace organizing. The twentieth racer, Mary Haizlip, still wasn't on hand. As the morning fog gradually burned off, the darkened outlines of nineteen wood and fabric birds at rest gradually revealed themselves as racing planes. Clover Field came alive.

Some aircraft had undergone various repairs after their flights in, and they needed to be test-flown. The women gave a last check of the rigging in flight. Moving surfaces such as the ailerons on the wings needed to be smooth in trail and in balance for maximum speed. Even a slightly drooping aileron would add drag and slow the aircraft down. (It seemed odd that so many of the airplanes' parts, such as ailerons, empennage, and fuselage had acquired French names. But France had been an early contributor to the development of powered flight.)

Many white-coveralled feminine figures were to be seen flat on their backs under the belly of their airplanes scrubbing off oil and dirt. Slick airplanes slip through the air faster. They wiped smashed bugs off the wings' leading edges and applied polish. Each pilot test-flew her airplane, confirming it was in absolute readiness. The fuel tanks were topped. There was an old aviation maxim that nothing was more useless than runway or fuel left behind. A pilot careless about fuel quantity would pay with a forced landing. And the pilots who started their takeoff run midfield could well wish they had the runway they'd left behind as they struggled to climb over trees or wires at the end of the field. Maybe that was why there always seemed to be a cemetery near the airport.

The pilots prepare for takeoff at Clover Field.

Once the airplanes were checked and rechecked, each pilot turned to her road maps and the new aeronautical charts. She had drawn a line the night before along the course she planned to follow, with a hash mark every ten miles, and applied the magnetic variation correction to her heading. Each pilot had studied the course carefully, and she even wrote notes alongside the course line—reminders of checkpoints to watch for. On this morning, each aviator folded the chart and tucked it in a safe corner of the cockpit to be stashed under her leg in flight, protected from the wind. It was difficult to fly the airplane while unfolding a chart in an open cockpit out in the breeze, so the en route unfolding was carefully programmed before departure. The racers loaded the required gallon of water and three days' food in each airplane along with a parachute—ready for any eventuality.

Unless they flew aerobatics, most of the women did not wear parachutes as a general practice. However, even the nonconformists followed the race rules and dutifully strapped them on. Back on October 20, 1922, U.S. Air Corps test pilot Lieutenant Harold Harris had worn one of the then new-fangled 'chutes to test fly a fighter plane with experimental ailerons. The parachute was not comfortable, and he very nearly took off without it—after all, the things had not yet saved anyone's life. But Harris dutifully 'chuted up. During a friendly dogfight with another pilot, the lieutenant's airplane broke apart, and he jumped. The startled man pulled three times on the ripcord before discovering he had been pulling on a leg strap fitting, but finally felt the canopy blossom at the last possible moment. Lieutenant Harris became the first person ever to have his life saved in an emergency by a manually operated parachute.

Leslie Irvin was the designer of the Army's parachutes and was, himself, the first person to voluntarily jump out of an airplane to test his design. After Harris's successful save, a newspaper reporter suggested a club for those who owed their lives to a parachute. The subsequent club became known as the Caterpillar Club, both because caterpillars lower themselves to earth on threads, but also because the parachutes were made of silk manufactured by caterpillars. Just a couple of weeks after Harris, another man, Lieutenant Tyndall, jumped for his life when his airplane's wings came off. The next person to have his life saved was a stunt jumper who dove out of an airplane with six chutes on, planning to open one after another. The first five became entangled, and the sixth saved his life. The first female member joined the club on June 28, 1925. Irene McFarland took to the silk using an emergency parachute when her primary failed to open. Irvin started keeping a record of the members of the Caterpillar Club.

By the end of World War II, the Irvin Parachute Factory had recorded twenty-seven thousand Caterpillar Club members. They had also received a telegram from Lieutenant General Jimmy Doolittle, whose life was saved by parachute three times in three years. It said, "Aeroplane failed; chute worked."

~

The Women's Air Derby pilots learned right away that their stops, and the accompanying festivities at each, were terribly overscheduled. This created a certain amount of friction between the women and the officials. The hosts at each fuel and timing stop tried to outdo the previous town in the hospitality department. The non-aviators planning the events, luncheons, dinners, speeches, and entertainment were appropriately filling the agenda. The fact that the pilots would want to supervise while their airplanes were serviced did not occur to the planners. Of course, the women would have preferred to camp under the wing rather than endure all the social obligations, but they were polite, not wanting to appear ungrateful for the hospitality. Yes, there was a difference between male and female air racers.

The racers paced the tie-down area, gave and took advice from each other, rechecked the weather, and practiced handling the persistent reporters. Each of the racers had been in the public eye before dealing with curious and adoring fans. However, only Amelia Earhart and Ruth Elder had any real idea of the reporters' aggressive behavior—ambushes veiled as "the public's need to know." Trying to play down the male versus female angle, Earhart said, "It's a sporting event and nothing else."

Still, these women were unintentional pioneers, their air race is one of the more intriguing chapters in the infancy of civil aviation, and the public *did* want to know. In the early twenties, Army General Billy Mitchell had preached against governmental neglect of military air power, spurring passage of the Air Commerce Act of 1926. Secretary of Commerce Herbert Hoover implemented improvements to airfields and safety, including a pilot licensing requirement by 1927, and airplanes were licensed two years later. Charles Lindbergh's solo flight from New York to Paris in May 1927 stimulated ardent interest in learning to fly and awareness of the great potential of air commerce. By 1929, just two brief years later, air racing was the rage, now even for women.

A crowd gathers near one of the Travel Airs.

Aircraft use grew more diverse with air ambulances, bush flying, crop dusting, and freight transport uses. Civilian aircraft manufacturers popped up, with Matty Laird in Wichita, Kansas, being one of the first. The success of the Laird Swallow biplane was catalytic. It attracted former military aviators Lloyd Stearman and Walter Beech, plus farmer Clyde Cessna to the business. The work of these men established a foothold in Wichita, a first step towards the city's claim to the title of Air Capital of the World. (Wichita would eventually count sixteen aircraft manufacturers to its credit.) Travel Air Company built 547 aircraft in 1929, no mean feat considering the technology of the day. And the Travel Air Company's open-cockpit biplanes dominated the 1929 air derby fleet. Stearman and Cessna soon left Travel Air to form their own airplane companies, and Beech then sold Travel Air to Curtiss-Wright, staying on to manage the company. Walter Beech resigned in 1932, and with $25,000 in capital, he formed his own company, which evolved into Beech Aircraft Corporation. His secretary, Olive Ann Mellor, became Mrs. Beech.

The nineteen planes on the tarmac that morning (with Mary Haizlip still missing) were disparate, and the wide variety of aircraft available to the competitors prompted the air-race sponsors to form two divisions by engine size. The first division was composed of aircraft with engines of 510-cubic-inch displacement or less, which included the Monocoupe, Fleet, Golden Eagle, Travel Air with the OX-5 engine, Moth, and Eaglerock—the smaller, lighter, sport planes, they called the CW class. The second division covered up to 800-cubic-inch displacement engines, which included the Wright J5 engine Travel Air, Waco, Swallow, Lockheed, Spartan, Rearwin, Curtiss Robin, and American Eagle. These were the heavier, working aircraft, or the DW class. Depending upon the engine, the Travel Air was competing in both classes. The cubic-inch displacement was defined by the sum total volume of all the engine's cylinders. Later, engines were differentiated by horsepower, but in 1929, cubic-inch displacement was the defining distinction.

Increased publicity buzz about the Women's Air Derby worked much to the benefit of the aircraft manufacturers. As aviation was becoming an exploding industry and manufacturers envisioned skyways like highways, it was in their interest to support a spectacle that proved anyone, "even women," could fly their planes.

Few really considered women as less capable pilots than men. They already had too much evidence to the contrary. But the bias of the times made patronage, however false, almost mandatory. Heck, they thought, women have something to prove, and in so doing will help business. They queued up to have their airplanes represented in the spectacle.

The press was quick to point out that of the eleven female transport pilots licensed by the United States government, seven were in this race. Barnes didn't mind pointing out that "those dumbasses got it wrong, as usual," since, actually, ten of the eleven females holding the prestigious transport license were racing, with only the UK's Lady Mary Heath missing—and she would be flying the pylons in Cleveland. Despite professional acumen on par with men's, the group was variously dubbed the Petticoat Pilots, Sweethearts of the Air, Ladybirds, or "Flying Flappers." These descriptions had the effect of trivializing their aptitude and the race itself. On the other hand, it energized the women to disprove the implications of these demeaning tags. Earhart claimed that a female spectator had even poked her with an umbrella "to see what these women pilots were made of!"

Reporters dug to find out why women wanted to trespass into the male domain. A woman clad in white coveralls, hair pinned back out of her face, hands showing evidence of engine oil rather than dish soap, tried to explain, "The glory of soaring above God's Earth and the satisfaction of taking the machine up and bringing it back to the ground safely, through my own skill and judgment, has melted away the boundaries of my life. Racing opens my door to the world. Don't cut me off from the adventure men have been hoarding for themselves in the guise of protecting me from danger." For this nameless spokeswoman and for the others, an airplane was obviously the badge of emancipation.

Nearly every news article had its share of asides—male opinions of the "little ladies" who dared to race airplanes, which the following typified: "Women pilots are too emotional, vain, and frivolous to fly and are hazards to themselves and others." While the press and the opposite gender whittled away at the women pilots' confidence, the contenders themselves were supportive of one another, but only up to a point. Their competitive spirit remained intact. Psychological games, designed to produce insecurity in other contenders, were underway. Crosson put a blanket over her shoulders and hunched over the elevator hinge on the horizontal tail, obviously making a secret adjustment in the up-and-down movement. As planned, her maneuvering did not go unseen, and the other racers and mechanics were soon buzzing, speculating which special elevator adjustment would make the airplane go faster. The brainwashing campaign started.

A tall and shy twenty-three-year-old local pilot by the name of Howard Hughes was watching, and he smiled at the charade and subterfuge. "Good luck, Miss Crosson," he offered. Crosson and the others couldn't have imagined where this handsome young fellow Hughes was going in aviation, though they all knew he was in the movie business.

Like Crosson and her brother, many of the women were half of a flying duo. Claire Mae Fahy arrived with her husband, a Lockheed

test pilot, Lieutenant Herbert J. Fahy, who had in May established a
new solo endurance record of nearly thirty-seven hours. Lieutenant
Fahy would follow his wife along the race route to be on hand to tend
to mechanical needs, which would undoubtedly arise along the way.
He preferred to worry from where he could see her, rather than from
a distance.

Herb Fahy called out to Crosson too, "Congratulations on your
altitude record!" She had established this on the same day as Herb's
own endurance record.

"What a team you and I would make," Crosson teased enthusiastically. "Did you hear that I got race number one?" she
exclaimed, as a huge grin took charge of her face. "Claire's going
to have to pedal hard to keep up with me, 'cause with that number,
I'm destined to get to Cleveland first." German pilot Thea Rasche
was not the only non-U.S. pilot of the group. Jessie Keith-Miller,
known as "Chubbie," though she was a tiny person and not
chubby at all, was Australian. Keith-Miller had met Captain Bill
Lancaster of the Royal Air Force while on vacation in England,
and she agreed to help him raise funds for a flight to Australia, the
first being in a light aircraft, if she could go along. She helped him
in an Avron Avian named the *Red Rose*, which departed London
in October 1927. A sandstorm in the desert between Palestine
and Baghdad brought them down for a precautionary landing,
at which time they picked up a passenger—a cobra. Once in the
air, the snake made a worrisome appearance, and Keith-Miller
dispatched it with alacrity, dropping the snake over the side of
the cockpit.

Chubbie Keith-Miller

Within five hundred miles of their destination Down Under, engine failure put Keith-Miller and Lancaster on the ground with a severely damaged airplane. During the three-month repair period, Bert Hinbler, an Avro Factory test pilot who was seeking the same London-to-Darwin record, passed them by. Nevertheless, the pair continued on to a tumultuous welcome. Now, instead of completing the first flight from London, they were the first flight from London with a passenger—and a woman passenger at that.

Keith-Miller was not then a pilot, but she caught the flying fever. Though each was married to another, she and Lancaster fell in love and became inseparable. They made their way to America, where Keith-Miller learned to fly. She resolved the little detail of her lack of flying credentials, and the press overlooked it. The media loved her, and their attention made her fame even greater in the U.S. than in her native Australia. The Bell Aircraft Corporation offered her a new two-place biplane trainer to race, rebuilding the cockpit around her tiny five-foot-one-inch figure. Though she was certainly inexperienced at piloting, she well knew the pitfalls of long-distance flying.

Takeoff at Clover Field.

By one thirty in the afternoon, nineteen airplanes were lined up for takeoff in two long rows. The adjacent Douglas Aircraft factory buildings were a significant reminder of the World Cruisers built for the U.S. Army and accentuated the historical importance of the event about to begin. Could the women withstand the stresses of competing with one another in these volatile machines of the air? Should they be home in the kitchen wearing an apron? Gladys O'Donnell responded defiantly to an insolent reporter, "My mother never gave me the keys to the stove!"

Crowds lined the sides and the end of the field. Somebody had said there were three thousand citizens out for the takeoff. Were they there to watch history or to see what kind of women would fly these machines? Were they ghoulish people who wanted to be on hand for a wreck? Each racer preferred to believe that the crowd was cheering for her alone. Clover Field's proximity to the movie studios ensured that plenty of celebrities were there to witness the takeoff. Cowboy star Hoot Gibson had personally offered many of the pilots a sincere "Godspeed." Author Edgar Rice Burroughs thrilled both Crosson and Thaden when he wished them luck and fun.

Marvel Crosson sat impatiently in her cockpit, wiping sweaty hands on her coveralls and checking the maps one more time. Just as soon as Crosson strapped herself in and the engine was cranked, and she awaited her turn to go, one obscure law of nature presented itself—as it often did. Crosson suppressed her need to run to the bathroom and forced her mind into another direction: "I wonder how many people are out there?" "Will Joe be waiting for me in San Bernardino?" "How many of us will actually make it to the finish line?" These diversions didn't work; they only made the need worse. But as the race got underway, Crosson forgot the "call of nature" altogether.

At last, at 2:00 p.m. a radio-relayed pistol shot from the Cleveland terminus signaled the flag drop, and the race began. There was finally action to dampen the racers' nerves as they concentrated on their immediate next job—a good, smooth takeoff and turn on course.

The race was 2,759 miles long, averaging just over three hundred miles per day. Starting in Santa Monica, California, the racers were to be in Cleveland, Ohio, by August 26 for the start of the Cleveland Air Races. At stake was nearly $25,000 in prize money, but even more important, the hope for fame and respect that could be leveraged into a job.

Louise Thaden couldn't block the memory of her carbon monoxide problem with the Travel Air. As the engine warmed up, she took regular whiffs of hot, outside air through the new cockpit air tube. She wondered why her engine was the only one putting out the killer fumes.

Thaden's larger engine put her in the DW "heavy" competition class. Walter Beech had gone the extra mile for Louise, and she had the new NACA-developed (National Advisory Committee for Aeronautics) full-engine cowling around the nose of her plane. The challenge had been to provide streamlining while simultaneously cooling the engine with baffles that moved the air around the cylinders. Smooth structure, instead of an open space or a sharp corner or a cylinder poking out, translated into speed. This one aerodynamic improvement was rumored to give her as much as a twenty-mile-per-hour advantage. Even sitting on the ground, the modified airplane looked substantially faster, smoother, and more streamlined than others that were uncowled. Though Thaden didn't have the benefit of Walter Beech's rumored Travel Air Mystery Ship, the new cowling was enough of an edge.

Even so, Thaden suspected she didn't have the fastest of the Travel Airs. Marvel Crosson had the special narrow fuselage model 2000,

built specifically for racing. Her brother Joe had added some weight
in the tail for a more favorable center of gravity. Insecurity mounted.
No question, it had to be faster than Thaden's.

Pancho Barnes's Travel Air 4000 had some hastily made changes
for speed; it too had a full cowling. The Travel Air factory had rated
for speed: Crosson number one, Thaden number two, Barnes
number three, and Noyes number four The rest of the Travel Airs,
new or old, were mostly standard.

Nevertheless, Amelia Earhart's beautiful, red, five-passenger
Lockheed Vega monoplane was the most feared competition. She
and Edith Foltz were firing up their enclosed cabin jobs, Foltz in an
Alexander Eaglerock Bullet with a Kinner 5 engine. Al Mooney's
Eaglerock design had encountered some problems, but its configu-
ration was the precursor to many later popular aircraft. Mooney was
soon designing airplanes in his own name.

Earhart was competing in the higher-powered DW class too, and
Foltz was in the alternate lighter CW. They had the luxury of flying
inside, out of the constant wind. Since the pilots couldn't hear the
engine sounds and the wind in the wires, skeptics said there would
be a danger of missing developing mechanical problems. Others
viewed enclosed cockpits as just an aberration. Foltz said to the
press, "Just watch; all airplanes will be enclosed someday, and the
landing gear will go up and down for flight efficiency and speed, just
like my Bullet."

Crosson, now first for a takeoff to the west, headed into the afternoon breeze off the ocean as she taxied into position. She wiped her
hands on her coveralls, carefully pushing her charts under her left leg.

Her heart pounded as she consciously breathed deeply and slowly. She peered around the nose cowling, since it was impossible to see over. As the flag dropped, Marvel applied full power smoothly, and the engine roared in response. She fed in right rudder with her right foot to compensate for the torque of the revolving propeller that made the airplane want to turn left. As she gathered speed down the dusty field, the tail lifted and she was able to see ahead. It looked as if the throng was all in front of her. Crosson said a quick prayer to the engine god, for if it quit now there was no place to go except into all those onlookers. Suddenly, she was over the fence and the crowd, building climb speed, and making a 180-degree turn back toward an easterly course.

Since Mary Haizlip didn't arrive in time for the start, only nineteen aircraft were flagged off in one-minute intervals—two minutes sometimes, to let the dust settle. A small coterie accompanied them in the air. Wiley Post flew escort in his Lockheed Vega named *Winnie Mae*, and Carl Lienesch flew along in the Union Oil Company's Travel Air.

Both carried extra luggage for the racers. All heads were turned skyward, watching the racers fly out of sight, imagining what they were seeing and feeling. The big, round engines had the roar of a group of motorcycles—powerful, resolute, brave. Will Rogers shook his head in admiration as the courageous pilots lifted off for Cleveland, each intent on being the first one to the finish line.

"It looks like a Powder Puff Derby to me," he exclaimed. The reporters wrote down Rogers's words, and, from that moment, the 1929 Women's Air Derby became forever the Powder Puff

Derby. Despite his seemingly sexist remark, Will Rogers's admiration was sincere. The women knew it and were grateful for his support. His newspaper and radio coverage—and gift for expression—helped immortalize their race and brought world-wide esteem for their efforts.

Thus, the Powder Puff Derby racers climbed free from the swirling dust, challenged the constraints of gravity, and with irrational confidence in their fragile aircraft and fickle engines, embarked on their great adventure.

SUNDAY, AUGUST 18, 1929

Race Day 1

SANTA MONICA TO SAN BERNARDINO
68 MILES

They are aviators, but they are still women. They had only been out sixty miles when they all struck and wanted to have it their way.

Yours, Will Rogers
Syndicated newspaper column

ATLANTIC
OCEAN

GL
O
MEXICO

The first leg was purposely kept short to leave time for all the media hysterics that preceded takeoff—all those rides to give, interviews, sponsor stroking, and airplane tinkering in the early morning. The first overnight stop, San Bernardino, was only sixty-six miles east. Marvel Crosson noted her takeoff time, made her turnaround, and took up a heading of zero seven zero degrees. There wasn't much reason to climb looking for a tail wind, since the distance was so short. She'd probably just get up into a helping tail wind when it would be time to descend. Crosson poked her head up outside the cockpit to locate the road that, according to Messieurs Rand and McNally, should take her to the foothills town of San Bernardino. "Look sharp," she admonished herself. "Get the right road. The basin is getting so crowded and confusing with orange groves turning into towns." Crosson, now accustomed to Alaska, would be more comfortable out over open terrain, always watching for a good field for landing in case of engine trouble. She slouched back down again, mostly out of the hot wind. As for the glaring California sun, there was just no way to avoid it. The current heat wave had their destination at 105 degrees.

Crosson could see a road and a railroad. She juggled the standard road map and new aeronautical chart, keeping them out of the wind while holding the control stick between her knees. The new government flying chart even indicated terrain, with the mountains off to the north. The sea-level departure point showed green, then the chart turned brown with increased elevation. The color white, which designated below sea level, extended clear from the Salton Sea all the way down to Calexico/Mexicali on the southern border. But there would be some high country to fly over first. Distinct navigational checkpoints such as lakes, rivers, towns, and railroads were noted on the new flying charts, along with compass variation lines, making navigating over unfamiliar terrain easier than it had been with only a road map. The visibility was pretty good, and if she headed right for that mountain notch up ahead she ought to stay right on course.

It was amazing that nineteen airplanes could be headed from Santa Monica to San Bernardino only one or two minutes apart, and she could see only a couple of them in the closest proximity. Barnes's position was worrisome. Should Crosson be farther north where Barnes was? Was she not compensating for drift from a northerly wind? "C'mon, Marvel. Why do you jump to the conclusion right away that Pancho's on course and you're not? Let's have some self-confidence here. Poor ol' Pancho is losing time by being a mile north of the course. That's it. I'm right on."

Pancho Barnes, who had taken off right behind Crosson, was

easing past her, then Louise Thaden did the same thing. Numbers two and four were passing her by. Those Travel Airs! Crosson was suddenly worried that she wasn't getting full power out of her engine. At least Blanche Noyes, in number three and also a Travel Air, had failed to gain on her. As Crosson looked back to see who might be coming up, she saw a Vega with number six on the side turning around. Amelia Earhart was headed back. "I wonder what her problem is," Crosson mused. She was holding altitude, so Crosson knew the engine must be okay. "I'd best pay attention to what I'm doing, and let Earhart take care of herself." She was slowly gaining on Thaden.

The light aircraft had taken off first, and with such a short distance there wasn't a lot of jockeying for position. The excited waiting crowd cheered as the light plane division's Phoebe Omlie arrived first at 2:32:15. The pack was pushing her.

Louise Thaden started descending smoothly for San Bernardino, speed increasing. She knew the swirling dust ahead had to mark the landing area. Her greatest fear was that someone else's mistake might cause her to lose time getting out of their way and going around. Everyone's nerves were as tight as a new corset. So far so good.

The men of the San Bernardino Exchange Club had gone so far as to paint an air marker for their important guests. After a noon luncheon at the California Hotel to plot and plan, the men had donned painters' caps, gathered up brushes, and with the help of the fire department, ascended to the roof of the Fox Court Street Theater. There, the men (whom the newspaper branded "alleged" painters) drew in twelve-foot-high aluminum-colored letters the

name SAN BERNARDINO, which would really put them on the
map. The names of air-marked towns were underlined on the new
aeronautical charts. Included in the air-mark sign was an arrow
pointing to the airport, another arrow pointing to magnetic north,
and a circle, indicating an airport at the end of the rainbow, or in this
case, in the direction of the arrow. A satisfied painter affirmed that
even "an aviator with the blind staggers couldn't miss it."

Aviators appreciated air-marked roofs for verifying their position,
along with towns that identified their water towers—except the
ones painted in the dark of night by teenagers glorifying their gradu-
ating class and said only "Senior Class of '27." Many an aviator had
dropped down to read a town's name on its water tower only to be
disappointed at high schoolers' handiwork.

The San Bernardino airport supporters took pride in Federal
Airport. Mr. R. H. Mack of the chamber of commerce pointed
out that the airfield was planted in grass, which would be sprin-
kled immediately prior to the first airplane's arrival. An on-site well
flowing one hundred inches of water was promised to ensure the
absence of dust.

Had the challenge to the sunbaked August turf been only nineteen
airplanes, Mr. Mack's promise could have been borne out. However,
excited citizens from town and adjacent communities flocked to see
the women aviators, driving onto the landing field and overwhelm-
ing the fragile new sod. As a result, swirling dust marked the landing
area better than any air marker.

Thaden could see that the uncontrolled crowds had left little room
for landing, driving their cars right up onto the field. The airplanes

were so close together that by the time someone landed and rolled out and off the center of the landing strip, the next plane that arrived had to maneuver to avoid overtaking the ship on the ground. Since no one wanted to pick up and go around in conflicting traffic with those being timed, there were some landings that were dangerously close. Pilots on the ground watching the show were impressed. These women knew what they were doing. They landed and got out of the way as fast as possible, both for their own safety and out of concern for their sister pilots. It was a dramatically staged ballet—until Opal Kunz arrived.

Kunz, the press always pointed out, was the socialite wife of Dr. George Frederick Kunz, a famous gemologist and vice president of Tiffany & Co. in New York City. She was also an outspoken feminist determined to work for equality within the pilot ranks. Though Kunz didn't favor war, she believed that "all women should learn to fly as a patriotic duty."

Within two weeks of receiving her pilot's license, Kunz suffered an engine failure, totaling her airplane in the ensuing emergency landing. She and her passenger, Verne Moon, emerged unscathed. The newspaper reporter could almost be heard to snicker in his description of Moon as "twenty-three, ex-sailor, who married a wealthy forty-six-year-old widow two years ago." As was so often the case in aviation, Moon was an "airport bum" who hung around the airport and who liked to ride in the airplanes. Quickly replacing her wrecked Travel Air, Kunz threw a formal affair at her hangar at which Mrs. Thomas Edison christened the new airplane.

Opal Kunz and Mrs. Thomas Edison

By the time Kunz landed at San Bernardino with Amelia Earhart right behind her, the visibility—due to the people, cars, and airplanes chewing up the sod—was terrible, despite the gallons of water poured on it. Opal couldn't see the exact landing area until she was right on top of it. She landed the airplane about ten feet above where she thought the ground to be and pancaked in, damaging the plane's undercarriage. If she could have laughed at that moment, she'd have remembered the old saying about botched landings: "It's the pilot's responsibility to periodically check the integrity of the landing gear." Later, Earhart overshot the appropriate touchdown spot, but the crowds parted at the end of the landing area, giving her adequate room to stop the airplane short of the fence. As it turned out, the damage to Kunz's Travel Air was confined to the shock absorbers, and the ship was repaired in time for the next morning's takeoff.

Bobbi Trout

Farther back in the pack, Bobbi Trout concentrated on her navigation—holding a heading, keeping the notch in the mountains beyond San Bernardino in the same perspective, and staying exactly parallel to the mountains to the north.

Trout had inaugurated 1929 by flying R. O. Bone's Golden Eagle monoplane into the record books. She had been demonstrating the airplane for the factory when Mr. Bone asked if she could fly it for twelve hours to beat Viola Gentry's eight-hour endurance record. Of course she could. Trout beat the sun up on January 2, 1929, staying aloft for twelve hours and eleven minutes. That meant landing after dark, her first night landing, giving Trout the longest night flight by a woman to that date as well. Trout was eighteen.

The spunky aviator was a media dream, always cheerful and had the gift of gab. The May Company department store in the Los Angeles area had lifted Trout's airplane to their roof for an aviation exhibit. The exposure for Trout and the store was immense. Reporters loved it that Trout operated a filling station to finance her flying, and they knew that she was always a good story.

The weather to San Bernardino was hot and clear with good visibility. As Trout passed over the little town of Montebello, she saw an airplane on the ground—it seemed to be taxiing back to the end of the pasture for takeoff. She wondered who had a mechanical problem.

Trout knew from her time, speed, and distance computations that she was coming up on San Bernardino. Everyone would be making a fly-by at the time clock, then fly a traffic pattern for landing. The racers were excited, but they would still have to stay alert to any nearby airplanes. Trout could see a field of dust dead ahead, and knew it must be the airport. Two dry lightning-set forest fires added to the lowered visibility. She opted for a powered descent so she'd lose no time in a glide. "Come on, sweet and steady. Keep the air speed up until we're past the time clock," she said to herself.

Bobbi knew the popular saying that a good pilot has a skinny neck, and she kept her head swiveling, looking for other aircraft. Even in that great big sky, two airplanes had been known to try to occupy the same space at the same time, and there were nineteen competing airplanes of fairly similar speed that seemed to form clusters and did not have the time to spread out.

It was still "each pilot for herself." The era of help from the ground in the form of another pair of eyes on radar was far in the future. Each pilot was responsible for everything—navigating, separating from other aircraft, keeping an eye out for emergency landing fields, and even resolving her own mechanical problems. There was no Little Miss Helpless to be found among this pilot corps.

"Well, nice of them to mark the airfield with a dust cloud so we can find it," mused Trout. She saw an airplane directly in front of her and hoped that made her second in line, since she couldn't see much else. The time clock was supposed to be at the approach end of the runway, and she dove for it to get as much speed as she could. In fact, the timers were positioned as advertised. The instant the propeller crossed the finish line, the first official signaled the second one with the watch, who noted the official arrival time to be forwarded to the chief timer. After crossing the line, Trout pulled up into a sweeping, climbing turn to come around and land, tracing a delicate curve in the sky.

Mary Von Mach was a Travel Air pilot, serene and cautious. Her mother's name, Mary Ann, was painted on the fuselage beneath the cockpit so that she could be with her daughter in spirit across the entire country.

Von Mach was the pilot Trout had seen on the ground near the little town of Montebello. The start of the race had drawn a few immature male show-offs who departed immediately prior to the women then lingered in the air ready to "escort" the racers on their way. Von Mach, one of the least experienced of the racers, had been a chance selection for the harassment. When a curious and reckless stunt pilot nearly hit Von Mach while buzzing her Travel Air, no way would she fight, but instead ran. The fellow decided that a little dog fight was in order, but Von Mach would have none of it. She chose to land the airplane, reasoning rightly that her tormentor would lose interest. It was a shame to lose time on the clock over such nonsense, but Von Mach was flying the race for experience and the joy of flying, never really counting on being in contention.

Von Mach was last to land at San Bernardino, along with Amelia Earhart, who had returned to Clover Field for a second start after a quick repair. The pilots gathered, giddy with relief to have the first leg safely behind them, then disappointed to learn that they couldn't supervise their aircraft refueling. For some reason, the fuel trucks wouldn't be out until midnight.

Edith Foltz models her famous Folzup suit.

The four thousand San Bernardino spectators couldn't get enough of the female racers—their airplanes, their hairstyles, their clothing. Edith Foltz was the clotheshorse of the group. She had designed and trademarked her lavender Folzup suit, a flying outfit that quickly converted to streetwear. The skirt pulled up and became a jacket, and knickers were worn beneath for climbing into the cockpit. Her unusual airplane and garb attracted a lot of attention. That is, until Barnes upstaged Foltz by lighting up her overpowering black cigar.

Many of the racers carried their own stopwatch and compared numbers with the official timers and each other. Several pilots had to admit that they'd been so excited that they'd forgotten to punch time on at the start. Unofficially, it looked like Phoebe Omlie was heading up the light plane class at thirty-two minutes, with Bobbi Trout about four minutes behind her. Chubbie Keith-Miller had wandered around for over an hour before landing at San Bernardino. Pancho Barnes and Louise Thaden were neck-in-neck in the heavies, within less than a minute between each other. Gladys O'Donnell and Marvel Crosson were just two minutes behind, and could easily move on up in the standings another day. All four were under thirty minutes. The leaders were happy, but they were quite aware that anything could still happen.

SUNDAY, AUGUST 18, 1929

Race Day 1

EVENING, SAN BERNARDINO

The "she derby" got off the ground and away in the air, and what is humorously referred to as the stronger sex went back to the kitchen sink and the radio. The husbands left by motor to go ahead and prepare proper food for their wives in each town. I tried to find a mother in the outfit. There was so many Mrs. I thought I might find one wayward soul. But all had no time for maternal worries. They had given their lives to the carburetors.

Yours, Will Rogers

Syndicated newspaper column

After cleaning up their aircraft and spending a few minutes with their sponsors, husbands, and mechanics (sometimes all three were the same person), the competitors were whisked off to what was to become the toughest part of the race—the banquets.

Their San Bernardino hosts would provide what was to become standard hospitality each evening of the race. The excited locals entertained their guests with a formal banquet, complete with fresh flowers and formal attire, though there seemed to be some unspoken rule at each stop that the entrée had to be chicken. To save weight, the racers didn't carry many clothes, pulling out their one wrinkled, dress-up frock for a long evening of dining, speeches, and small talk with their hosts. The evenings dragged on—first speeches and entertainment, then in San Bernardino, a movie titled *The Flying Fool*, starring the flying of their comrade Pancho Barnes. Barnes facetiously denied that the title referred to her, while her cohorts applauded loudly, proud of Barnes's success in the movies.

It was past midnight before the contestants finally met to discuss the next day's events. The racers unanimously agreed that the evening entertainment combined with the late-night pilot meetings then a predawn wakeup call was excessively brutal. Without adequate rest, their sleep debt would compound.

Monday's route would be 144 miles to Calexico for a stop, then another 204 miles to Phoenix for the night. The racers who had flown the course backward en route to the start in Santa Monica were concerned about the Calexico stop. They thought the airfield was too short for the heavier aircraft. It was an unnecessarily danger-ous stop when Yuma was an easy and close substitute. Barnes, whose plane was one of the heavies, led the revolt, demanding that Yuma be substituted for Calexico. Their hastily prepared petition read: "We, the undersigned, pilots in the Women's Air Derby, hereby declare we will go not farther than this point (San Bernardino) unless routed by or through Yuma instead of Calexico."

The women also drafted and signed a second petition allowing Mary Haizlip to compete, despite the delay waiting for her airplane in Santa Monica. The petition, dated August 19, read: "We, the undersigned pilots of the Women's Air Derby from Santa Monica to Cleveland do hereby wholeheartedly consent to the entrance of May Haizlys (sic) in this event, her start to be made this date from Santa Monica." They either didn't consider that the timers had already left Santa Monica or just decided to let the race officials work that out.

Their insistence was supported in part by anger that they had not been furnished with a definite routing until a few hours before takeoff. Some had already arranged for fuel in Yuma, and Thea Rasche had forwarded aircraft parts to Yuma, believing the race would stop there.

At 2:00 a.m., local race committee chairman Dr. L. W. Ayers flatly refused to allow any deviation from course and announced that those so doing would be disqualified. The final authority, Floyd Logan, the air race chairman in Cleveland, had cleverly left his telephone off the hook. It looked like a showdown until someone eventually roused him. Logan allowed the pilots a compromise. The en route landing could be in Yuma, but all racers were required to fly over and be identified at Calexico. At 2:30 a.m., the racers finally went to bed for two hours' sleep in anticipation of their 6:00 a.m. departure. Some stayed up even later reworking their charts.

Petition to allow Mary Haizlip to compete in the derby.

Only the *Daily Sun* reporters got less sleep than the pilots. Their impressions filled the front page of Monday's paper:

> In the light plane class, Bobbi Trout, a trim young girl with a daredevil look in her eye, finished second in an elapsed time of thirty-six minutes and twenty-three seconds. Mrs. Keith-Miller, flying a Fleet plane in the light class, completely lost her bearings near the end of her jaunt and went clear to Redlands before she discovered her mistake. She could have made it about as quickly in an automobile.

Actually, Redlands was only a ten-mile overshoot. Chubbie Keith-Miller had either wandered further than that, wasn't flying with full power, or had a really slow airplane—or she wasn't volunteering exactly where she'd been. She'd averaged fifty-six miles per hour. By comparison, Bobbi Trout had made good at 113 miles per hour.

> Amelia Earhart, flying a big Lockheed monoplane, finished eleventh (sic) in an elapsed time of forty-three minutes flat. Amelia, sometimes known as the "Lady Lindy," had a lot of hard luck at the start, and had to turn back to Clover Field soon after the takeoff because of motor trouble. She furnished another thrill when she overshot the runway in landing, causing the crowds to jump hither and yon looking for something to crawl under.

Opal Kunz pancaked her ship about ten feet above the ground and crashed, wrecking the undercarriage. But Miss Kunz' mishap brought out some of the prettiest flying feats seen during the afternoon. Coming into the field directly behind Miss Kunz when the accident occurred was Miss Neva Paris of Great Neck, New York in a Curtiss Robin Challenger plane. Miss Kunz' plane bogged down right in the middle of the runway, and, swerving her ship, Miss Paris came in diagonally at high speed and managed to set her craft down perfectly, despite the handicap.

Women may be fliers, but they're just women after all. This was conclusively demonstrated yesterday as one by one the pilots landed and were summoned to have their pictures taken. "Just a minute," was the invariable response. Then out came compact boxes and lipsticks and only after their application would the girls consent to face the camera.

"This is the first real test of women's ability to fly," said pretty Ruth Elder, who tried to fly the Atlantic, fell into the ocean and later into the movies.

The women rejected being lumped together, insisting that Ruth Elder was the compact queen.

The en route press coverage was colorful and as accurate as could be expected on the fly. Reporters didn't necessarily know much about airplanes, especially with women flying them. The racers learned to count on and look forward to Will Rogers's daily national column to relate their adventure in his down-home humor, with a true understanding of their mission and appreciation for their quest to be considered serious aviators. Rogers could skewer the politicians in his sly hillbilly style and simultaneously support aviation and the pilots he admired. The women were glad he and Wiley Post were along with them, and treasured their friendship.

Amelia Earhart and Mary Von Mach were well down in the standings the first day due to their unplanned stops en route. Neva Paris and Vera Dawn Walker had not made good time in their Curtiss Robins. The Robins had already revealed themselves as slow airplanes, and Paris and Walker were to lag throughout the race.

Vera Dawn Walker

Tiny Vera Dawn Walker had been working in the movies as an extra and a stand-in for Tom Mix. The cowboy actor loved flying and talked her into going for an airplane ride, leaving her amazed that she loved it. Walker became determined to learn to fly. She finally found a flight school that would take on an under-one-hundred-pound, four-foot-eleven-inch student, only upon her guarantee to release them of all liability. She heard about and signed up for the air derby as a pilot with eight months' experience.

Movie mogul Howard Hughes encouraged Walker to fly, but he agreed that she needed more flying hours before taking on a cross-country race. She was already working two jobs, one in the movies and one selling real estate, to pay for her flying. Hughes supported her successful search for a company to give her a little experimental "racing job" in which she could both prefly the race and gain some experience.

Howard Hughes (left) and Roscoe Turner

Total logged flying hours were a strong indicator of flying knowledge, though the definition varied. Some pilots spent a lot of time in the traffic pattern, doing what the Brits colorfully called circuits and bumps. It meant going 'round and 'round the airport practicing takeoffs and landings. Other pilots logged more flying hours actually going somewhere—learning navigation, terrain, weather, and density altitude firsthand. Obviously, the latter would prove important in the Women's Air Derby, and Walker's aviation mentors saw that she was as well prepared as her limited flying time allowed.

Walker's little borrowed racer proved unreliable while she was building flying hours prior to the air derby. Engine trouble led to a forced landing on unsuitable terrain. The only flat surface within gliding distance as the engine gave up the ghost was soft sand, where she dug in, nosed over, and broke three ribs—hers, not the airplane's. She would fly the race with her ribs taped—shades of Chuck Yeager who years later broke the sound barrier with ribs taped.

Walker's fabric and wood airplane had been quickly repaired, as was often the case in 1929, and she hurried to be ready for the start of the race. Her troubles were compounded when her repaired airplane didn't pass inspection at the start. It was not legally airworthy. The Curtiss-Wright Corporation was holding a competition to select a pilot to sponsor. Walker hurriedly competed against a dozen other girls flying a much bigger ship than she was used to and prevailed. She was awarded a Curtiss Robin in which to race the air derby. The company included the required parachute, with Walker learning later that the oversized chute was usually reserved for Charles Lindbergh. In her spirited fashion, the pint-size pilot displayed gallon-size guts.

Two sets of race timers flew the route also, leap-frogging to keep ahead of the competitors. Just as soon as all the race airplanes were off in Santa Monica, those timers jumped into a race official's airplane headed straight for Calexico, skipping San Bernardino. Wiley Post and Will Rogers carried a load of racers' luggage to Cleveland, but their primary task was to pick up the San Bernardino timers and deliver them to Yuma after the last airplane departed their first race stop, then on to Douglas while the first group timed Phoenix, and so on. The timer airplanes could stay ahead of the racers since they could fly direct, without the interim stop. Since the racers departed each new day (except the last) in the reverse order of their arrival, it kept them closely bunched, convenient for the timers, press, and arrival crowds. This method of timing explained why racers who fell behind but elected to finish the race anyway, went on untimed. The timers had to keep moving and couldn't wait for stragglers.

The press at San Bernardino mobbed Phoebe Omlie and Pancho Barnes, leaders in their respective classes. Omlie was quoted as saying, "Just before I reached the line, I nosed my plane down with the motor wide open. I was hitting about 130 miles per hour, I believe."

A happy Barnes said, "It's some feeling to have arrived first. I'm sure glad my 'whoopee' made such good time. From the time I hopped off at Clover Field until I arrived here, I never saw any of the other contestants, and here's hoping I get to Cleveland in the same position." To add to the festivities at San Bernardino, a squadron of army airplanes from March Field demonstrated military maneuvers. A powerful broadcast system with microphones at the finish line and amplifiers strategically placed kept the crowds informed.

~

In the skies elsewhere, the giant airship *Graf Zeppelin*, with its forty crew members and twenty passengers, was floating silently over the islands of Japan six hundred miles from Tokyo, moving steadily toward its immediate destination. It was on an around-the-world flight from and to Germany, the Cleveland Air Races a must-stop on the itinerary. The Kamui Lighthouse on the southwest coast of Hokkaido Island radioed weather conditions of fog and rain as the *Graf* altered course due to the weather, continuing at sixty miles per hour. The *Zeppelin's* dogleg passage over the Tartar Straits was necessary to avoid the Manchuria district with Russian and Chinese troops engaged in battle. The citizens of Tokyo grasped at any news of the great German dirigible's imminent arrival.

Although the *Graf's* aerodynamic engineering was imperfect, that didn't interfere with the purpose of the world flight that generated intense public interest, including that of bankers who agreed to finance four more dirigibles. The plan was to run two ships each way across the Atlantic weekly carrying mail and freight. The Goodyear-Zeppelin partnership planned to later run ships across the Pacific to Hawaii and the Philippines.

There was other world news: the bullish stock market was soaring to new price records with "steel, communications, and chemical shares raging unchecked." From the Holy Land: "Thirty-eight were killed in rioting over worship at the Wailing Wall." The women's accomplishments were news, but the world did not hold still.

FIRST LEG STANDINGS
SANTA MONICA TO SAN BERNARDINO, 68 MILES

Light Planes

RACE #	CONTESTANT	ELAPSED TIME	AIRCRAFT & ENGINE
8	Phoebe Omlie	32:15	Monocoupe, Warner
100	Bobbi Trout	36:23	Golden Eagle, Kinner
54	Claire Fahy	44:11	Travel Air, OX5
61	Thea Rasche	46:30	Gypsy Moth, DH Gypsy
109	Edith Foltz	52:55	Eaglerock, Kinner
43	Chubbie Keith-Miller	1:12:59	Fleet, Kinner K5

Heavy Planes

RACE #	CONTESTANT	ELAPSED TIME	AIRCRAFT & ENGINE
2	Pancho Barnes	27:21	Travel Air, Wright J5
4	Louise Thaden	27:50	Travel Air, Wright J5

RACE #	CONTESTANT	ELAPSED TIME	AIRCRAFT & ENGINE
105	Gladys O'Donnell	25:19	Waco 10, Wright, J5
1	Marvel Crosson	29:23	Travel Air, Wright J5
3	Blanche Noyes	31:15	Travel Air, Wright J5
16	Ruth Nichols	32:50	Rearwin, Ken-Royce
66	Ruth Elder	34:40	Swallow, Wright J5
18	Opal Kunz	38:36	Travel Air, Challenger
11	Margaret Perry	40:19	Spartan, Wright J5
23	Neva Paris	41:22	Curtiss Robin, Chlnger
6	Amelia Earhart	43:00	Lockheed Vega, Wrt J5
113	Vera Dawn Walker	51:04	Curtiss Robin, Chlnger
5	Mary Von Mach	not available	Travel Air, Wright J5
76	Mary Haizlip	not yet started	Amer Eagle, Phantom J6

MONDAY, AUGUST 19, 1929

Race Day 2

SAN BERNARDINO TO CALEXICO TO YUMA
220 MILES, 165 MILES

Biggest news in the papers today was that
Colonel Lindbergh had won the horseshoe
pitching contest out in the Black Hills of
Virginia, at Camp Hoover. What's the matter
with this country when an aviator can walk off
with a horseshoe pitching test? Is there no limit
to this man's cleverness?

Yours, Will Rogers
Syndicated newspaper column

As the women arrived at the airport predawn, people were already out, wiping bugs off wing leading edges and the last traces of oil that had collected under the planes' dirty bellies. Many were unknown to the racers, simply citizens who wanted to be helpful and were curious about the race. The women were wary about men helping them and were a little embarrassed about their ambivalence toward their generous volunteers. They wanted to make a statement of their own and resented the hurdles the other sex created for women in aviation. They began talking of meeting at Cleveland following the race and forming some sort of organization for women pilots so they could network for jobs.

Takeoffs that morning were in reverse order of the previous day's landings, putting Vera Dawn Walker off first and Phoebe Omlie last. Louise Thaden was only twenty-nine seconds behind Pancho Barnes. Those Travel Airs were the ships to have! Today's legs were much longer than the day before, and the group would undoubtedly spread out more.

Some racers were fueling out of their personal supply of the new Shell aviation gasoline. The U.S. Army was experimenting with assorted gasolines. For some time, pistons stressed for higher compression had increased airspeed by boosting horsepower, but the pistons quickly burned out. The army learned that the Pennsylvania gasolines were high in paraffin content with a low knock rating that burned pistons rapidly. The California gasolines, high in aromatics, had a high knock rating, and they were kinder to higher-compressioned pistons. A few racers were lucky enough to have some of the new Shell California 100 octane aviation gasoline shipped to each air derby stop.

Ruth Elder came over to Louise Thaden in an agitated state. "Those so-called mechanics they so kindly provided for us might delay my takeoff indefinitely," she said.

"What's happened?" Thaden asked, as she looked over at Elder's two-place open-cockpit biwing Swallow. Mechanics were draining its fuel tanks.

"They put five gallons of oil in the gas tank. Those guys are either terminally stupid or brain-dead." Elder was too irritated to stand still and stomped over to the next racer to vent her anger.

Thaden immediately thought of Thea Rasche's warning of sabotage. But it couldn't be. Had it been intentional? Probably not. Anyone would know the pilot would check the fuel and catch the discrepancy. Still, everyone was a bit paranoid. Some women didn't know who to doubt more—men or each other. Thaden reloaded her small overnight bag along with her required food supply. She had chosen to bring malted milk tablets and beef jerky.

A crowd was gathering around Edith Foltz's Alexander Bullet. The plane's appearance was quite radical alongside the other aircraft in the lineup. Few people had seen a low-wing ship like hers, with the landing gear actually retracted up into the wings after takeoff. Some folks looked askance at such a different airplane, but there was no doubt of its speed. The factory had had serious flat spin problems in their test program, giving the airplane a questionable safety reputation. An airplane spinning with the nose pointed down was almost always in a recoverable maneuver. However, when the Bullet got into a flat or horizontal spin, as a toy top spins, sometimes the pilot could not get the spin to stop and the airplane "spun in," or spun to the ground. In fact, the Bullet had not yet been awarded a type certificate by the government and was in the experimental category. (This model aircraft never did receive a standard certificate, which restricted its use. In defense of the Bullet, its design was innovative and progressive—a major step forward in aeronautical engineering.)

Edith Foltz poses with her plane.

Thaden carefully and contentedly preflighted (inspected) her beautiful blue and gold Travel Air nearby. She confided her euphoria about her splendid airplane to a reporter: "I'm going to get every last bit of speed out of this jewel and navigate with perfect precision over the rough terrain we have ahead. Being here to race with these women is the happiest time of my life."

Vera Dawn Walker cranked up to taxi first for takeoff after the six light planes were in the air. As Opal Kunz climbed into the high cockpit and prepared to race, she waved to Ruth Elder in her Swallow, whom she would follow on takeoff. Elder's engine appeared to be running smoothly in spite of its "oil-down." Louise Thaden S-turned carefully to see where she was going and joined the line of racers. There was no sense taxiing into a hole and damaging the prop.

The starter finally flagged Thaden into position, and she concentrated on her course out of San Bernardino. She kept the 120-degree heading in mind and checked her few instruments as she listened attentively to her engine, always attuned to any signal that it was not working well. In takeoff position, Thaden held the brakes while starting to add power, but she did not throttle up to full power, which would stir up rocks and damage the prop. If the timing was right, she would achieve full power just as the flag fell. The flag dropped, and Thaden was on the roll for Calexico.

At six o'clock in the morning the air was smooth, and Thaden had decided to take the direct route to Calexico rather than fly through Banning Pass and travel on the east side of the San Jacinto range where the valley was lower. Thaden was a good navigator and felt she could hold a steady heading just west of the San Jacinto, then the

Santa Rosa mountains until the high valley dropped off. She would then see the large Salton Sea, the now landlocked extension of the Sea of Cortez, to the east. From there she would simply hold a heading to Calexico/Mexicali. She wished they would put a big fence up on the Mexican border just so she could fly to the fence and turn left.

She started a long climb to seven thousand feet, an altitude necessary to clear the high valley terrain, while ever alert for engine overheating. Achieving altitude was always a struggle with the horsepower they had available, and the racers flew most of the route from five hundred to one thousand feet above the ground. The official schedule showed 144 statute miles to Calexico, then another 204 to Phoenix—which, of course, wasn't correct. The racers had had to scramble to redo their flight plans with the course change. Thaden's plan was to fly by the Calexico timing line, then to Yuma for fuel and to be timed. If she didn't wander, Phoenix should be just about three hours' flying time from San Bernardino.

Visibility was good, and Thaden could fly parallel to a road. She lifted her head above the cockpit so that she could see where she was going, then back down to look at the chart and compass to verify her heading. Even perched on the seat parachute beneath her, Thaden needed a cushion to sit high enough to see out without having to unstrap her seat belt every time she needed to observe the terrain beneath her. The road made a left turn off through Banning Pass as expected. She was right on course. She would snuggle up to the mountains on the left, and see the town of Hemet on her right. She had drawn a red course line on her chart, and as the preselected checkpoints, or prominent features on the ground, came along exactly as they appeared on the chart, her correct position was confirmed. After Hemet, the barren desert country wouldn't provide much to navigate by until the mountains slid into the Salton Sea, then it was downhill to Calexico. There would be one little bump at Superstition Mountains, a 759-foot hill as compared to 10,804-foot San Jacinto.

Louise Thaden with her plane.

Gazing down, Thaden was struck at the audacity of pioneers who had found their way through this vast country in covered wagons.

Imagine taking children on that quest. What brave souls were their mothers. Thaden imagined that if she went down in these tall foothills, it might be a long time before anyone found her. Bad thoughts, she chided herself. Her airplane was running well.

Even so early in the morning, a slight breeze from the west gave the racers a little lift on the windward side of the mountains. As the moving air encountered the mountain, resistance forced it up and over, just as breakers act on ocean waves. Soaring with the help of the natural lift gave low-powered planes a boost. Thaden barely outclimbed the terrain without having to circle and lose time, and at seven thousand feet, she almost rolled her wheels on the sugar pines below at the high point. In another twenty miles the terrain lowered abruptly, the forest giving way to the rocky decline into the Mohave Desert. She wished she knew more about geology and what forces had made these mountains rise so high above the valley floor—and what caused the ground to tremble sometimes like a terrible miles-long dog shaking his wet fur.

While Thaden was making good time and staying exactly on course, several of the pilots flying the lower horsepower aircraft elected to fly on east through Banning Pass and head south on the eastern side of the mountains. The climb to clear terrain on the western slope in their underpowered airplanes meant they would have to circle, which would take too much time. Trading off the time to climb for a little extra distance would prove a good gamble. Those kinds of decisions were what racing was all about.

Claire Fahy was her husband's student. Learning to fly from a spouse was just as hard as having a relative driving instructor. A man's wife couldn't be just an average student pilot; after all, he'd married her, and she was smarter than the average pilot-to-be. The relationship between the student and instructor couldn't help but be personal rather than detached, putting stress into an already difficult classroom. Lieutenant Herbert Fahy was a Lockheed Aircraft Company test pilot and the holder of altitude and speed records. Claire learned well from her husband, but she couldn't possibly gain his experience level in the year she'd been flying. Though she loved the challenge of flying alone, Claire was glad that Herb was following close behind.

Claire Fahy

Claire Fahy was flying a Travel Air with the OX5 ninety-horsepower engine, putting her into the low horsepower, light aircraft class. Hers was a biwing open-cockpit airplane with a pair of upper and lower wings. The dope-tightened fabric wings were braced for strength with metal struts. Diagonal brace wires ran from the upper-wing outer edge to the lower-wing root, further intensifying the integrity of the wings. Rough air currents, acrobatics (especially when poorly executed), and hard landings all conspired to find the aircraft's weakness and pull it apart. The designers and manufacturers used all their knowledge to make their products strong, yet compromises were necessary to keep aircraft light enough to lift a load, the pilot, and fuel.

There was a sensory advantage in these open-cockpit airplanes, a oneness of pilot with wings, like a bird. Fahy had been taught to listen to the wind in the wires. As air flowed over and under the wings, vibration set up a humming in the wires whose voice changed with angle of attack, the relationship of the wing to the relative wind. As the airplane climbed or descended, the wires spoke differently, just as the hammer struck different tones from a piano wire. An experienced pilot used all her senses, including her ears, to know what was going on with the airplane.

When Fahy heard a sharp "twang," she knew it was trouble. Her heart thumped as she saw two separated wing wires dangling back sickeningly in the wind. She had no idea how much extra strength had been built into the airplane or if her weakened wings would give up and fold back. Fahy thought of her parachute, but she immediately rejected a jump from such a low altitude—she was only about five hundred feet above ground.

Fahy brought the power back, thinking to ease the pressure on the struts by slowing down. She started looking for any field on which to land, but with just a few miles to go to Calexico, went on. After her initial scare, anger took over. Wing wires don't just break. Someone must have sabotaged her airplane. Fahy eased on down for a landing while keeping a sharp eye out for her fellow racers flying the Calexico timing line. The first airplanes had commenced timing by shortly after 8:00 a.m., and Fahy's day was already bad enough without adding a midair collision if someone were in the vicinity. Instead of flying the timing line at Calexico and going on as the other racers did, Fahy landed.

She jumped out of the airplane as the engine died, and she was so agitated that she could hardly speak. Not expecting anyone to land, the timers knew something was wrong even before questioning her. Fahy anxiously examined the broken wires, then said, "You can see these wires have been eaten through with acid. My airplane has been sabotaged. Seeing the wires parted in the air made me wonder if I had any chance of landing in one piece. Who could do such a despicable thing?" She was near tears.

The stunned officials and onlookers couldn't believe the race planes could have been tampered with at either Santa Monica or San Bernardino. But here was evidence of serious trouble. Claire Fahy declared herself out of the race. When Fahy didn't show up at Yuma, her husband would come looking for her.

Mary Von Mach's Travel Air also made a stop at Calexico, but she went on. Mary Haizlip, who had a late start and was trying to catch up with the other racers, arrived in the Calexico area at dusk. The lights of the American city Calexico and Mexico's Mexicali ran together as one city, and in the fading light it was impossible to pick out the border from the sky. Haizlip became uneasy as she lost time searching for the airport, having trouble pulling it out of the haze. What a relief to finally spot an open area that had to be the airport.

Haizlip made a smooth approach over the end of the landing strip to be timed just at nightfall. She came around and landed, happy to be catching up with her fellow racers.

Only after landing did Haizlip realize she'd overshot her mark and was on the south side of the border in Mexicali on the Baja Peninsula. The Mexican officials were kind but firm that all the forms dealing with an improper incursion into Mexican airspace, and use of the Mexicali airport without permission, be completed in triplicate and stamped by the government representative. Several hours spent cutting red tape preceded Haizlip's short flight back across the border after dark, with explicit instructions on the location of the Calexico airport. After a night in Calexico, Mary Haizlip hastened to join her sister aviators who were still nearly a full day ahead of her.

Race Day 2

YUMA TO PHOENIX
158 MILES

It was a warm sultry night and Dr. Eckener of the *Zeppelin* didn't know if that still air would raise him high enough to get over the mountains, so Los Angeles had a banquet and twenty local townsmen spoke. They rushed from the dinner to the field and the ship raised so fast they had to throw fourteen typewriters and two radio announcers overboard to get it back to a flying level.

Yours, Will Rogers
Syndicated newspaper column

Marvel Crosson, never seen without a huge grin that spread to her luminous dark eyes, was in perfect position to see the Yuma airport. She just couldn't pick it out of the shadow. She suspected that all the racers were cutting across a tiny corner of Mexico as she was to save a few miles to Yuma. This desolate dune country was like the Sahara, requiring only a little wind to drift a blanket of sand across the fields, hiding any clue of the airport. For Crosson, the lack of differentiating color defining the terrain reminded her of flying in Alaska in the snowy winter. Crosson had learned not to become fixated on where she thought the landing field should be, but to keep her eyes moving, scanning a wider area.

Searching the ground, she caught what looked like the tail of an airplane rising awkwardly above the wings. Someone had either made a forced landing in a farmer's field or a troubled arrival at the Yuma Airport. Crosson gambled on the latter and headed for the crippled airplane. As she approached the field, Crosson could see people surrounding the airplane to bring the tail down and pull it out of the landing area. The airfield was low, only two hundred feet above sea level. It was pretty much a 160-acre square. She flew west to east across the field to be timed alongside a small building, then tear-dropped back around to land west, facing the building rather than coming in over it, or alongside, in burbling, difficult wind currents. With the whole field available and not constrained by a runway, Crosson could land directly into the wind.

Concentrate, she reminded herself. The windsock showed a strong wind shifting between the west and northwest. Crosson could feel the airplane wanting to drift south. She turned the nose into the wind to stop the drift, straightened out, and dropped the right wing to eliminate any side load on the landing gear. At the same time, she endeavored to land well short of the disabled plane. She took a small bounce, then the front wheels wanted to dig into the soft clay, risking the same fate as the wrecked aircraft. Crosson held the stick back into her gut to keep the tail down, wishing she had a load of bricks in the tail end to help. It was easy to see how the other pilot could have dug in and gone up on her nose. Crosson maintained some power to keep the airplane moving and to avoid bogging down. Then the accomplished pilot quickly taxied out of the way for the next aircraft.

The bent airplane had a number six on the tail—Amelia Earhart again. Earhart must be jinxed, Crosson thought. The man who flew to the West Coast with her was killed on his return east, Earhart had a jammed starter on the race takeoff and now some sort of problem in Yuma.

It turned out that Earhart had landed long, nosed the plane over, and broken the propeller, but there was no other serious damage to the Vega. She called to have another prop flown in from Los Angeles, and the other pilots, in an unnecessary but quite feminine act, decided to wait with Earhart until her airplane was repaired. Earhart's accident occurred around 8:00 a.m., and as they arrived, the women lounged in the only shade they could find—under their airplane wings—as the temperature quickly climbed to over one hundred degrees. The kind people of Yuma went home to bring cold drinks, sandwiches, and ice as the women roasted in the intensifying heat. They finally flew out around noon when Earhart's new prop was on, little suspecting that their act of support for Earhart was to have disastrous consequences.

Meanwhile, Pancho Barnes was following the pilot's friend, the iron compass—railroad tracks. The men who laid the tracks naturally ran them from town to town, where the freight and passengers needed to travel.

Pilots flying over desolate country depended upon the iron compass when nothing else was available to navigate by, or even as a backup to verify position. However, often multiple tracks left a town in several close directions, and it was always possible to take the wrong set of tracks. When the only navigational aid was a highway map—and the next town came up on the wrong side of the tracks or a lake ran north and south instead of east and west—it was easy to convince oneself that the mapmaker had just made a couple of errors. The tracks had to be right. Since self-doubt was not in an aviator's genes, even the most experienced pilot could fly far down the wrong track before admitting to personal error. The pilots all agreed that they were never lost, simply momentarily disoriented.

Pancho Barnes

Sure enough, Barnes was unknowingly following the wrong set of railroad tracks across the desolate country into Mexico. Totally disoriented with nothing but cacti and alkalized desert scrub below, Barnes searched for any kind of definitive landmark. Her compass was bouncing like a rubber ball, but the averaged heading didn't seem right. Was she north of course or south? Which way should she turn? Should she hold her present course and hope for a water tower with a name on it? When Barnes spotted a homestead, she instantaneously slowed her throttle to descend. The desert would make for a rough landing field, but she needed to find out where she was and not throw away her lead in the race. Later, she related her landing and reception. "When I raised the nose for landing and dropped into a pasture among some disinterested steers, the dust was so thick I could hardly see to dodge the sagebrush. I spotted a homestead and taxied over that way." Barnes gained the locals' attention, but she would have had a tough time understanding them. "When they got close enough that I could hear them, they were yelling, 'Hola! Hola!' Hell, that's Spanish. I wheeled that air machine around, goosed the throttle, and got outta there."

As it turned out, Barnes, and Mary Haizlip before her, were not the only visitors to Mexico that day.

The ladies' delayed afternoon flight from Yuma to Phoenix combined with all the worst conditions from Mother Nature's repertory. The extreme heat bred thermals that lifted from the desert floor creating a roiling sea of air, its waves unapparent until they buffeted the airplane. The now 120-degree temperature was debilitating, and the air so rough that Louise Thaden seriously questioned if her airplane could possibly stay together. In clear air, Thaden ran full speed into invisible severe turbulence. She felt like batter in an eggbeater that first churned her then spat her out. *Bang, twist, slam, sink.* Her plane repeatedly slammed the invisible thermal walls. At that moment, Walter Beech was God, and her fate was in his hands. If the airplane Beech provided was strong enough to withstand the beating it was taking—the sudden wild ride up followed by stomach wrenching descent—it could withstand any maneuver a mere pilot could inflict upon it.

Even with her seat belt cinched tightly, Thaden lifted almost completely out of the cockpit. She struck her head on the windscreen, shattering her flying goggles and then, regaining her senses, flew into a momentary calm. The worst was anticipating the next hit. When it came, ugly waves of terror washed over Thaden's soul, depositing globules of fright. Then the next wave rolled in, and another. A reservoir of courage and pride, mixed with that measure of fear, begat tenacity. Thaden set the fear aside and went on. A mist of engine oil bathed her sweaty clothes and exposed skin, adding filth to her miseries of soreness and exhaustion. Thaden was not alone in this inferno. Nineteen other pilots clung to their determination. Thaden and many others later said that they spoke to God about their wish to make it to Phoenix.

Despite the time clock's inexorable progress, some racers would likely have landed had there been a decent spot to do so. There seemed to be no alternative to riding it out. There was nothing below but desert, sand, low hills, scrub brush, and wind. The choice between the almost certain disaster of landing in that inhospitable terrain and remaining in the hellish air persuaded the pilots to go on…except for Ruth Elder.

Tired and frightened, the starlet pilot opened her map wider to search for some sort of checkpoint. The wind grabbed the map from her hands and sent it on its own flight over the side. Exhausted by the rough ride and completely lost, Elder decided to take a chance with the terrain. She became obsessed with parking and getting to her water to both drink and pour over her head. She found a pasture near a ranch house pretty much into the wind and put her Swallow down. Careful, easy, wing down, straighten the nose, stick back, success!

As luck would have it, she had picked a field with grazing bulls. Suddenly, all Elder could think about was the red color of her airplane. Fortunately, the ranch wife working at her washtub outside took a woman pilot dropping in from the sky in stride. She marched over to the airplane and oriented Elder in short order. Elder was disturbing the cattle. Ranchers don't want their herds dispersed, losing weight, and scattered in uncertain directions through broken fences. The Hollywood pilot was entirely out of her element. She never shut the engine down. Forget the water; she swung the tail around and was on her way. Elder's encounter with the bulls became one of the classic, and most embellished, tales of the derby.

Ruth Elder shakes hands with her instructor George P. Haldeman.

When the main body of racers departed Yuma, Claire Fahy, Bobbi Trout, and Thea Rasche had not yet arrived. All were known to have departed San Bernardino. The consensus was that their fuel was exhausted, and they were on the ground somewhere.

German pilot Thea Rasche drew special attention from a fascinated public due to her connection, by nationality, with Germany's giant dirigible *Graf Zeppelin*. As Rasche flew alone in her fragile aircraft toward Cleveland, the *Graf*, with its crew of forty, silently proceeded around the world toward the same destination in Ohio. Rasche was determined to uphold her country's honor.

Thea Rasche

Thea had learned to fly in 1924 in Germany, becoming the country's first female aerobatic pilot. She became a popular and well-known figure in the United States when she came over to fly air shows. It was not a surprise that the Moth Aircraft Corporation asked Rasche to represent them by flying a Gypsy-Moth airplane in the air derby. She was pleased to do so.

Rasche's sponsorship by Moth Aircraft became somewhat muddled when their promised racing plane was not ready on time. Instead, she took loan of an older two-place open-cockpit Gypsy-Moth biplane, which had a hole in the fuel tank. The airplane was repaired so hurriedly that there wasn't even time for a test flight before the start of the race.

Just out of Calexico, Rasche had experienced intermittent engine problems, then total stoppage. She made an emergency landing near Holtville, California, that damaged her airplane. The locals were intrigued with this woman pilot and her German accent, and they were certainly sympathetic to her problems. They were outraged that she'd be assigned such a mechanically deficient airplane from the factory. After repairs were accomplished, Rasche proceeded on to Fly Field in Yuma the next day with the following document. It had been drafted by a mechanic and the sympathetic bystanders who were suddenly her friends and supporters.

We the undersigned were present when Miss Thea Rasche was forced to land at the Thiesen ranch near Holtville and saw her take off gasoline clarifier which contained scraps of rubber, fibre, and many other impurities. I also examined the gas tanks and found them both to have plenty of gasoline but the gas line had some obstruction in it that refused to let the flow come thru. I picked up the pieces of sediment from the clarifier and found them to be the same as stated above. The engine had been missing sometime and finally went dead altogether which sounded like lack of gasoline to me.

Signed, Gilbert Morgan, and
three other witnesses

Rasche suspected foul play. She told of the telegram from New York about her experience, the warning of sabotage, and also pointed out that her airplane had not been guarded in San Bernardino. However, it was entirely possible that a careless fuel cell repair could have left foreign objects in the tank.

Lieutenant Herbert Fahy's airplane arrived in Yuma the next day along with a disappointed Claire Fahy. Adding to the string of mishaps, the wheel of the plane struck the edge of a concrete marker in the middle of the landing field, smashing the landing gear and a wing.

The pall put on the competition due to Claire's broken brace wires continued. Herb stated publicly, "The wires show evidence of being burned with acid. I am convinced that there is something rotten in this race. I'll do everything in my power to have it called off."

Bobbi Trout, though missing, was within sight of Yuma, but piled up in another country. Like Crosson, and probably all the other racers, Trout had taken the shortcut across the corner of Mexico heading for the Yuma Airport. Her new Kinner engine had been cutting out, and within six miles of Yuma, it quit. She was too far out to glide to the airport. Trout looked for a smooth landing site, thinking she'd clear some dirt out of the carburetor and be on her way.

She glided her open-cockpit Spartan to a promising-looking field, which turned out to be near the town of Algadones on the Mexican border. Too late to change her course, she realized she'd be landing across deep, plowed furrows. When the wheels struck the furrows, the beautiful Golden Eagle came to rest on its back. Trout had run out of gas, but now she had a more severe problem.

Trout's factory support came to her rescue in Mexico, but it was three days before the airplane was flyable again. Mechanics partially repaired it out in the field. Trout marshaled a team to tow the airplane across the border to the Yuma airport where it was hastily rebuilt. Trout's family came to lend their support during the repair, then she continued the race. Though breaking in a new engine, three days behind, and with no timers left to time her, Trout was determined to fly to the finish line—much to the satisfaction of her fellow racers and an admiring public.

By dark, seventeen race planes had landed at Sky Harbor Airport, a rectangular sod field on the outskirts of sleepy little Phoenix, a town waiting to blossom with the proliferation of air conditioning. All the missing airplanes were accounted for, except Marvel Crosson. Another racer had seen her not far past Yuma as they were coming up on the wild Gila Mountains country near Wellton, Arizona, then lost track of her. You couldn't miss Crosson's Travel Air with the big number one painted on the side. But where was she now? Nightfall ushered in its characteristic weariness and doubts. The beleaguered aviators had had a big day, but fatigued as they were, their anxiety for Crosson mounted, with speculation of the most hideous sort.

PACIFIC
OCEAN

DOUGLAS

TUESDAY, AUGUST 20, 1929

Race Day 3

PHOENIX TO DOUGLAS
208 MILES

The women's air derby started from right close to my shack, and Fred Stone and I were over to the field quite a bit. We met and had a long chat with this Marvel Crosson that was killed. We both talked at the time of what a fine wholesome type of girl she was, no riding boots or riding breeches or spurs or anything but just a neat gray suit. She had a great record as a flier.

Yours, Will Rogers
Syndicated newspaper column

While Marvel Crosson's friends and fellow competitors had been struggling with their awful fears for her safety, Crosson's body was resting in trackless backwoods, no longer suffering from the heat and turbulence of the air race. Crosson had fought off growing feelings of illness, determined that her will to fly the airplane was stronger than her malfunctioning body. Her nasty headache could be expected in such awful air, but soon her stomach joined the rebellion. She unfastened her seatbelt to rise and vomit over the side. Her world went gray as she leaned up and forward, and when she lost consciousness, the airplane responded to the airplane's center of gravity, moving forward as her body did, and without a pilot's hand on the stick, it plunged to the earth.

Anticipating the outcome of a story that was still only speculative, the newspaper front-page stories on the morning of August 20, 1929, read something like WOMAN FLYER REPORTED IN DESERT SMASH-UP.

The *Yuma Morning Sun* announced what the fliers had feared all night long:

While the eyes of an anxious nation are turned toward Wellton, Arizona, where the plane of Marvel Crosson, woman flier, crashed into a Mesquite jungle in the Gila River Valley yesterday afternoon, United States Department of Commerce agents last night launched an investigation of ugly charges that several of the airships had been deliberately tampered with to put them out of the woman's air derby.

The fliers, who had managed to get a little sleep, woke to the near certainty of Crosson's death. Louise Thaden and Gladys O'Donnell were particularly close to Crosson. They alternated tears with unfounded optimism. Crosson's friends gathered to share the rumors and newspaper reports generated during the night.

FOUND KILLED

Plunging from an altitude of over 2000 feet, Marvel Crosson, champ woman high flier, is believed to have dropped into a mesquite jungle on the north bank of the Gila river, about five miles from Wellton. Three eye-witnesses saw the plane go into a nose dive and a spin. Through the thin desert air, the faint sound of a crash reached them. Posts are now scoring the jungle.

**News of Marvel Crosson's death reached her
fellow pilots the next morning.**

Distraught, Louise Thaden read, "Several posses combed the dense thicket on the north bank of the Gila all last night seeking trace of the lost plane. Three witnesses saw it go into a nose dive yesterday afternoon and crash to the ground. The searchers are combing an area of one hundred square miles."

"Don't forget how unreliable witnesses are," Thaden added, unrealistically reminding the group.

Vera Dawn Walker commented, "The radio said four ranchers saw her flying at about two thousand feet, wobble in the air, then spin in. They said they could even hear the sound of the crash. That seems like a pretty detailed witness description to me. On the other hand, she was less than twenty minutes out of Yuma and two thousand feet seems pretty high."

Gladys O'Donnell had heard that four airplanes would be searching that morning since the dense riparian growth was impassable in many places. "Sometime last night the searchers had to abandon their horses and crawl on their hands and knees. They say this is the worst section in Arizona." O'Donnell added morosely, "There's even a report that the race will be halted at Phoenix until the investigation is completed."

Chubbie Keith-Miller and Amelia Earhart had shared a room the night of Crosson's death. They talked about public perceptions that if a male pilot were killed, it was just a sad part of the job. On the other hand, the death of a female pilot was not acceptable—the same reason women couldn't go to war. They agreed that the public would have to get used to the idea of women taking risks in the air.

Surprisingly, the gentle Mary Von Mach took a leadership role in rallying the distraught group.

"If I had crashed and were unable to go on, my worst nightmare would be that I had caused the race to stop," she said. "I would want my friends to honor me by carrying on my mission to prove the abilities of women pilots and the modern airplane. Would Marvel want us to mope around, wring our hands, and consider calling off the event? Oh, no. She would tell us to carry on where she left off." Von Mach paused, then, looking around at her friends, she added, "Our pain shall become her tribute."

Her companions were moved by the homage to their friend. The group came to consensus even without speaking. Their hearts went out to Crosson's brother Joe. The race would go on, each pilot more strongly dedicated than ever to fly well, compete fairly, and make a good showing for Crosson.

Von Mach called out, "Ladies, start your airplanes!" as they headed for the airport.

Mary Von Mach

Despite the anxiety and confusion over Crosson, the Phoenix RON proved an oasis—a fertile spot in the desert with cool shade trees and top-grade mechanical sustenance for their "steeds." After landing, the pilots had remained at Sky Harbor to clean plugs, wipe down engines and airplane surfaces, and change oil and fuel for the next leg. Policemen and Boy Scouts kept the friendly spectators away from the aircraft while essential tasks were accomplished.

Friendly people, a hot bath, and an extra two hours of sleep in a comfortable hotel rejuvenated the exhausted racers. The takeoff had been moved from 6:00 a.m. to 8:00 a.m., and those two hours meant everything. The women preflighted their ships, signed autographs, and responded carefully to reporters' questions. Only three days out, they had already fallen into a tempo and pattern. The women lined up to take off in reverse order of their arrivals. Their top standings, from Santa Monica to Phoenix, were led by Pancho Barnes in the heavy aircraft class, followed by Louise Thaden and Gladys O'Donnell. The leaders in the light class were fronted by Phoebe Omlie, with Edith Foltz and Chubbie Keith-Miller right behind her.

After the unbearable heat of the midday takeoff out of Yuma, everyone pressed to get airborne in Phoenix's cool morning air. The regular morning weather briefing—a dubious science at best—called for typical afternoon cloud buildups with increasing westerly winds, but the morning forecast predicted winds light and variable.

Phoenix's Sky Harbor Airport was just that, a safe harbor for roamers of the sky. Though Phoenix was hot in the summer, the air was clear and dry, and cool palm trees sheltered travelers. Most weather reports across the country did not report visibility greater than fifteen miles even when it existed, but Phoenix loved to casually brag, *Visibility, eighty miles*. Phoenix could just as well have been named Oasis.

Louise Thaden had studied her 208-mile course out of Phoenix into Douglas with its initial heading of 120 degrees. She strapped her small overnight suitcase into the two small front seats and settled into the aft cockpit. Amelia Earhart had generously offered to carry some of the women's larger suitcases.

Vera Dawn Walker unkindly remarked, "She needed the baggage for ballast. She really did. Amelia is really a grand sport, but there are dozens who can fly rings around her."

Thaden had nothing critical to say about Amelia Earhart. Earhart was always a meticulous flyer and cautious. She liked the limelight but never failed to promote all women pilots, and she was invariably flying something new, perhaps one step ahead of her current skill level. Wiley Post was carrying luggage for racers too, as were other officials flying the route.

The race director had cautioned the pilots to follow roads, railroads, and known landmarks and not try to dead reckon, that is apply computations of airspeed, course, heading, wind direction, ground speed, and elapsed time. Dead reckoning is a mathematical formula, and the old truism "Garbage in, garbage out" was genuine. Without accurate upper winds in the formula, dead reckoning can be an unreliable form of navigation. Nevertheless, Thaden was trying a combination of pilotage, keeping known landmarks in sight, and backing it up with dead reckoning. Once she left Phoenix, she kept the Superstition Mountains to the east and the low San Tan Mountains immediately west of course, skirting the tallest peak. She was coming out of relatively low country with the Phoenix area averaging about a thousand feet above sea level. Her direct course took her right into the mountain/desert country where she would need to detour the higher peaks. The sun was not yet high overhead, and it painted the eastern hills a peachy pink, with the western sides lightening from mossy green. God's crayon box contained at least five dollars' worth of different colors for the desert.

The visibility was good, making it easy to see Newman Peak, an isolated 4,500-foot hill and the road and railroad coming from the west leading into Tucson. Just north of Tucson, Thaden eased to the east of Mount Lemmon, which at nearly ten thousand feet was too high to overfly comfortably. She picked up the almost dry Santa Cruz River that led her down a nice, wide, high valley in the direction toward Douglas. Thaden's heart picked up the pace as she entered the high country. All pilots had learned to keep a constant lookout for good emergency landing fields, and the choices were slim in southeastern Arizona—no good pastures, no low-growing row crops, no wide roads, all good for off-airport landings. The only crop that seemed to be in good supply here was rocks.

Thaden verified her position by crossing the road and railroad southeast of Tucson, threading between Rincon Peak, at about eighty-five hundred feet, and Mount Fagan, just over six thousand feet. Both were coming up right where the chart said mountains that size were supposed to be. She aimed just to the east of what had to be Apache Peak poking up at seventy-eight hundred feet. The valley floor was generally about four thousand feet above sea level, which meant flying between forty-five hundred and five thousand feet mean sea level, five hundred to one thousand feet above the ground. These mountains all showed up "as advertised" by the chart, and in the right relationship to each other, giving Thaden confidence that her heading was valid.

Thaden idly thought it would be nice if some of those kids who climb water towers to write names would identify some of these mountain peaks with big white letters too. The light winds gave her the opportunity to gain a little altitude where she could see better and keep track of her bearings. By the time she went past Tucson, Thaden had pretty well established that holding approximately 130 degrees on the compass, when she wasn't detouring around a mountain, would bring her to Douglas. It would get easier. Everybody was nervous first entering the high country, but it would get less stressful with time.

Thaden finally had a road to follow as she flew over the old mining town of Tombstone. The road soon veered off to the right, threading through a pass in the Mule Mountains. She was close enough to the mountainside to see holes outlined in timber—old abandoned mines. She fully expected an ancient, bearded miner to wave to her from the door of his claim, a mule tied to a scrawny tree down his namesake hillside. She did spot a family of deer who gazed at her as she sped by, but they didn't seem concerned. Thaden wondered how many thousands of deer she had flown over but didn't possess the hunter's eyes to see. She kept the Mule Mountains to her west, then went on into Douglas and the Sulphur Springs Valley, a 4,150-foot airfield. Her trouble-free leg over the incredibly desolate American desert boosted her confidence, but not all the racers found that leg so easy. It was a day of forced landings in godforsaken places.

Vera Dawn Walker's only instrument, a compass, was not reliable, so she resolved to fly from one town to the next via the highway map rather than try to navigate with it. She had been advised that once over Tucson, she would see smoke from the smelters in Douglas and could follow the railroad tracks right to the airport. However, she took the wrong set of tracks heading east, the ones that were northeast instead of southeast. Finally realizing her mistake, Walker straggled into Douglas after backtracking a long way around the high Chiricah Mountains, the great circle route.

The tiny flyer later told the other racers, "I knew I was going the wrong direction when I saw those dry salt beds near Lordsburg, New Mexico. I said to myself that I'd better land while I can, so I did, and refueled at some isolated burg. I wasn't there three minutes before the entire town was at the strip crowding around my plane.

"I got started again and was going southwest this time towards Douglas when I hit this cumulus thunderstorm—it wasn't near anything. I fought with those controls, and battled that storm, and finally just dove to get out."

Walker had made a classic beginner's mistake. Seeing what she thought was an isolated summer shower, she skirted it too closely and found herself immediately drawn into the thunderstorm as it swelled. Even though she was in an enclosed cabin, the rain sounded like hail, and visibility no longer existed. With no reference outside because of the heavy rain, it would be impossible to maintain level flight without a horizon. Walker didn't know up from down, and the normal "seat of the pants" signals for right-side-up flight were gone.

Vera Dawn Walker

She explained, "I couldn't tell where in the world I was in that storm. I lost flying speed and, like I said, just dove to get out. The controls finally responded, or that would've been it for old Vera Dawn." When she fell out the bottom of the storm, or spun or spiraled out, she could see again and righted the airplane. She was lucky to be high enough to regain control before exploding into the earth.

"'Course I had to put the plane down in this cow pasture," (undoubtedly until she could breathe again), "and I did that all right, but I was surrounded by cattle. Y'know they'll eat the fabric right off your plane, so I had to stick with the plane."

Walker got that right. What beast could resist fabric impregnated with dope, a glue mixture. Dope dried on linen made for strong wings, and cows considered airplane fabric dessert. Any pilot who left her airplane alone in a pasture with cows would be looking at bare ribs when she returned. Then when old Bessie had her fill, she would lean up against the rudder and massage her back. The big scratching post would be bent up all over and naked if the pilot left it for long.

Walker's method for fending off the curious cows was to glare at them. "They just looked at me, and I stared at them until finally some man came walking by with Chubbie Keith-Miller—she'd crashed right nearby—and they got me out."

Walker had landed to regain her composure after her scare in the weather, and had plenty of fuel to go on. The men with Keith-Miller shooed the cows away for a clear path for Walker's takeoff. They directed her to Douglas.

Keith-Miller had run out of fuel and was down at Elfrida, Arizona. Someone reckoned she had walked eighteen miles for help, then she spent the night helping repair her damaged airplane. Ranchers out in the middle of nowhere were fascinated to have a woman drop down from the sky. Even more astonishing, the woman was flying in a transcontinental air race! The ranchers were isolated, used to repairing farm machinery, and had the tools on hand to do so. What could be different about an airplane engine, filing out a bent prop, or patching a torn wingtip? They weren't afraid to jump right in and help, cheer for their new friend, and hope she would win the race. Someone always seemed to be on hand to help after a forced landing.

Opal Kunz made a forced landing as well, because she was out of fuel. Kunz was a big city girl used to sophisticated, bustling Manhattan. She was awed by her country's great Southwest. How could so few people live so far apart with no theater or deli or shopping or even real trees? Though the country had an austere charm, it was devoid of luxuriant vegetation. In fact, the cacti personified its neighborhood, hardy and prickly, yet intriguing in its own form of resplendent beauty.

Blanche Noyes

Irrepressible Blanche Noyes, who had learned to fly only six weeks before the derby, had wandered off course, landing in Cananea, Sonora, Mexico. She had an imaginative tale to tell.

Noyes described her adventure in the evening's "hangar flying" session. "I ran into a bad ground fog, mostly factory smoke, and lost myself completely. I thought I had better land and get my bearing. It was an orange grove, I think."

"Blanche," the always forceful Vera Dawn Walker interjected, "there's no oranges down there on the border. You had to be in mesquite."

"Well, then, there were horses and cows. And then suddenly, from every direction, Mexicans began to appear. I never have seen anything as mysterious as the way those Mexicans bobbed up."

Noyes went on, "I asked them questions but couldn't get a thing out of them. All they could do was shake their heads and say, '¿Quién sabe?' I asked where the United States was, but got nowhere with that, so I pulled out my map and showed it to them.

"They knew what a map was, but for the life of me, I couldn't get any directions out of them. Just then a lot of Mexicans rode up on horses with fancy trimmings. So, I thought it was time for me to get out of there. I took off and flew north about twenty miles, then I hit Douglas."

By the time the women arrived at Douglas, Marvel Crosson's ghastly fate was no longer speculative. The wreckage and her body had been found. Twelve miles north of Wellton, four Arizona ranchers had seen an airplane similar in description to Crosson's plunge into a grove of distant cottonwood trees. They did not see a parachute open. Though searchers had looked for the spot all night, they couldn't locate it in the dark, rough country of willows and mesquite. Interspersed with the tall, rangy cottonwoods, the mean catclaw acacia was enough to stop anyone in his tracks. At first light, Deputy Sheriffs Victor Gael and J. C. Livingston, serenaded by the haunting song of the cactus wren, located the aircraft wreckage, and two hundred yards away, Marvel Crosson was found with every bone broken. The men said that she had been killed instantly, speculating that she had been thrown from the airplane with the parachute pack rupturing upon impact with the earth. Others theorized either she had jumped too low for the parachute to open or that it had malfunctioned.

Louise Thaden couldn't help but wonder if Crosson had experienced the same carbon monoxide poisoning that she had in her Travel Air. She felt a sudden fear for the other women flying Travel Airs. Was the problem in the airplane?

Editorial writers were not shy about expressing their opinions of the Air Derby in light of Crosson's death. The *New York American* thought it might be too late to call off the race, but it should be the last of its kind.

"The air is not yet safe for racing, and it is undermining public confidence in aviation, as the coming and best of all means of transportation, when human life is needlessly sacrificed in such ill-advised contests as the women's air derby. A fine young woman has been called as a sacrifice on the altar of a premature competition. Air racing for women should be discouraged as a far too hazardous adventure." A self-righteous, pretentious Oklahoma oilman by the name of Erle P. Haliburton was succinct and certain: "Women have conclusively proven that they cannot fly." His newspaper quote went on, "Women have been dependent on men for guidance for so long that when they are put on their resources they are handicapped."

The racers and their supporters, grieving over Crosson's death but still confident, were angered by the patronizing commentary. Race manager Frank Copeland, as outraged as the racers themselves, responded, "We wish to thumb our collective noses at Haliburton. There will be no stopping this race."

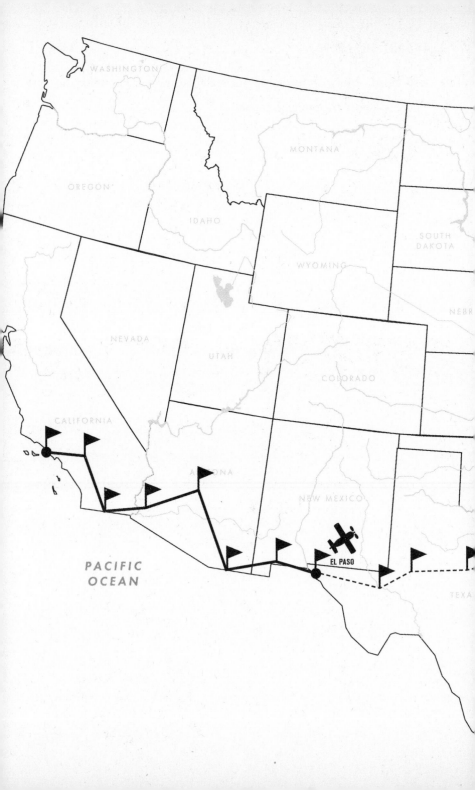

WEDNESDAY, AUGUST 21, 1929

Race Day 4

**DOUGLAS TO COLUMBUS TO EL PASO
118 MILES, 65 MILES**

Got a lovely invitation from Henry Ford to come to Dearborn tomorrow and hear Mr. Hoover tell Mr. Edison what the electric light had meant to him before becoming a Republican. Was headed over there and ran into a thick fog and had to come back here. Chicago might be wicked, but that lighted field looked mighty good at night, and I sure want to thank Mr. Edison personally tomorrow for inventing those little things.

Yours, Will Rogers
Syndicated newspaper column

Louise Thaden awakened with a dreadful headache. *Where am I,* she thought. *This is Wednesday, I must be in Douglas, Arizona, flying in an airplane race across the United States of America.* Suddenly, she remembered that her friend Marvel Crosson was dead.

Before she had even rolled out of bed, she heard a knock on the door. She presumed it was the hotel wake-up, but Amelia Earhart's voice called out gently, "Louise, are you up?"

"Not really. Give me a second to wash my face."

Thaden scurried around trying to make herself presentable, then opened the door to Earhart.

"I was just thinking of Marvel, Amelia," Thaden said distractedly. "All this seems so unimportant with her life squandered. What are we doing here?"

"Oh, Louise, I know how upset you are, but this race is to prove to the public that airplanes are the transportation of the day and the future, and that women have as strong a right to fly them as men," Earhart reminded her. "Marvel is cheering each one of us on. You mustn't be discouraged."

Earhart's positive words were just what Thaden needed to hear to get past the immediate tragedy and on to the business at hand. Earhart handed Thaden the morning paper with Marvel Crosson and the other racers prominently pictured on the front page above the fold. Seeing Crosson's face with its dark curls was painful. Thaden quickly set it aside.

"The weather looks great," Earhart said. "There will probably be normal thunderstorm activity late in the afternoon. Volunteers are already wiping the oil off the belly of your airplane. I'll go with you to the airport when you're ready."

Earhart gave Thaden a quick hug and was out the door. Thaden thought, leave it to Earhart to make the rounds to raise the morale of the troops. Thaden took a quick minute to reflect in her journal: "When the foreordained time for death comes, how better could one choose than this: 'the spirit flying free, knowing no transition from the lower fringes of Heaven into its wondrous infinity.'"

Each of the women handled Crosson's death and the continuing challenge in her own way. Pancho Barnes had bounced back from the malaise infecting the racers and was already at the airport, painting her airplane. She had strayed into Mexico en route to Douglas and, with her sense of humor intact, was painting in large white letters on the fuselage of her Travel Air: MEXICO OR BUST. Might as well tell the world—especially since today's leg ran right along the Mexican border. Someone would surely stray across. Too bad the real border wasn't a red painted line as it appeared on the new sectional chart.

The racers gathered by their airplanes. Ruth Elder's Swallow and Gladys O'Donnell's Taperwing Waco had mechanics' help from the start of the race. The others had sporadic assistance from husbands or sponsors or were dependent upon local mechanics to troubleshoot the inevitable mechanical problems that developed along the way. Not surprisingly, the women became good shade-tree mechanics themselves. Thaden and Earhart arrived at the Douglas Airport along with the dawn, and they greeted the other racers.

"Hi, Edith. Your airplane looks fast even tied down. Good luck."

"Morning, Opal. Hope we find a good tailwind today."

"Pancho, does 'Mexico or bust' mean you're going or have already been?"

And the race went on, each pilot more determined than ever to fly her airplane well and to finish the race.

The racers were a diverse group with little in common save their love of flying. For example, Edith Magalis Foltz, the woman with the big, friendly smile, had stumbled into aviation by accident. She had somehow invested in an OX5 Eaglerock, and, leaving her toddler to be cared for at home, she barnstormed in it. Foltz then took out a state transport license so she could carry passengers for hire. She flew copilot in a trimotor Bach with Western Air, the first West Coast charter transport between Seattle and San Francisco. Foltz snubbed her nose at transport companies, which invariably said they couldn't hire women pilots because "women passengers wouldn't trust another woman."

Foltz had made it a point to ask the women who flew as her passengers on Western Air how they felt about riding behind her, and she said they all seemed pleased. When Western Air was sold to United Airlines, that was the end of her career as a budding airline pilot. Some people said that Foltz's brush with transport carriage made her the world's first female airline pilot. Nearly a dozen others eventually made that same claim.

No one dreamed that it would be more than another four decades before the airlines would hire female pilots. They never would have believed that it would take until the early seventies for the airlines to open their membership to women. When the Department of Commerce proposed grounding professional female pilots for one week each month to ensure safety, one faint (female) voice brought up the delicate problem of enforcement. A study ensued, which apparently became lost and forgotten. However, the subject was not finished. As it evolved, women pilots were forced to retake all their pilot certificate and rating exams after recovering from the "illness" of childbirth. Other countries were even more discriminatory. Early on, Canadian female airline pilots were required to ground themselves the moment they suspected they might be pregnant. Crosson's death added impetus to an ongoing effort to ground women to keep them in their place.

Edith Foltz had endured some critical comments in the air derby by competing in an eccentric airplane, the Alexander Eaglerock Bullet. Foltz retorted that retracting the gear on an airplane and enclosing the cockpit wasn't odd, it was state of the art. And the Bullet was fast. She was holding her own in the CW class, standing right behind Phoebe Omlie. Foltz was right that the Bullet was an engineering breakthrough.

Edith Foltz

It was time to fire up and go. Foltz suffered standard pretakeoff nerves as she taxied out. The luxury of an enclosed cockpit allowed her to spread out her charts on the right seat and open the air vents for as much air as she wanted.

She could reach around the seat and swig some water as the cockpit temperatures spiraled, and she had jettisoned the helmet and goggles needed for flying open cockpit. Foltz loved the Bullet, though she conceded sometimes its Kinner engine was less than reliable. She was careful to stay far away from slow airspeed in a tight turn, a maneuver approaching a spin entry, because she knew the factory test pilots had declared a flat spin likely unrecoverable in this airplane.

The route out of Douglas to Columbus was sixty-six degrees on the compass. Again, flyers cut through a tiny corner of Mexico.

Douglas was close to 4,200 feet in elevation with higher terrain on the Arizona–New Mexico border, where it was necessary to cut between a 6,900-foot peak and an 8,565-foot peak and across dry river beds. Edith Foltz noted that all the roads seemed to go north out of Douglas. Did nobody have reason to drive east? A little town named Paradise was up in the nearby mountains, and she wondered what old prospector would consider that dry, empty country paradise. Taking the shortcut a few miles through Mexico, Foltz finally picked up a road running right into Columbus. The so-called Columbus Airport seemed to be a repeat of Douglas—high, hot, and desolate. The heat rose off the desert floor in visible ripples. It took the air away. Most of the racers, having not bothered to dig out their water, found it difficult to even walk upon deplaning. They thought they were too tough to worry about dehydration, but their debilitation was a reminder that they were mortal. The excited air-race spectators seemed to be of an independent bent, hardworking ranchers and miners, and they were generous to the women with snacks and cold drinks, pleased to have this brush with history. Without meaning to give their admirers short shrift, the racers were in and out of Columbus in record time, just long enough to refuel and restart a hot engine.

The Columbus–El Paso leg was an eighty-degree heading and about seventy statute miles right down the border fence. The ground was simply bare, save a skinny gratuitous road, a bare thread below, paralleling the border. It was tempting to fly with one wing in Mexico and the other in the United States. Were their brains going soft? Wasn't fuzziness just supposed to happen at altitude? Maybe this oven boiled their brains, too.

When Foltz spotted the Rio Grande River and a lone hill just west of El Paso, she knew she was getting pretty close to the airport. The brown desert floor gradually turned green as she progressed. Water plus brown equals green. Gradually, the dusty nothingness gave way to cotton fields. These led to the grazing cattle and the prosperous-looking farms of west Texas.

The city had been named El Paso del Norte (the pass of the north) by Spanish explorers. An 1848 treaty following the Mexican-American War established the wide, wandering Rio Grande River as the Mexico–U.S. border, and the northern part of the city became El Paso, Texas, while the south was renamed Juarez. The Rio Grande River ran right through the center of what was still largely a farming community settled along the chief route between Mexico City and the Spanish colonies in New Mexico.

A storm blew in with the first of the racers. The whistling wind demanded some impressive crosswind landing techniques. The women's acumen did not go unnoticed. It was noted by the local airport bums, as they were affectionately named. Some of the pilots discovered that the crosswind component exceeded their airplanes' capabilities, and they landed across the designated runway area to put down safely. Once on the ground, it was impossible to turn sideways to taxi without the wind picking up a wing. The spectators who knew enough about flying to realize what was happening grabbed the upwind wingtips to walk the airplanes to the tie-downs. The first airplanes into El Paso were lucky to get into hangars. The latecomers were obliged to tie their wings down tight out in the open, and the pilots secured the controls so the fabric-covered ailerons and elevators wouldn't be destroyed by flapping up and down in the brutal Texas wind. The racers and volunteers covered all the openings they could, knowing full well that it was impossible to keep the whirling dervish dust particles from gnawing away inside the engine cowling and underneath the fabric-covered surfaces.

Louise Thaden and Gladys O'Donnell

Number 105, Gladys O'Donnell, taxied in, struggling with the buffeting crosswind. Thaden's good friend Gladys O'Donnell was tall, flying in once-white coveralls, and she sported a white frame around her brown face when she removed her flying helmet. With the help of some local volunteers, the tired pilot secured her Waco. A race official sought her out with a telegram from Long Beach. Since telegrams were invariably serious business, O'Donnell perched on the wheel of her airplane out in the wind to read it immediately. Lynn Owen, age twenty-nine, a pilot for the O'Donnell's flying school, had been killed when he got lost in heavy fog and crashed. His student was uninjured.

Flight schools of the day were like fraternities or private clubs, where all present were intimate friends. O'Donnell was overwhelmed. She had been contending with navigating in the heat and the wind at a less-than-minimal experience level, with only forty-eight minuscule hours in her log book. The young, brave novice was bone tired, and her mind was still burdened with Crosson's fatal crash. News of the death of this fine young man, a member of their airport family, was now more than O'Donnell could bear. She dropped her head in her hands and sobbed. She couldn't stop.

The day came grinding to a halt in El Paso. With the wind howling, going on to Midland was out of the question, and the rest of the leg was aborted. A furious sandstorm reduced visibility to a quarter of a mile. The wind made a high-pitched shriek as it circled around the buildings. El Paso hosts scrambled for overnight accommodations for their unexpected RON guests.

Exhausted pilots, the unexpected hostages of this weather's particular hell, took time to assess their progress. The unofficial standings at El Paso put Louise Thaden in the lead of the heavies. Amelia Earhart had the best time on the El Paso leg, but Thaden was still ahead overall. The light aircraft class showed Phoebe Omlie with a substantial lead. In fact, her lead was so strong that some thought she should have been in the heavy class. More likely, her airplane's performance put her squarely between the classes. Bobbi Trout, not yet arrived, was considered out of the race at this point, and the early stop timers shut down their operation without her. The race officials obviously didn't comprehend Trout's tenacity.

An imposing figure paced the ramp, steadfast in the mounting wind, awaiting Thea Rasche's arrival in El Paso. F. K. Baron von Koenig-Warthausen, taking time from his world tour in a Klemm aircraft, had diverted to Texas to encourage his fellow countryman.

Unfortunately, Rasche was running a lap behind and did not pass through El Paso until the next day. The derby's managing director tried to placate the German, speaking admiringly of Rasche and telling the Baron that she had exhibited rare skills.

Margaret Perry had been ill at the start of the race and flew through the fourth day with an unremitting high fever. She looked awful in El Paso, but she was determined to continue.

Margaret Perry

Newspapers were following the race intently and were full of information about the sabotage investigation, as well as following up on Crosson's sad fate as described in this United Press dispatch:

> The district attorney's office today questioned those who handled the airplanes of the competitors in the women's air derby of the National Air races in an attempt to learn whether some ships were tampered with during the first overnight stop of the derby.
>
> Field guards, the men who serviced the planes, and race officials were called to the office of Chief Deputy District Attorney Thompson, in charge of the probe.
>
> Thompson said he intended to prove or disprove the sabotage accusations.
>
> Claire Fahy, forced down at Calexico, contended that acid had been placed on the struts of her plane, making it necessary for her to leave the race. Thea Rasche, German aviatrix, asserted that dirt had been placed in her gasoline. She went down near Holtville but reentered the competition later.
>
> The opinion prevailed among officials that the sabotage charges were not well founded. It was admitted, however, that preparations for the handling of the planes of the derby had been inadequate.

It was tempting for newspapers to editorialize about this rare occasion with its unexpected calamities. The *Midland*

Reporter-Telegram speculated that weather wasn't the women's only impediment in El Paso, but that the race had been halted to inspect and ferret out weaknesses in various airplanes. This was not true, but it was a way to assuage Midlanders who had anticipated the pilots' arrival that evening, and were disappointed the racers couldn't get there for hospitality and to spend the night. The paper pointed out that "the contract held with race officials will have automatically been broken—though through necessity." People on the ground were learning what the aviators already knew—that everything in flying is ultimately dependent upon weather.

Louise Thaden was writing a daily commentary for the *Wichita Eagle* under the byline Louise McPhetridge von Thaden. She wrote from Douglas, Arizona:

> We are all determined to carry on with the pioneer spirit that blazed early-day trails in spite of misfortune and trouble. The other entrants join with me in expressing sympathy for Miss Crosson's relatives, and even though we are busy preparing for the next hop, there is clearly a wholehearted depression as a result of the bad news. We participants know nothing of the terrible rumors out regarding sabotage, which has been given such widespread publicity in the papers. We have implicit faith in each other and there is a spirit of camaraderie being shown that will keep us near to each other years after this racing event is forgotten. There have been numerous instances where little acts

of kindness have cemented friendships that will live always in our memories.

In Wichita, Kansas, considered the aviation capital, seven of the eight columns on the front page of the *Wichita Eagle* talked about aviation. In fact, the paper's own Travel Air would be aloft to greet the racers as they neared Wichita. Marvel Crosson's picture was captioned, "the first fatality of the women's air derby." It was somewhat disturbing that they inferred there would be more deaths. On one side of Crosson's picture was a self-congratulatory piece about how well the Travel Airs were doing, then on the other side, news, or more accurately no news, of the missing Swiss ocean flyers Kaesar and Luscher that had last been sighted crossing the Azores on a Lisbon/New York attempt. In reference to speculation about the great *Zeppelin*'s attraction to American investment capitalists, Will Rogers hadn't been able to resist remarking that "the *Graf*'s sixty people were going around the world in less time than a congressman can make a speech." The *Graf* was just leaving Tokyo for America's West Coast.

In eastern Oklahoma, multiple forest fires had broken out, filling the sky with smoke and cinder that would affect visibility for the racers if not doused quickly. There was no rain expected. The newspaper plugged their coverage of the big air race and said, "Follow the 'Ladybirds' in *The Eagle*." They reported that in Wichita, all the airplanes would be guarded by soldiers detailed from Camp Jones to patrol the field.

Since El Paso was an unplanned overnight stop, the tired pilots did not have to endure another banquet. A little side trip across the bridge to Juarez, Mexico, was in order. Louise Thaden's favorite drink during Prohibition was orange soda pop spiked with two ounces of vodka. She brought a cold jug of the concoction to maintenance crews before calling it a night.

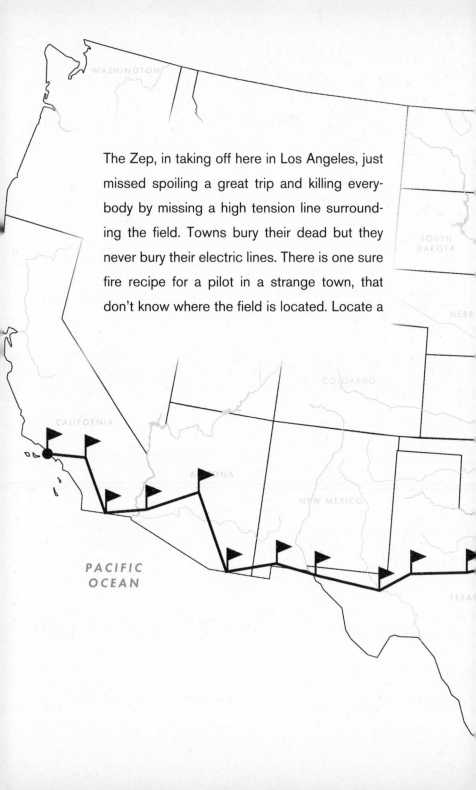

The Zep, in taking off here in Los Angeles, just missed spoiling a great trip and killing everybody by missing a high tension line surrounding the field. Towns bury their dead but they never bury their electric lines. There is one sure fire recipe for a pilot in a strange town, that don't know where the field is located. Locate a

Race Day 5

EL PASO TO PECOS TO MIDLAND TO ABILENE TO FORTH WORTH
165 MILES, 100 MILES, 140 MILES, 138 MILES

high tension line, follow it till it crosses another higher tension one. There is almost sure to be a field there. If not, follow it till it comes to an intersection of three of more lines and there will be located the city's municipal field. It's as sure as the sure fire method of locating a speakeasy by following the town's leading citizens.

Yours, Will Rogers

Syndicated newspaper column

T he racers had taken on a mantle of certainty by their fifth race day of nine. They had gained confidence in both their airplanes and themselves, having successfully negotiated the high desert country of the great Southwest. The women were bonding into a cohesive corps of woman power.

Louise Thaden reveled in the beauty of the El Paso takeoff. She wrote in her Wichita newspaper report, "When we took off this morning at El Paso the [mountains] were blue with low, wide clouds crowning them and surrounding them with the shimmer of reflected morning light." The El Paso to Pecos leg was not anticipated to be a difficult flight, with the air all washed out and visibility good. It was simply going to be a long day adding on all the miles not completed the day before due to the sandstorm. The route still crossed high desert, but the morning air was not yet manufacturing its jarring, invisible potholes and bumps.

Nevertheless, adventures were to be had.

By the time she reached Pecos, poor Mary Haizlip knew her American Eagle, specially built for racing, carried only two hours' fuel total. Due to its last-minute delivery, she'd had no prior chance to test fly the airplane and to determine its exact fuel capacity. Though the airplane had a Department of Commerce license, it had been purposely designed with limited tankage to keep it light for pylon racing. Her fellow competitors carried at least three or four hours' fuel, enough to get to the destination plus a little reserve. Haizlip had come into four timing stops completely dry. In fact, she had had to get out and push the airplane out of the landing area at El Paso. Since Haizlip was afraid if she mentioned her limitation she might be disqualified, she did not complain. With no reserve of any kind, Mary Haizlip's silent resolve displayed an extraordinary amount of courage.

Ruth Nichols in her airplane.

Ruth Nichols led the way into Pecos across more of the "nothing" country—nothing much to navigate on and nothing growing, but it was a desolation of special beauty. This leg was the last of the high country, where the ground had been four or five thousand feet above sea level and low-powered engines were challenged to climb over the adjacent mountains. Sometimes, the pilots decided to divert off course around a mountain rather than huff and puff over it. The high, rough country also caused some apprehension about emergency landing fields. The pilots were always on the lookout for a good spot in which to put down in case of engine trouble, such as an alfalfa field or a pasture, and the desert country didn't offer much.

Nichols was acclimated by now, and the conditions didn't bother her. There were some 5,500-foot mountains just east of El Paso, with a lower pass she could take just south of the direct course. She was searching for some salt flats up against the Guadalupe Mountains and should be flying over the south end, which came up right on schedule. Several roads funneled into Pecos, which was only 2,600 feet mean sea level. This meant the end of the high country.

The rising sun could blind the pilots, but the low shadows it cast caused Nichols to wish for a camera and the time to circle and shoot some spectacular photos. She held up her hand to shield her eyes from the penetrating sun, scanning for the Pecos Airport. Everybody started looking for the airport from farther out than they could possibly see it. It was just human nature to anticipate. Nichols caught sight of the field teeming with cars.

Louise Thaden, realizing a Travel Air was close behind her, kept looking over her shoulder coming up on Pecos. She landed and quickly taxied out of the way of the oncoming plane. Good sportsmanship dictated not interfering with someone else's approach, though Thaden had the right of way. Pancho Barnes pressed on, landing hot on her tail.

Barnes's quota of luck was about to run out. Contrary to speculation, the incident that occurred as she landed had nothing to do with the previous evening's excursion. She, like the others, had gone from El Paso across the Rio Grande into Juarez. There, the Mrs. Reverend Barnes had obligingly answered a challenge and chugged a pitcher of beer. Despite what people might have said, the problems that arose at Pecos was due to the race manager's inability to control the crowd.

The town's three thousand citizens had done their best to clear enough mesquite and sagebrush to make a narrow landing strip for the racers. But on race day, seemingly every car in town was parked along the edge of the strip for a good view of the women and their airplanes. There was no safety margin remaining. It made for some very near misses and one hit, Barnes's.

Few realized that when pilots raise the airplane's nose for landing, they are virtually blind to the front and maintain their momentum straight down the runway by way of their peripheral vision. In Pecos, a fearless and foolhardy citizen drove too far into the landing strip, so when Barnes descended, she landed right on his car, bashing in its top and demolishing both the Travel Air's upper and lower right wings. Barnes was not injured, but the airplane was so badly damaged it could neither continue to fly nor be easily repaired. An irate, boisterous, swearing Barnes was out of the race.

The dust had not yet settled from Barnes's arrival when Thaden spotted Blanche Noyes, the pretty actress turned pilot, circling low overhead. Her plane looked like a wounded duck with a broken wing and badly crippled legs.

"It's going to be a crack-up!" Thaden yelled, shutting down her engine and leaping out of the cockpit. "Get fire extinguishers, call an ambulance!"

The crowd was milling about the landing strip, unaware of their danger. "Get them back," Thaden shouted, and she waved her arms at an advancing group of reporters.

Noyes somehow executed a normal approach, then put the ship down with perfect precision on the right wheel. As it lost speed, the beautiful, crippled Travel Air settled easily onto the broken left wheel and slowly ground-looped, pivoting on its broken leg. Cameras flashed. As the wheels touched and the engine died, Louise ran toward Noyes. "Are you all right?"

Noyes's face was sooty black. Silently, she lifted two shaking, scorched hands. "I'm okay," she said.

The other pilots gathered around, and Thaden leapt up onto the leaning wing. She stood still a moment, then she pressed poor Noyes's head to her.

"What happened? You're a mess—but it was a great landing. We all thought you were going to crash."

Tears made white rivulets down Noyes's cheeks, but she tried to smile. "It was a good landing, wasn't it?"

She said breathlessly, "I smelled smoke from the cockpit about thirty miles short of Pecos. Of course, I'm terribly afraid of fire, for heaven's sake, it's a wooden airplane with wings covered with dope on linen. But there's no way I was going to try out that parachute and jump. Can you see me explaining to my bridegroom why I lost the airplane? And even worse, I'd miss the rest of the race."

She continued, describing an incident that included an emergency landing in the desert. "I looked for the source of the smoke, turned around, and saw it curling up from the baggage compartment beyond my reach. I remembered Dewey's [her husband and flight instructor's] advice to sideslip away from fire, keeping it away from my face and lungs. Dewey taught me that quick descent maneuver well. That's how I avoided the dangers of a dive. I raised the nose, lowering the airspeed. But I was careful to keep enough speed to avoid a stall. That's when I deliberately crossed the controls, stick all the way over to the left with the left wing down and full right rudder. That controlled the degree of turn into a field with the rudder pressure. I side-slipped down two thousand feet turning just enough to miss the worst of the mesquite."

The women and reporters who heard her seemed spellbound. "When I got on the ground and stopped, I leaped out of the cockpit and yanked on the fire extinguisher fastened to the floor, but I couldn't get it out. I was frantic. I don't know where I got the strength, but I ripped the whole case right out of the floor. The wooden flooring came up with it. After all that, I couldn't make the damned thing work.

"I just grabbed the burning valise with my bare hands and threw desert sand on it to put the fire out. It was hands or the ship. I guess a mechanic must have dropped a cigarette or ash on top of my packed clothing and it smoldered.

"There I was, out in the middle of nowhere, and I needed to get on to Pecos 'cause the clock was running. I had never cranked my own airplane, but, boy, I could and I did. I turned that crank for four minutes, at least, before it got going.

"All I could think about on the takeoff was to do as little damage as possible plowing through the mesquite. That old pilots' saying that any landing you walk away from is a good one applied to my takeoff in the desert. I tore holes in the bottom of the fuselage and wings, and damaged the landing gear, but the blessed machine flew. I headed straight for Pecos. And here I am—both me and the airplane in one piece."

Noyes's adventure captured the front page that day. Everyone, and the racers most of all, were proud of her grit and obvious flying skill.

Noyes failed to ferret out an airplane mechanic at Pecos, but she did find a man who would weld her landing gear together. Heavy tape was good enough to patch the fabric skin. Noyes crossed her fingers, ready to head on her way, knowing the gear had to hold for only three more landings until she could have a new apparatus installed at the factory during the Wichita stop.

Noyes had ordered one of the new NACA-enclosed cowlings, and, in the midst of her temporary repairs, the new cowling reached her halfway across the continent. She was sure that little item would give her another twenty miles per hour, and make her competitive with the other Travel Airs. Noyes and all the racers fueled up for free in Pecos, courtesy of the Burford Oil Company, and they were on their way.

They pressed on to Sloan Field in Midland, Texas, happy to be moving into lower terrain. Navigation was easy on this short leg, with a road and railroad delineating the course. Now, a new spectacle appeared below them: oil wells. Small clusters of oil rigs grew into forests, their vertical arms keeping rhythm up and down, up and down. This worthless-looking land was one of God's jokes. It was as though He had submerged pools of black gold in nowhere, then patiently awaited the invention of the internal combustion engine.

Walter Beech's factory crew—test pilot Pete Hill and his teenage son Pete Jr., along with a mechanic—waited for the Travel Airs at Midland. Led there by concern for the safety of the Travel Air pilots, they were to provide maintenance support for their covey of racers along the rest of the route. The men had their own suspicions about Marvel Crosson's loss, and Louise Thaden agreed with their conclusions.

Though numerous theories had been advanced for the cause of Marvel's accident, the factory crew suspected that she had suffered from the same carbon monoxide poisoning that had affected Thaden before the race began. She was too good a pilot for any other explanation to make sense. There was evidence that Crosson had vomited over the side, and it was likely she was no longer lucid enough to fly the airplane. They rejected the speculation they'd heard that she had bailed out, despite the distance of her body from the airplane wreckage. Her parachute pack probably burst upon impact and tangled around her body because of the force of the collision. Bearing in mind the potential for further calamity, the Beech men would follow the racers to Fort Worth, ready to make any modifications necessary.

Midland was a quick in and out, even including lunch. If Midland didn't have its honored guests for a banquet and overnight, they would at least take them to town for a first-class luncheon. The ever-polite racers expressed their appreciation to the locals. However, they were eager to be on their way since as the day wore on, as the sun beat down on the earth and thermals initiated their predictable spirals, turbulence and discomfort grew with the heat.

The women flew as low as five hundred feet above the ground when they had an iron compass, the railroad tracks, to follow. The penalty of that perspective was sparse topographical checkpoints, so occasionally they'd climb up to a thousand feet, or even higher, for a better view. They had drawn their course line on their Rand McNally road map or aeronautical chart with slash marks every ten miles to facilitate the time and distance computation. As they flew, their index fingers traced along the lines on the charts. This "finger flying" seemed vital to keep track of position and what to look for ahead. When learning to fly, the women had discovered what a dreadful classroom the airplane was. It was hard to think in the noisy, three-dimensional, constantly moving schoolroom. And one couldn't park for a few minutes of contemplation. In those days, before instruments and electronic navigation, pilots would continually review their charts and computations before taking off.

Each pilot clamped the control stick between her knees to keep her airplane on course, thus freeing her hands for folding out the chart. In order to view the terrain for a defining town, mountain, or river, each flyer would have to scoot high in the seat and poke her head out the side into the wind, enduring the blast of hot air. Even a "skid," moving the big cowled engine out of the way to one side with the rudder would occasionally prove necessary so that the pilot could see ahead. The constant thuds as the airplane bounced through the afternoon air's pounding surf was wearing, and the turbulence made it difficult to read a compass.

Holding a predetermined heading while applying appropriate correction for the crosswind—flying west to east, most often a tail wind—proved a challenge when relying on the dancing compass that was floating in alcohol and riding the same waves as its host. The compass would respond to every thump. It naturally aimed downward at the ground, because north was in the earth, not up in the air parallel to the nose of the airplane. The compass would lead and lag at turning north and south. The racers had to keep in mind variation corrections from true north to apply to the heading calculations, an exercise that kept them busy.

Cross-country was any flight from departure point to destination, no matter how far or close. Flying cross-country, pilots were quite used to being "momentarily disoriented." But part of the fun of flying was the challenge of navigating, not so much a science as the application of experience, wits, and curiosity. Looking over the side and trying to match lakes or towns or railroad tracks with their same relative positions on the chart was a sort of game. There were many fewer towns and roads in those days. It was easy to talk oneself into believing that the town you were seeing with the lake at the north end was really the same as the one on the chart, but they moved the lake. Then the pilot would come to her senses, thinking, "I'm lost, er, momentarily disoriented." On the other hand, unlike now, there was never anything wrong with landing in some smooth-looking pasture and asking the farmer the location. The farmers loved it, and pilots met someone new. By the Abilene stop, 138 miles short of Fort Worth, the now exhausted racers were clearly hanging onto a vision of the day's end at Fort Worth. Refreshments were available at Abilene under a large tent, but even better, the thoughtful hosts had placed some cots on which the grateful pilots could rest for a few minutes. No bumps, no noise, no sun. What luxury!

Vera Dawn Walker had grown up in a town near Abilene, but she hadn't been there for many years. A flock of relatives had heard of her exploits and came out in force to greet her. In the excitement of Walker's arrival, they swarmed the airplane. Impossible as it seems, even with the noise, when people couldn't see the whirling propeller, they forgot that it was there. Pilots were ever alert that if a stranger to airplanes got close to the prop, they might walk into it, a usually fatal accident that occurred often. The man out in front of the group greeting Walker seemed totally oblivious to the danger of the propeller. She frantically shut down the engine, which is not instantaneous, and suddenly realized that it was her father who was about to walk right into her still-spinning propeller. An alert bystander grabbed him back as the propeller slowed to a stop. Walker almost fainted, coming so close to killing her own father.

Gladys O'Donnell made a rough landing, and she took a little wingtip ding and fabric tear as the wing dipped to the ground. There was no serious damage to the airplane, and a patch sufficed to send her on her way. Since the bottom wings were close to the ground and it didn't take much to drag a wing, ground loops and a little wingtip rash were not uncommon.

Edith Foltz and Margaret Perry both ended their day at Abilene without continuing on to Fort Worth. Foltz was happy with the mechanics she found there and decided to have her landing gear, which had been damaged at Pecos, repaired. Perry was ill, as she had been for the entire race. She simply ran out of steam and knew she needed some good rest immediately. Both intended to catch up with the main body of racers in Wichita the next night.

The investigation of sabotage charges overtook the racers in Texas. The newspapers declared that Deputy District Attorney C. O. Thompson of San Bernardino announced that he had issued subpoenas for Mr. and Mrs. Herbert J. Fahy, requiring them to appear in court to explain their assertions that someone had meddled with Mrs. Fahy's airplane. The district attorney had questioned eleven witnesses and had not been able to find a single instance of sabotage. "We are told the field was guarded adequately and that mechanics of the various oil companies interested in the race were with the planes all night." Dr. L. W. Ayres, chairman of the San Bernardino race committee, issued a statement denying charges that the planes had been tampered with. "I think Mr. Fahy's declaration is one of the most unsportsmanlike things I have ever seen," he said.

Amelia Earhart's Vega was more comfortable than the open-cockpit biwing airplanes, since it was heavier and more stable. She was able to fly protected from the weather. Nevertheless, she too had had about enough of the long day from El Paso. The country they were flying over was certainly more interesting than the desert. They could view farms and towns, and could fly even lower now since their destination was less than a thousand feet above sea level. Earhart kept a careful eye out for her fellow racers as she let down approaching Fort Worth.

Like the rest, she buzzed the timing line fast and low, then came around for a smooth landing, happy to have the long day done.

Earhart's shiny red Vega was easily recognized, and the popular aviator was instantly mobbed by the excited spectators as she taxied in at Fort Worth. The thirty policemen who were there were unable to contain the crowd. All the racers were bone tired, dirty, deafened by the engine noise, hungry, and straining to stay awake for the inevitable banquet. Happily, they thought, Fort Worth was beef country.

FRIDAY, AUGUST 23, 1929

Race Day 6

**FORTH WORTH TO TULSA TO WICHITA
253 MILES, 130 MILES**

Claremore, Oklahoma [Will's hometown], has grabbed off another distinction it being the only town between Santa Monica, California, and Cleveland, Ohio, that those Cleveland race officials haven't made those poor girl aviators stop at.

Yours, Will Rogers
Syndicated newspaper column

The exhausted racers' arrival in Fort Worth had been engulfed by some twenty thousand spectators. The pilots did their duty mingling with their kind hosts despite the challenges of the previous days. The women enjoyed each other's company and that of each local aviation community, but the aviators almost lost their good manners and began to laugh when the evening's lavish Texas spread turned out to feature, of all things, another chicken evening.

Their host, Amon G. Carter, was dressed like a dime-store cowboy in silver spurs, bandana, leather chaps, and a pair of pearl-handled pistols, all while sporting an enormous cowboy hat. But he wasn't all show. A stroll through the ranch house revealed original Remington and Russell paintings hanging on the walls and other beautiful western art. How did Carter's clownish getup jibe with his tasteful abode?

The group turned to Vera Dawn Walker who always had an opinion and was a Texan, to boot. "Who is Amon Carter?"

She explained that he was a newspaper publisher, but not just *any* publisher. He and his *Star* newspaper were Fort Worth's biggest boosters. The slogan above the masthead bragged "Where the West

Begins," which his friend Will Rogers had helped to promote nation-wide. Walker related the infamous "elevator incident."

"Amon Carter was dressed in his cowboy getup while attending a gathering at a big hotel. While on an upper floor along with a crowd waiting for the elevator, it went on by without stopping. Carter whipped out one of his pearl pistols and fired through the door. Nobody was hurt, but it sure fed the Amon Carter lore," Walker said.

In fact, Amon Carter was an extraordinary entrepreneur who started out peddling sandwiches to railroad passengers as a teenager, then he sold picture frames door to door. Upon moving to Fort Worth in 1905, Carter borrowed $250 and started a newspaper, later buying the *Star*. A lucky oil strike turned Amon Carter into not only a community booster but also a philanthropist, who, as time went along, became instrumental in bringing what was to become American Airlines and General Dynamics to Fort Worth, and he helped establish Texas Tech in Lubbock and Big Bend National Park.

In typical Amon Carter fashion, on the evening of the derby stop, he made a grand presentation of a colossal cowboy hat to the group's representative, Amelia Earhart. It was large enough to take over the back seat of her Vega. His guests politely controlled their laughter at the rendition of a schmaltzy song titled, "Sweethearts of the Air."

The next morning's paper followed the lead of Will Rogers's daily piece, needling their own renowned publisher who had hosted the festivities: "Those race officials have those girl aviators landing at every buffalo wallow that has a chamber of commerce and will put up a hot dog sandwich. They even made 'em eat with Amon Carter."

Poultry or bust, another dawn had arrived, and today would be the

Tulsa to Wichita leg. Everyone anticipated Wichita as the highlight on the route. Many of the women's aircraft were built in Wichita. As the "Air Capital of the World," the city would attempt to prove it when their special guests arrived. Plus, the national publicity had begun to capture the imagination of the American public. Already, each stop drew larger and more excited crowds to the airfield.

Louise Thaden was hanging onto her lead at Fort Worth by twenty-one minutes, with Gladys O'Donnell, Amelia Earhart, and Ruth Nichols all close behind now that Barnes was out. Everyone knew that anything still could happen. Phoebe Omlie had only one real challenger left in the light airplane class. Elapsed total times from the start in Santa Monica to Fort Worth were:

HEAVY PLANES

Louise Thaden	11:04:30
Gladys O'Donnell	11:25:52
Amelia Earhart	11:46:52
Ruth Nichols	11:51:08
Mary Haizlip	12:24:06
Ruth Elder	13:35:03
Mary Von Mach	15:12:32
Neva Paris	15:55:10
Opal Kunz	18:44:27
Vera Dawn Walker	21:30:15

LIGHT PLANES

Phoebe Omlie	13:28:30
Thea Rasche	16:20:31
Chubbie Keith-Miller	24:56:15

Blanche Noyes was running behind due to her makeshift landing gear repair in Pecos, but the determined ingénue aviator soon caught up. Margaret Perry buckled to her illness and was out of the race at Fort Worth. The high temperature and general lassitude that had afflicted her since the start of the race was finally diagnosed as typhoid fever, and she was hospitalized.

Others continued to fly, even though they were hopelessly behind. They had resolved to finish this race in Cleveland. Thaden wanted desperately to be the first into Tulsa, but especially Wichita, where her entire family and her sponsor would be waiting. However, Thaden was not without regard and admiration for her sister pilots. She observed, "Were there a prize for tenacity, Bobbi Trout and Mary Haizlip surely would be in an uncontested tie for the award."

Trout had been scheduled to fly a ninety-horsepower Golden Eagle Chief in the derby, but in light of the competition, a one-hundred-horsepower Kinner engine was installed to make hers the fastest airplane in the lower horsepower class. After her mishap, while the others were leaving Fort Worth, Trout was blistering along in an attempt to catch up.

Bobbi Trout's crew had worked feverishly for twenty-four hours in 120-degree temperatures to repair her Golden Eagle in that plowed field south of the border. Kindhearted residents had leveled off a provisional takeoff strip for Trout. Then a mechanic noticed serious undiscovered damage to the underside of a wing. They gave up, removed the wing, and towed the airplane to Yuma to finish the repair inside a hangar. Trout was close enough to home so that her family could join her to lend support. Finally, on Thursday, August 22, the day of the El Paso to Fort Worth leg for the rest of the racers, Trout got into the airplane and flew out of Yuma, intending to catch the racers by Saturday. Since she was now breaking in a new engine, a Kinner representative flew wingman beside her in a Vega. Trout declared the rebuild splendid. She was out but not down.

In a dispatch the *Associated Press* gushed:

> Miss Trout has been hailed as the most popular woman flier in the west. She has the appearance and voice of a seventeen-year-old boy, being slender with close-cropped brown hair and a gift of spontaneous and unconscious expression. She is unassuming, and with half a hundred people standing about eager to do something for her she did nearly everything for herself, then thanked everyone present for their assistance. She expressed absolute confidence of making Fort Worth by Friday night and of catching the derby sometime Saturday.

Another reporter wrote succinctly, "She looks like a boy, flies like a man."

Evelyn Trout, her actual name, was always more interested in boys' things than girls', even taking manual training in school and becoming an adept mechanic. She was the first girl in her high school to have the trendy new hair bob, acquiring the nickname Bobbi.

Trout was actually operating her own service station when she discovered flying, and she immediately sold it to pay for flying lessons. She didn't stop with the private pilot certificate but went on to earn a transport license. The vivacious and talented young pilot was spotted by the Golden Eagle company and hired to demonstrate their product—with the same reasoning as always for women pilots. "After all, Mr. Customer, if this little lady can fly our fine airplane, then you can too." The company's motivation was irrelevant to Trout. She got to fly airplanes and was paid for it, while at the same time making record endurance flights. Could life be more perfect?

Bobbi Trout

Departing to the northeast out of Fort Worth, the racers moved into different terrain. Now closer to sea level, they could fly at lower altitudes than they had been able to do and the engines performed better, no gasping for breath like people at the mountain tops. The section lines began to straighten themselves out into one-mile squares, the same pattern that Thaden had benefited from on her queasy journey with Walter Beech just a few days prior. Instead of navigating toward a peak or mountain range, the racers from now on could cut section lines at an angle, and hold that angle consistently. The geometry was as good as a compass. With the miles of healthy crops as far as the eye could see, Trout wondered how anyone in the world could be hungry. There seemed to be so much.

Crossing the Red River had meant farewell to Texas, and suddenly below them was red earth. The dirt roads were red, the plowed fields were red, even the barns were red. Ah, it must be from the historical trail of tears, mused Thaden. Had the dispossessed shed blood through their tears? The pilots had entered Oklahoma, Will Rogers country.

Even in August, the river flow was still high enough to give Thaden the urge to learn to fly a seaplane someday, to explore all the little inlets and fish off the floats—wouldn't her husband Herb love that? The farmers seemed to take pride in their properties, no junk out behind the barns. She did have to chuckle at the regional dump, hidden behind a line of trees where no one would see it. Louise Thaden could see it! She spotted the minuscule Arbuckle Mountains near Ardmore, remembering how differently she had felt the last time she came by here from the other direction, from Tulsa to Fort Worth, only a week before. Reminded of the carbon monoxide, Thaden took a quick, thankful whiff of outside air through the cockpit pipe.

As the racers progressed into southern Oklahoma, visibility gradually decreased. Smoke and haze rose over to the east toward the little town of Broken Bow, where forest fires were incinerating what was to be twenty-five thousand acres of trees and brush. At Tulsa, the women would learn that game warden W. A. Ward had his own earthbound drama. When he came upon the man who started the fire, the arsonist fired three shots at Ward and fled.

Bad luck and a flat tire delayed Gladys O'Donnell in departing Fort Worth. Some were obliged to make some extra landings for other reasons before their luncheon date in Tulsa.

Ruth Elder's map disappeared over the side in the wind again, as it had when she met the bulls, and the west wind carried her a little off course to the east over the Ouachita Mountains. Elder knew she was easing over toward Arkansas and corrected back to the west. There were lots more little towns now, and they were confusing without a map to establish their identities. She held her heading as best she could, but she decided to land and find out where she was. The landing was just fine near Muskogee, Oklahoma, where she was able to determine her position east of the desired course. It would be a short hop to Tulsa. However, the takeoff presented a slight problem, her path impeded by a recalcitrant herd of cows. The starlet had grown impatient with their special attention and managed to chase them away, swinging her motor crank overhead. Inexplicably, after firing up, she left the essential starter crank behind. Most of the Tulsa airport crowd waited for her late arrival and gave the glamorous pilot a big ovation.

Mary Haizlip was forced down twice in Oklahoma by her plane's dirty oil line, and Vera Dawn Walker made a precautionary landing to cool her overheating engine.

The Tulsa stop included a chamber of commerce luncheon and an address by William Martineau, president of the State Press Association. His theme was "newspapers' difficulty in determining and discriminating between good and bad publicity of aviation." The women were asked to respond—which several did. Ruth Elder's comment that American women would be fighter pilots in a future war was quoted widely. She was right, though she probably didn't envision it would take more than sixty years.

Erle P. Haliburton, who had provided an earlier statement to the press as a self-appointed authority, was on hand to elaborate on his chauvinistic views:

> The women's "On to Cleveland" air derby is contributing nothing to aviation. It should be canceled immediately.
>
> Women are lacking in certain qualities that men possess, just as men are lacking in certain qualities that women possess. Handling details essential to safe flying is one of the qualifications women have not mastered successfully.

Amelia Earhart took time to respond. She sat in the cabin of her airplane talking soberly to Mr. Haliburton for fifteen minutes. Earhart's credentials gave her some measure of credibility.

After lunch and the speeches, the Tulsa society ladies took the racers to the Mayo Hotel for yet another reception. The aviators recognized these events as public relations duties connected with their objective of promoting aviation and women in aviation, and they attended in good spirit.

At last, it was time to check that the airplanes had been fueled, give them a good preflight, and take up a northwesterly course for Wichita, just about an hour away. Mary Von Mach didn't get very far out before returning to Tulsa. She was ill, but after a short rest she was off again. Though the race route had left the desert behind, brutal heat now included high humidity. The pilots were required to carry water during the race. However, for most there was no way to stash it where it could be reached during flight.

As dark storm clouds gathered before and above them, the pilots prayed for a cooling wash down from rain. The racers encountered their first showers between Tulsa and Wichita, near Ponca City, or Punkin' Center as the residents sometimes joked. Flying means you are one with the elements as well as their victim. Those in the open cockpits were attacked by thousands of sharp needles of rain each time they exposed their faces for a navigational peek around the windscreen through the moist, gray veil. They would remove the goggles for sharper visibility, or just keep wiping them. The white silk scarf worn by aviators wasn't just an affectation. It had a practical purpose as a goggle wiper for rain and the all-too-frequent, inevitable engine oil mist.

Two modern aviation breakthroughs occurred departing Tulsa. It was the only time during the race that the pilots were given a chart of the winds aloft, compiled from special balloon observations of the upper air. The winds aloft information helped the racers select an en route altitude with either the best tail wind or the least damaging head wind. Heretofore, the weather information had been so inaccurate as to be useless. The current government weather map showed showers in Kansas City, Kansas, and heavy rain in southern Illinois and Kansas City, Missouri, hopefully to end the next day.

Arrangements also had been made for a live, in-air radio broadcast from an army airplane equipped with a shortwave transmitter. It rendezvoused with the fliers as they approached Wichita, broadcasting a running account of the event. Thaden wasn't keen on having a stranger fly formation on her, but she supposed these trained army aviators knew what they were doing.

A shortwave receiving set in a downtown studio picked up and amplified the broadcast. The program was sent out over telephone wires to the station and broadcast on their regular wavelength. A Topeka station normally broadcast on the same wavelength cooperated with the Wichita station, and they agreed to stay off the air. Ground-bound listeners were, for the first time, privy to the thrill of flight. The crowds' excitement increased as they heard the army observer's voice over the loudspeakers describing Louise Thaden's beautiful blue and gold Travel Air approaching Wichita.

The *Wichita Eagle* newspaper, which had devoted substantial resources to the derby stop, conspicuously sent their own airplane to greet the arriving racers. The racers were pleased at the excitement and special attention their arrival generated. On the other hand, while they were concentrating on maintaining their speed and keeping track of and avoiding other racers who might be close by, they were less than thrilled to have the army and the newspaper buzzing around in their midst.

Wichita was organized, and its committee had the advantage of knowing the various hazards and glitches in the guise of hospitality already experienced along the way.

For a start, spectator viewing planned for some ten thousand people at the airfield offered a clear picture of the arrivals but no access to the airplanes. The turf airfield was well sodded, and airport lights had been installed, should someone arrive late. A large, new hangar was reserved for the race aircraft, with a mechanic assigned to each airplane both for maintenance and security. Accommodations were provided for the accompanying fleet. No more landing in a sea of dust. No more dodging cows and cars. The planes finally got the velvet-glove treatment they deserved, and the ladies were cosseted like the visiting dignitaries they were. Each racer had her own assigned hostess who housed and chauffeured her in a car with her name on its side. Festivities were arranged from the 3:30 p.m. arrival time until conclusion of the dinner and dance. The sympathetic local officials promised they would let the women get some rest by 9:00 p.m. sharp.

As spectators gathered, awaiting the racers' arrival, the local manufacturers showed off their ships with an impromptu air show. The spirit of aviation swelled to a fever pitch. Local flyers were ordered down shortly before the racers were due by an airplane launched with yellow letters on the side reading LAND AT ONCE.

Louise Thaden approached first at 3:17 p.m., registering utter disbelief at the scene below. The new municipal airport located southeast of the city and a mile square in size was overrun with automobiles; roads for miles around were blocked bumper to bumper. An almost physical aura of welcome engulfed her from the ground. Thaden's blue-and-gold airplane, washed by the en route rain, returned to its city of birth and an explosive cheer from not ten, but twenty thousand throats. They claimed Thaden as their own child returned safely home.

Determined to make a good showing for the home crowd, Thaden made her timing flyby, then a perfect soft drop onto the healthy green sod. Once on the ground, she was besieged by reporters. Thaden said in her radio interview on KFH, "Today really brought up the most beautiful part of the trip so far, but one of the most welcome sights we'll see will be that fine, big landing field at Wichita. Can't help mentioning one thing more before I close tonight. That's about this 'sabotage' business. To be short and sweet, it is 'the bunk.' Nothing to it."

One by one, the broadcaster announced a pageant of the nation's state-of-the-art aircraft, many manufactured in Wichita. The crowd appreciated not only fine aircraft, but national heroines making history—marked by the throaty bark of their powerful engines. All of the women were flattered and, in turn, impressed with the advances of modern broadcasting technology.

The radio announcer filled in with other aviation news of the day between arrivals.

The Navy is continuing tests on the dirigible *Los Angeles* carrying as many as six hook-on airplanes at one time—Captain Roscoe Turner took off from Glendale, California, with passengers and landed nineteen hours and fifty-three minutes later validating transcontinental passenger service—a bevy of U.S. marshals and Prohibition agents arrested thirty-two people on charges of selling liquor—eighteen pursuit planes and two Sikorsky amphibians carrying forty-five United States Navy fliers en route to the national air races at Cleveland passed over Wichita, the largest such fleet ever seen—nine men departed Portland, Oregon, racing to their first stop at Walla Walla en route to Cleveland— Anne Morrow Lindbergh made her first solo flight in Hicksville, New York, after nine hours of instruction from her husband Colonel Charles A. Lindbergh.

Thea Rasche received disappointing information upon her arrival in Wichita. There, officials were notified that her federal license had expired, and she was grounded, crushing news considering how far she had come and her determination to show well for her country. However, negotiations with the Department of Commerce proved successful. Her license was renewed locally, and she was allowed to proceed. Undaunted, Rasche was an enormous hit with the crowd. "I'm glad to be here looking for more speed. Everything is going well, but not as well as I would like it to go for me."

As they pressed everyone, reporters besieged Rasche with questions about feelings between the flyers and about sabotage.

Rasche insisted, "There are no poor sports flying in this race."

Newspapers overflowed with descriptions and observations from whoever would make them. Wichita was abuzz.

Mrs. M. C. Naftzger, a resident of Wichita, was quoted as saying, "The derby will stimulate interest in aviation, doubtless. I think the women are plucky and the excitement helps them to stand the strain." The race director Frank D. Copeland couldn't leave public-statement-prone Erle P. Haliburton alone. "To hell with Haliburton!" he exclaimed.

The National Exchange Club of Wichita, along with Steffen Ice Cream Company and other sponsoring firms, took out a full-page newspaper ad. They said, "The object of this race, to stimulate interest in aviation, to aid long distance flying, and to further the Exchange Club's program of establishing Airports and Air Markers is being fulfilled. Wichita welcomes you, aviatrixs of the Woman's Air Derby, and extends to you the keys of the city. Wichita has 113,000 hearts and every one beats for Aviation."

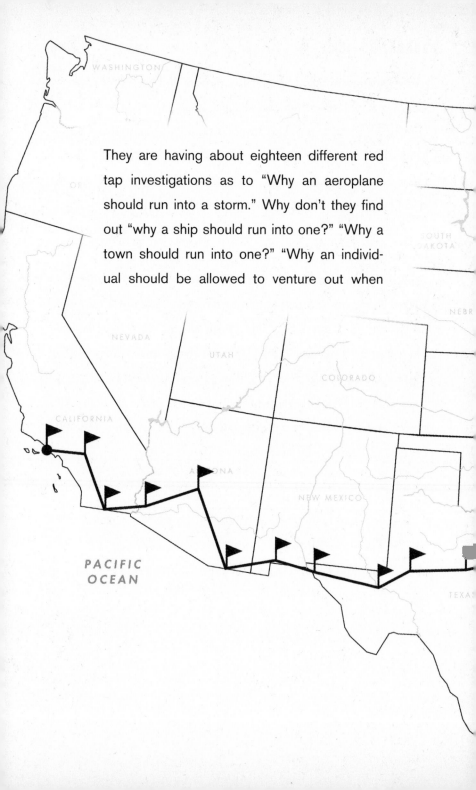

They are having about eighteen different red tap investigations as to "Why an aeroplane should run into a storm." Why don't they find out "why a ship should run into one?" "Why a town should run into one?" "Why an individual should be allowed to venture out when

SATURDAY, AUGUST 24, 1929

Race Day 7

WICHITA TO KANSAS CITY TO EAST ST. LOUIS
175 MILES, 250 MILES

EAST ST. LOUIS

he knows there is one at large some place?"
In fact let's all get together and by the aid of
our chambers of commerce, pass a resolution
denouncing storms. You can only defeat the
elements by organization, so let all government
and civic bodies get together with the real old
man thunder and lightnin' where he stands.

Yours, Will Rogers

Syndicated newspaper column

An airborne traffic jam erupted in Wichita Saturday morning. Not only the Women's Air Derby departed, but all the newest factory products were being flown to Cleveland for "show and sell." Planes took off one after another, like a long-segmented worm with propellers. Soon the sky between Wichita and Cleveland was dotted with every type of plane.

Olive Ann Mellor, a Travel Air executive (and soon-to-be Mrs. Walter Beech), announced they were sending three "speed jobs," including the much-anticipated craft Walter Beech would be flying. Now referred to exclusively as the Mystery Ship, the Model R had been designed and constructed behind covered factory windows. Building the mystery airplane in secret garnered a great deal of publicity, more than could have been bought through the trade journals.

Swallow sent two Kinner-engine trainers for the trade show during the Cleveland Air Races. Cessna would enter one Wasp-powered plane to be flown by Colonel Art Goebel, the famous Dole mainland-to-Hawaii air race winner. Stearman was expected to send several models with various-sized power plants.

Walter Beech had taken Thaden aside, asking, "Would you like to fly our new low-wing Travel Air with the Chevrolet engine in the races at Cleveland?" Thaden realized that he meant the new Model R.

Ecstatic, Thaden replied, "Are you kidding? Wow. I'd give you my right arm to race that airplane." She was already committed to racing the derby Travel Air 4000 in Cleveland, and now the new model also.

Thaden maneuvered into takeoff position, added power at the flag-drop, and started rolling, then as the tail rose, waited for enough speed to lift off. As always, despite distractions, she savored that moment of flight as she lifted free of the earth. She wondered what she had ever done to deserve the gift of flight.

Thaden turned to a heading of 42 degrees, cutting the section lines at almost a 45-degree angle for 175 miles to Kansas City. The continuing leg on to East St. Louis would be 250 miles. No longer clear and blue, the sky turned a gray overcast. Thaden knew from having climbed up through holes that the tops of the clouds were a fluffy, marshmallow-like white. All those ground pounders only saw a gray day. Thaden knew that it was sunny and bright just a couple thousand feet above the surface. After all the desert country, this was the first weather the racers were to encounter with lowered visibility and ceilings. There was an advantageous quartering tail wind out of the west, increasing in velocity with altitude. However, since the racers had to stay under the solid cloud layer, they couldn't ascend to the more favorable winds.

The departures from Wichita were not without excitement for the huge crowds. The racers taking off to the south made steep turnouts to the left toward Kansas City, except Ruth Elder, who made her turn to the right, skimming the cheering crowd before turning on course. Instinctively, she couldn't help seeking fanfare. And the public loved *The American Girl*.

When Gladys O'Donnell added power for the run-up, the right wheel found a soft spot and dug in with a thump. Her airplane went up on its nose dinging a prop tip. Her assigned mechanic was there in a flash and filed the ding. She was off in just a few minutes. They didn't worry too much about prop balance or impairment of the prop's integrity. There were a lot of things they didn't know to worry about or didn't yet have the technology to fix. O'Donnell and the mechanic agreed that the damage was too minor to warrant a new prop.

Telephone reports came in of an airplane down northeast of Wichita near Andover, then an inbound Western Air Express pilot said he saw a plane down near El Dorado, though his passengers observed a subsequent takeoff. Whoever it was went on, for searchers found no one there.

Neva Paris, who grew up in Kansas City, was as excited on this leg as Thaden had been going into Wichita. Like everyone, she was flying in lowering ceilings and rain showers, straining to spot her checkpoints. Unless the showers started merging and forming thunderstorms, she was okay. When the college town of Lawrence came up on the left, Paris knew she was right on course, and the airport would be easy for her to spot despite the intermittent pelting of rain.

It was Neva Paris's turn for the spotlight. She proudly received her hometown's homage and was on center stage for the newspaper there. "Could any woman learn to fly?" a reporter asked.

"Yes, indeed. As much so as they can learn to drive a car. The way they are making planes today, there's no great danger. That's just what this women's derby hopes to prove—that women are as much at home in the air as men."

"Do you still get a thrill out of flying?"

"Oh yes, I always will—it's a sport of the gods. I enjoy takeoffs the most. They never seem to lose their allure. But I am getting the greatest thrill of my life right now in this air derby. I've never been so interested in anything before… I want to see if it goes over big. It'll do wonders for aviation."

The Kansas City stop was quick, for fuel and a bite to eat, with some of the racers not even leaving their aircrafts. Those who took advantage of the luncheon at the Art Goebel Flying School liked the chance to clean up best of all. Neva Paris ran from airplane to airplane to tell the competitors of a meeting planned under the grandstands in Cleveland. She was the beacon lighting the way for a formal organization for women pilots.

The society reporters seemed to dominate the duty roster that day for the *Kansas City Star*. They especially loved Chubbie Keith-Miller's Australian accent.

"Aye, your blithering deserts," they quoted Keith-Miller, "do I like them? I sat down in one for ten hours the other day. Naow, I shall not leave my plane until I see it serviced. Bring on your oil and gas. Fill up the extra tank, please, and look you that it runs cock-full. Overflowing, quite—do you catch me?"

Typically, the reporters seemed more interested in pilot appearances than race results. Some of the copy read like a fashion report:

The boyish looking lass in white unionalls is Gladys O'Donnell. Mary Von Mach of Detroit wore a black shirt, corduroy breeches, and high-tops, and looked quite fit for a hunting trip. Her face was brown as an Indian's.

What a contrast, that skin, with Phoebe's. Phoebe Omlie of Memphis, of course, leader in the light plane class. Mrs. Omlie doesn't tan—she burns. She wears a cloth hat, not a helmet, and unlike Mrs. Miller, who was light as a jockey aboard her little ship, Mrs. Omlie goes in for a solidifying weight. It keeps her little Monocoupe steady as it tears through atmosphere with that sturdy purr.

That orange Lockheed is Amelia Earhart's—Amelia, with the calm air. She freckles and tans, and looks a bit weary. Thea Rasche, buxom German fraulein, was last to arrive in a slow plane. Ruth Elder landed with the wind behind her, but smiled down her embarrassment at the blunder.

So much for the beauty pageant. The reporter did manage to include one technical quote from Mary Haizlip having to do with wind correction: "I allowed five degrees coming over, and I smacked the field right on the nose."

A prominent column on page one of the *Kansas City Star* broke the story of Ruth Elder's matrimonial plans under the headline, FLYING TO HER WEDDING. Walter Champ Jr. proposed just before the Santa Monica takeoff, and Elder had made up her mind by the

first stop. The groom was somewhat perturbed at the instant publicity, not yet having advised his mother of the approaching nuptials.
He would learn that his life had taken a public turn. Sharing page one
alongside the happy news was the exposé of an ambitious farming
operation cultivating a marijuana crop large enough to supply the
entire southwestern United States. The policeman assigned to burn
the crop declared the smoke made him "light in the head," and he
beat a hasty retreat.

The racers had traded the awful bumps of the desert for smooth
air, but they also gave up unlimited visibility for haze. The midwest-
ern flyers knew this was a normal sky condition and acknowledged
that the luxury of great visibility was over. They generally followed
the Missouri River most of the way on over to St. Louis, crossing it
twice, then keeping the flowing landmark on their right wing until it
led them into East St. Louis. St. Louis deserved a salute as the racers
sped by. The city had had the foresight to sponsor Lindy.

There were several minor mishaps along the way. One unnamed
racer spotted the capitol building in Jefferson City, which meant she
had strayed, losing some time being south of course. Mary Haizlip
landed in Washington, Missouri, with a broken fuel line that she
repaired herself. A farm youth offered to help her crank the airplane
for takeoff, but when he couldn't manage, Haizlip cranked it herself.
That took fancy footwork, grinding on the crank then scrambling up
into the high cockpit.

Only the year before, Oliver Lafayette Parks, a Chevrolet salesman
who had opened a flight school on Lambert Field in St. Louis, decided
to relocate onto his own airfield. He selected some bottomland on

the east side of the river in Cahokia, Illinois, calling his operation
Parks Air College. Though a mile and a half from the Mississippi
River, protective levees had not yet been built, and the land was
swampy. But the flight students arrived in generous numbers, living
in dormitories on the field. Ever the ultimate salesman, Parks sold
128 Travel Air airplanes in his first year as Parks Air College.

Lafe Parks required his students to fulfill one hundred hours
of "work time." One of the jobs was to distribute coal-oil railroad
lanterns around the perimeter of the field at dusk and light them,
only to extinguish and gather the lanterns up again at daylight.
Before the end of 1928, Parks the innovator had his field lighted by
floodlights and a beacon, more modernized than St. Louis's Lambert
Field. Parks's four hundred flight students made his flight school the
largest in the United States, and the field was selected for the racers'
St. Louis stop.

Finding postage-stamp-size Parks Airport on the Illinois side
of the Mississippi River in low visibility was a strain. Landing an
airplane on it and stopping short of the fence turned out to be an
even bigger challenge—good practice for students, scary for a first-
timer. Additionally, the airport conformed to the unwritten law Will
Rogers described—landing fields are obliged to have obstacles such
as telephone lines and tall trees at both ends. City fathers and airport
owners were not yet dedicating any land as an obstacle-free approach
path to an airport.

The problem posed by trees or power lines was the inability to
land at the approach end of the field because of the slope of the
descent, while leaving plenty of landing area for rolling out and

stopping. When the wheels put down halfway down the field, little room was left for stopping. Pilots learned pretty quickly to diminish the lift, side-slip to shorten a horizontal distance, and accelerate the vertical until safely past the wires.

Blanche Noyes and Neva Paris both suffered landing gear damage after intentionally ground-looping to avoid running off the end on their landing at Parks Field. Thea Rasche was still contending with dirt in the gas. Bobbi Trout, catching up to the main body of racers, welded a loose exhaust pipe before moving on. These were all too typical malfunctions and normal field repairs. All were repaired in time for the Sunday morning takeoff.

National Exchange Club officials flying along in support of the racers in their personal airplanes were appalled to be groping through the haze, straining to see Parks Airport even though they knew it had to be immediately east of the river. Luckily, they arrived after most of the racers and spotted the airplanes, several parked at the edge of the field, one landing and another scrambling to get out of the way. Contending with the same challenges as the racers, their admiration for these women grew. Exposure to women who had dreams and pursued them, some even in life-threatening situations, caused flying sponsors to examine their own sometimes too-cautious path through life.

It was always possible to get an airplane into a field with no chance of getting out. Obstacles at the departure end inhibited the climb out. A low-powered airplane with engine performance further diminished by summer temperatures might not be able to climb above wires or trees that bordered a short field, especially in afternoon heat. Sometimes, a farmer would be asked to take down a fence. Pilots accepted the hand they were dealt. Curiosity along with daring and defiance all added up to the challenge and fun of flying air machines.

Meanwhile, growing tumult over the *Graf Zeppelin*'s 'round-the-world flight engulfed the racers and the public. The behemoth was flying at over sixty miles per hour out of Tokyo toward the American mainland. Every airplane and balloon in southern and central California was booked to watch the great airship's arrival on the continent from the air. The appearance from the north would be broadcast in four languages, while a naval flight patrol circled the airship to ensure its safety in the airplane-saturated sky. The Weather Bureau advised the *Graf* to abandon plans to approach the American continent via the great circle route as far north as Seattle. Volatile head winds were forecast. The *Graf*'s passengers, when crossing the date line in the Pacific, got a kick out of riding through two Saturdays in a consecutive forty-eight-hour period.

The 1929 flight was completed safely, and the *Graf* continued ferrying passengers across the Atlantic. However, only eight years later, the landing disaster of the giant zeppelin *Hindenburg* led to the class of airships' extinction, and long-range airliners took the *Zeppelin*'s place.

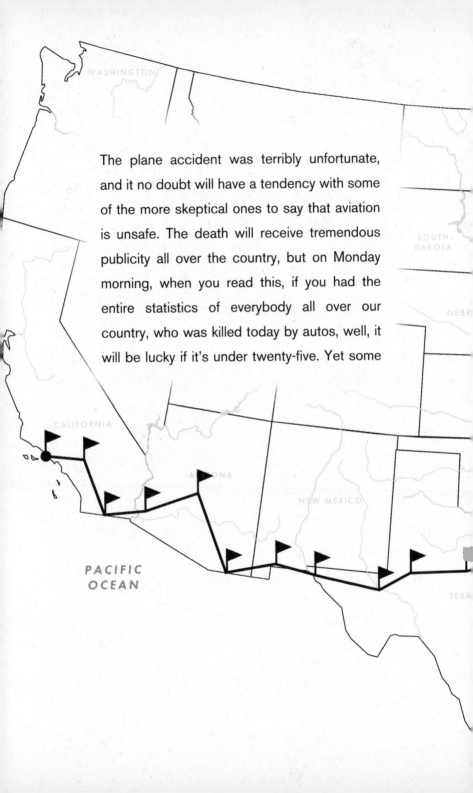

The plane accident was terribly unfortunate, and it no doubt will have a tendency with some of the more skeptical ones to say that aviation is unsafe. The death will receive tremendous publicity all over the country, but on Monday morning, when you read this, if you had the entire statistics of everybody all over our country, who was killed today by autos, well, it will be lucky if it's under twenty-five. Yet some

COLUMBUS

ATLANTIC
OCEAN

of their deaths will never be published beyond their own country newspapers. Yet every one of them is just as dead as those on the plane. So, sir, travel by air is here to stay, and all the doubt in the world can't stop it. And accidents by plane will be taken the same as we take the news that a train at a grade crossing has killed a truckload of people just a matter of fact.

Yours, Will Rogers
Syndicated newspaper column

Fog did not deter the racers from hustling to the airport at dawn Sunday morning. The Cleveland Aeronautical Exposition was opening that day, and the All Women's Air Derby would terminate on Monday—if the fog ever lifted in St. Louis. Over one hundred thousand people were already on hand in Cleveland for the event's opening ceremonies, and the crowd was expected to swell ten-fold by the finish. Elsewhere, three cross-country derbies were underway, the women from Santa Monica, plus two men's derbies from Portland, Oregon, and Miami Beach, Florida. Captain Roscoe Turner with his flying companion, a lion named Gilmore, was still attempting, despite some delays, to set a new record for a one-day east-west transcontinental flight. An outstanding pilot, Turner also knew how to exploit publicity to support his racing activities. When Turner noticed that the Gilmore Oil Company used a mascot lion to advertise their product, he acquired a lion cub that flew with him. He named him Gilmore, and it drew attention like a magnet.

At that late date, the racers' standings were solidifying. With only 536 miles left, it would be hard for anyone to make up enough time to overtake another racer. Any changes in standing now might be dependent upon forced landings or pilot mistakes in the next two days.

In the DW class, Louise Thaden was ahead with 16:27:57 elapsed time, Gladys O'Donnell was next, Ruth Nichols was third, and Amelia Earhart was fourth. The slower CW class had tightened some, but Phoebe Omlie was undoubtedly the winner, unless she ran into trouble. Omlie's elapsed time at St. Louis was 20:23:32. Edith Foltz was two hours behind her, Chubbie Keith-Miller another hour, and Thea Rasche yet another. This race was Omlie's to lose.

Phoebe Omlie

Blowhard Erle P. Haliburton continued to offer his opinions, which the newspapers continued to report:

All the pilots should have been forced to fly over the course at least four or five times. One plane was not even licensed. The death of Marvel Crosson, one of the best women pilots today, was needless. If it hadn't been for her fear and confusion regarding the course, she would have been leading now.

The women were outraged by Haliburton's remarks. Marvel Crosson was one of the most experienced pilots and had practice-flown the entire course prior to the race. The man's blatant prejudice was appalling.

The women completed their preflights in the gray, damp morning air. Mary Haizlip had suffered six emergency landings so far, and her fuel lines were drained, with all sorts of foreign debris removed.

The pilots had time on their hands while they waited for the fog to burn off. Travel Air mechanic John Burke passed the hours doing additional engine inspections. He was stunned to discover that Thaden's magneto points seemed to have been tampered with. Though Thaden doubted someone had done that, he thought it was an act of sabotage. That night in Columbus, he slept with the ship.

The rising sun quickly consumed the fog, and the racers were impatient to get on toward Cleveland. It was a beautiful day for flying, with a nice road and railroad tracks to follow all the way to Terre Haute, Indiana. Thaden had fuel siphoning out through her fuel cap, but she still had enough left to reach her destination. The siphoning fuel stained the wing due to a missing washer necessary to keep the cap tight.

Bobbi Trout was catching up, arriving at Parks Airport just a few hours after the main body of racers departed. She fueled quickly and was on her way. She was no longer being officially timed, and when she had landed at Wichita, three newspapermen were the only people on hand to greet her. Determination itself, she was entered in several racing events at Cleveland and was intent on finishing the race, timed or not. The *Wichita Eagle* wrote, "Bobbi Trout is considered one of the greatest fliers of her sex. It is plain that there are a lot of men who are determined that women shall be barred from the air. If anything was needed to put them into planes that would do it."

Thaden got a kick out of flying along a major road and seeing how many cars and trucks she could pass. It was tempting to drop down and buzz a car to scare the driver and thrill the kids. But that wouldn't be a smart thing to do because she would lose a few minutes climbing back up to cruise altitude. She thought the farmers in southern Illinois appeared to be prospering with healthy-looking crops. The corn was in. "Oh my gosh, there's a train," she observed. "Let's count the cars. I'm overtaking a train." Thaden kept an eye out for a good emergency landing field. The eventuality of engine trouble was always in the back of any pilot's mind.

The Terre Haute Airfield was not hard to pick out just south of town. It was only 485 feet mean sea level and not of generous size. The field met Will Rogers's criteria for a modern airport with obstacles scattered around the perimeter. There were pole lines and radio masts along with high stacks a thousand feet northeast of the field. The racers who had preflown the route in reverse shared the notes they had made describing the airfield, obstacles, and the general condition of the landing area. They were competing for speed, but supported each other for safety.

Unlike Wichita, the crowds at Terre Haute were poorly controlled. Consequently, the pilots stayed close to their airplanes to protect them from the throng. It turned out the fuelers were an equal hazard. They must have been recruited right off the street, and they had little idea what to do with a fuel nozzle. One fueler unscrewed Thaden's oil drain plug. Refreshment tables were laden with cheese and chicken sandwiches. The hosts were puzzled why only the cheese disappeared.

Following a quick radio interview, the racers headed out.

Since the next stop, Cincinnati, had been a last-minute add-on; even those who reverse-flew the course hadn't been there. The owners of the airfield, the Lunken family, had less than a year before incorporated the Aeronautical Corporation of America (Aeronca). Influential and well-respected community leader Robert A. Taft was a director of the company, ensuring both financial and political stability as aviation, and the country, headed into the Depression. Their Aeronca C-2 model, called the "Bathtub" because of its bulbous fuselage, was powered by a small, inexpensive, two-cylinder engine. Priced at a reasonable $1,495, the airplane became a popular trainer, with subsequent models in production for decades. The name is still respected as a trainer and is popular today.

The racers struggled to find the airfield, since not many prominent checkpoints along the route aided them. A road and the wandering Ohio River funneled into Lunken Airport, just barely in Ohio—across the river from Kentucky. Lunken was hard to see down in the river bottom. In fact, it was called "Sunken Lunken" because it was down in a hole, protected from the river water by dikes. Thousands of people swarmed the airport to see the women racers, about double the crowd that had gathered for Lindbergh just two years before. The *Cincinnati Enquirer* described Louise Thaden as "America's Queen of the Air." Well, there are worse things to be called, Thaden decided.

Edith Foltz never found Lunken and went on to Columbus, untimed. Poor Bobbi Trout was down again, making a dead-stick landing in a little field near Greensburg, Indiana. Without even partial power to stretch her glide to a better field, Trout had to put it in a fenced field with her approach between tall poplars. She sideslipped to squeeze in, but knew there wasn't enough stopping room, so she purposely ground-looped to halt before she tore into the fence. Trout's right aileron dragged over the fence and suffered a large hole. She used a piece of tin can and some bailing wire for a patch. An electrician from town did the engine repair, and she was on her way.

Each of the racers felt a sense of relief on their last leg of the day into Columbus. It was an easy leg, despite low visibility. A prominent road led directly from Cincinnati to Columbus with a string of towns all along the way. One farmer with a sense of humor, and apparently with some flying experience, had plowed out a huge arrow in the middle of his harvested corn crop, pointing toward Columbus. Thaden rocked her wings in salute as she went by. Thaden's husband, Herb, had been in Wichita and now was waiting for her in Columbus. Chubbie Keith-Miller was down within twenty-five miles of Columbus, at Xenia, Ohio, with engine trouble.

The Columbus Airport was in the process of building concrete runways, but the edges were unfinished and there was a ten-inch drop-off to a soft shoulder. The racers had been cautioned to stay in the middle of the runway on landing and not to turn off until they saw a flagger indicating a safe off-ramp. They were on the alert. More used to landing on sod, those with metal tail skids were surprised at the trailing shower of sparks.

The racers greeted each other in Columbus almost deliriously, they were each so happy to be so close to the finish line and still in the running. It was almost over.

Herb Thaden, with Louise at the Columbus banquet that evening, had chuckled at the sight of the flyers in their formal evening gowns. Their brown arms turned stark white around the elbows, then the tan color appeared again for a V-neck and face that was trimmed white around the eyes where the goggles had been. Louise confided to Herb her sadness that the race was nearing the end, "We have helped each other, worried together, laughed over mistakes, silently wept and endured in community, recognized our strengths, and combated weaknesses. We never mentioned the afraid times—anticipatory on the ground, actual in flight."

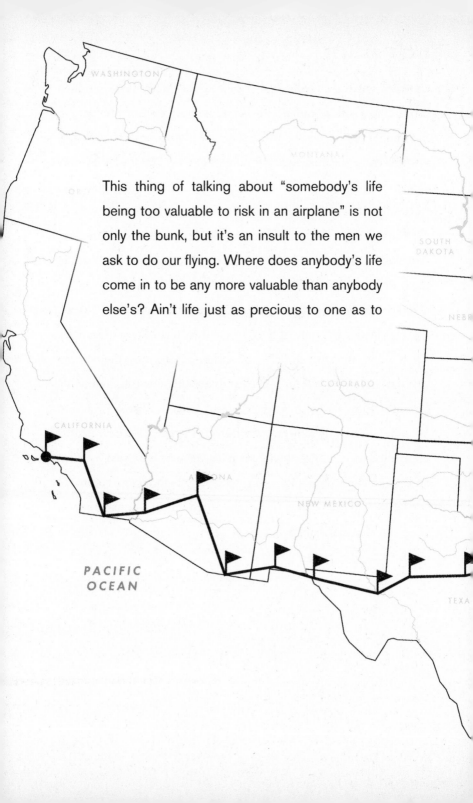

This thing of talking about "somebody's life being too valuable to risk in an airplane" is not only the bunk, but it's an insult to the men we ask to do our flying. Where does anybody's life come in to be any more valuable than anybody else's? Ain't life just as precious to one as to

Race Day 9

COLUMBUS TO CLEVELAND
120 MILES

another? If flying is dangerous pass a law and stop it. But don't divide our nation between a class that should fly and one that shouldn't. Aviation is not a fad, it's a necessity and will be our mode of travel long after all the people who are too valuable to fly have met their desired deaths by the roadsides on Sunday afternoons.

Yours, Will Rogers
Syndicated newspaper column

Since takeoff for the last lap into Cleveland would take place late, the racers enjoyed the best night's sleep in a week. Nevertheless, all were at the airport midmorning to find the souvenir and autograph hunters about in full force. They commenced to check over their airplanes for flight. Takeoff was scheduled for 1:00 p.m.

As they did so, they heard an airplane overhead and looked up, as flyers always do. Ruth Nichols, whose whole race had gone relatively smoothly, had had some maintenance done on her Rearwin. She made an early test flight, and the other racers watched her landing—their natural reflex. The first portion of Columbus's new concrete runway was still closed, forcing the pilots to land "long" over the closed part as they had the previous afternoon, touching down only at the beginning of the usable portion. That morning, a large steam-roller worked back and forth at the edge of the runway, just about where the usable portion began.

As Ruth Nichols descended over the closed runway, she seemed to drift a little in the crosswind as she came to the usable part. It was like a slow-motion picture of the inevitable—as if the two machines were drawn together by magnets. Nichols hit the steam-roller and somersaulted, coming to rest upside down on the soft dirt. Observers could see her crawl out from the wreckage as they raced to her. Miraculously, she was unhurt, but her third-place standing had dissolved in those ill-fated seconds.

For such a senseless tragedy to befall one of the most experi-enced pilots of the race simply proved that bad luck could reach out to anyone. Ruth Nichols, of the striking blue eyes and calm demeanor, was the holder of the second transport license issued to a woman in the United States. She had discovered airplanes on a family trip to Miami when her father bought her a seaplane ride, which had long-term consequences. When she returned to Wellesley College, the wealthy debutante discarded her track toward medicine, determined to make a career in aviation. Her mother had been nonplussed with Nichols's decision to study medicine, but the aviation alternative horrified her. Upon Nichols's graduation from college in 1924, the fledgling aviatrix promptly soloed and became the first female seaplane pilot in the United States. In 1928, Nichols flew along with her mentor on a nonstop record flight from New York to Miami. Just because the press had dubbed Amelia Earhart "Lady Lindy" did not prevent them from attaching that title to Ruth Nichols too.

Amelia Earhart and Ruth Nichols

Nichols helped establish aviation country clubs across the United States. Promoting the concept with a "Sportsman Air Tour," she wore all-white or all-lavender flying suits with matching helmet and goggles, and the shy Quaker girl learned the value of publicity to sales quickly. She toured ninety cities in forty-six states without a single forced landing. This achievement occurred in the day when flight plans usually carried the cryptic note "Arriving G.W.W.P." (God willing and weather permitting). Nichols had quietly flown the entire air derby well, without fanfare or drama. But now she was a victim of random fate, probably helped along by a moment of inattention.

The Columbus takeoff was the first time in the whole race that the competitors departed in one minute intervals in the order of their standing, rather than the reverse. Conceivably, this would allow them to arrive in Cleveland in about the same order. Louise Thaden and Gladys O'Donnell lined up side-by-side first on the runway. With

Ruth Nichols out, Amelia Earhart moved into third place, and Blanche Noyes followed. Though the aviators did not much like the side-by-side takeoff arrangement with that severe drop-off along the edge, no one objected. All the racers were flying conventional-geared airplanes with the third wheel at the tail as opposed to the modern design where the third wheel is usually placed in the front like a child's tricycle. As a result, the pilots sat low in the boxy airplanes behind a huge round engine with the cylinders lined up in a circle. It was impossible to see out until the tail came up. The pilot was forced to lean out the side to be able to go straight down the runway on takeoff. Wedged between an airplane on one side and a drop-off on the other, there was little room for a miscalculation or drift. Sobered by Ruth Nichols's fate, they all rose to the occasion. All Louise Thaden could think about was how easy it would be to lose the "guaranteed" first place she so desired.

Cleveland was only 120 miles away, plus or minus an hour in the various airplanes. Nonetheless, Ruth Elder did manage to get lost once again, landing in Akron. But the flashy pilot persevered and finally arrived in Cleveland as officials were considering a search. Edith Foltz had engine trouble not far outside Columbus, landed, then with characteristic grit, resumed the race. Bobbi Trout, officially out and not being timed, was determined to fly herself into Cleveland and did so. Considering the repairs along the way, she was flying a totally different and new airplane from the one with which she'd started. Proper clothing was the farthest thing from her mind, and she arrived sans luggage, borrowing a clean white blouse to go to the banquet in the same dirty pants she had worn for a week. For Louise Thaden, the last leg felt a little anticlimactic. Yet, as she listened contentedly to the hum of the engine and gazed at the heavens above, she knew no greater pleasure.

Finish at Cleveland.

As she approached Cleveland, Thaden thought the green earth seemed stationary beneath her wings. Her sweating right hand tried to choke the stick, her eyes moving constantly watching for traffic and for checkpoints. She told Herb later that her concentration was so intense that "there were seconds when I forgot to breathe." She wanted to be in Cleveland and win, but at the same time, she didn't want the exhilaration of her great adventure to be over.

Excitement was simultaneously heating up in Cleveland for the *Graf Zeppelin*. The airship had completed its spectacularly fast seventy-hour crossing from Japan to the Golden Gate, then cruised slowly down the coast, circling Los Angeles for four hours awaiting dawn for landing. More than one hundred airplanes flew convoy for the dramatic colossus. The *Zeppelin* was to draw the world together in 224 hours and 24 minutes. The only female passenger, Lady Drummond-Hay, described her voyage as "trackless adventure through pathless space—a new trail blazed by the meteor-like *Zeppelin*"—almost indescribable, certainly unforgettable.

A chemical company, rather than an oil company, refueled the leviathan of the air. A bevy of chemists measured out six hundred thousand cubes of natural and chemical gas mixed. Navigators plotting the *Zeppelin*'s course appeared to be following the women's' derby trail through Yuma, El Paso, Oklahoma, and Kansas—the lower, southern route to their destination in Lakehurst, New Jersey via Cleveland.

All told, each of the derby pilots was flying the last leg with singular concentration, yet they were also reflecting on the past week. There had been trials and challenges, grief and exhilaration, but the camaraderie of the women generated sustenance that would extend well into the future among all women pilots.

Louise Thaden spotted the airfield and grandstands through the light haze fifty-four minutes out of Columbus, picked out the timers at the edge of the field, and dove for the line. Thaden arrived over the finish line first from Santa Monica, just over 2,700 official miles (not including some route changes), over 9 days, logging 20 hours, 19 minutes, and 4 seconds of flying time. She crossed the white chalk line in a 170-mile-per-hour powered descent, thunderstruck at the thousands of people cheering and pulling for her. She could feel their exuberance physically. Gladys O'Donnell and Amelia Earhart thundered in right behind her. The frenzied crowd rose to their feet and swarmed Louise Thaden's blue and gold Travel Air, forcing her to shut the engine down in the middle of the field to avoid endangering anyone with her propeller. Her eyes swept the crowd for Herb, and the sudden emotion of her accomplishment surprised her. Throngs of reporters and photographers engulfed the airplane. A horseshoe of roses was thrust upon the pilot's neck—with thorns intact. Thaden suggested diplomatically that the flowers really should adorn the winning airplane, and they were transferred to the nose of her loyal ship.

Louise Thaden waves at the finish.

A radio microphone was shoved in front of Thaden, and she graciously performed as she had all along. The *Cleveland Plain Dealer* described her:

> As she faced the microphone, her teeth were very white
> against her brown cheeks. Her eyes are gray. The lids

looked heavy. Wind had been hitting them. She wore a white shirtwaist which had black stripes in it; perhaps it was one of her husband's, for it looked like a man's shirt and was open at the neck. Mrs. Thaden's neck is long and tanned. Her brownish hair is bobbed. When the wind strikes it, it falls over her high forehead. She brushes it back with her hands. Her face is thin. As she talked to the crowd through the microphone, she held a 20-for-15 cigarette in her right hand.

"Hello, folks," she said. "The sunburn derby is over, and I happened to come in first place. I'm sorry we all couldn't come in first, because they all deserve it as much as I. They're all great flyers."

Thaden with her decorated plane.

The *Plain Dealer's* Roelif Loveland waxed ecstatic about what he was seeing:

> These women started a week ago Sunday from Santa Monica, on the Pacific Coast. When this reporter used to study geography, the Pacific Coast seemed an awfully long distance away. It was, in fact, entirely too far away to be taken very seriously. They grew oranges out in California, and that was about all it was necessary to know, for nobody had much chance of ever getting that far away.
>
> Well—the National Exchange Clubs having offered prizes for the first women's cross-nation race in history—twenty women started. In a former generation they would have been darning socks and getting dinner and breakfast and supper and putting the kids to bed and reading, perhaps, of the wonders of South America in the *National Geographic Magazine*. Instead of that, they pulled on their tricky aviator's suits and flew to Phoenix, Arizona, thence to El Paso, Texas, thence to Fort Worth, Texas; to East St. Louis, Illinois; to Columbus, then to Cleveland.

Their triumph did not convert all the world to esteem pilots of the "weaker" sex, despite their finishing the perilous route in fragile craft. As the arriving derby pilots descended upon the welcoming Cleveland crowd, a reporter asked Colonel Lindbergh, "Is aviation a woman's game?"

He answered sourly, "I haven't anything to say about that. I'm sorry."

Certainly, Lindbergh was not alone in his skepticism. The bias can be found in isolated venues even today.

Still, at that moment, all the world was caught up in the exhilaration of the airborne gender revolution. The *Plain Dealer* wrote enthusiastically:

> Young, small for the most part, and pretty, these women of our century wear goggles instead of knitted shawls. They burn up distance in a way which is ridiculous. Just imagine your dear old grandmother hopping in a plane, tossing away a cigarette butt, pulling goggles over her eyes, giving the ship the gun and heading from California to Ohio.

Writing in the *Wichita Eagle* newspaper, Thaden said, "There is one big pleasure I will get out of winning. I'll now be able to make good my promise. I have won the cup for Marvel Crosson, and it will be inscribed with her name and turned over to her people."

A reporter noted, "There has not been a race like the Women's Air Derby before." There was never one like it again. It was a first. And it was a sisterhood.

Air derby contestants stand arm-in-arm at Parks Airport, East St. Louis, Illinois. Left to right: Mary Von Mach, Chubbie Keith-Miller, Gladys O'Donnell, Thea Rasche, Phoebe Omlie, Louise Thaden, Amelia Earhart, Blanche Noyes, Ruth Elder, and Vera Dawn Walker.

Sixty-two years later, female astronaut pilot Eileen Collins flew the space shuttle into outer space around the planet Earth. Astronaut Linda Godwin, saluting the women whom she believed paved the way for her, had already carried Louise Thaden's cloth flying helmet into space and returned it to the Ninety-Nines Museum of Women Pilots, the organization Louise Thaden and the other racers founded at the end of the 1929 derby. On another magical day at Cape Canaveral, derby racer Bobbi Trout was there, and watched as her Orville Wright–signed pilot certificate, entrusted to Eileen Collins, blasted upward until invisible in the black of space.

Bobbi still can't understand why she couldn't go too.

Final standings

HEAVIER AIRCRAFT	LIGHTER AIRCRAFT
Louise Thaden	Phoebe Omlie
Gladys O'Donnell	Edith Foltz
Amelia Earhart	Chubbie Keith-Miller
Blanche Noyes	Thea Rasche
Ruth Elder	
Neva Paris	
Mary Haizlip	
Opal Kunz	
Mary Von Mach	
Vera Dawn Walker	

OTHERS

Pancho Barnes—out, wrecked

Marvel Crosson—died

Claire Fahy—out, separated wires

Ruth Nichols—out, wrecked

Margaret Perry—out, illness

Bobbi Trout—finished untimed

Pylon Race Results

Women's Race (510–800 cu. in.)

Event #28 (of 35) at Cleveland

August 29, 1929 | 5 miles, 12 laps

PLACE	PILOT	PLANE	ENGINE	SPEED
1	Gladys O'Donnell	Waco Taper Wing	Wright J6	137.60
2	Louise Thaden	Travel Air	Wright J5	131.43
3	Blanche Noyes	Travel Air	Wright J5	127.77

Pancho Barnes and Ruth Nichols also competed but didn't place.

Women's Australian Pursuit Race

Event #30

August 31, 1929 | 5 miles, 12 laps

PLACE	PILOT	PLANE	ENGINE	SPEED
1	Gladys O'Donnell	Waco 10	Wright J6	138.21

RACE GEAR

A saddle on a motor
Burnin' dynamite for gas,
As a little liftin' surface
As will hike it off the grass,
A thousand roweled horses
With a feather for a girth
Three hundred miles an hour
Fifty feet above the earth!

The breed o' man who rides 'em
Is an optimistic guy
With magic in his fingers
And a telescopic eye,
A throttle bendin' genius
With 'is neck upon 'is nose,
His nervous system sweetened
With intestinal repose.

An autumn day of shadows
With the wind across the lake,
A bonus for a record
And a fortune for a stake;

But hell is in the makin'
And the devil sets the pace
When they tangle out at Cleveland
In the Thompson Trophy Race!

—GILL ROBB WILSON, 1938

EPILOGUE

Pancho Barnes grabbed a ride to the finish of the derby at the Cleveland Air Races after her accident in Pecos, arriving just in time for the start of the pylon races. It was a dangerous sport wherein the planes roared around pylons practically on the deck, in close proximity to one another. She loved the excitement of being there—all the new airplane models and the deep-throated roar of mighty engines. No one would have believed it had they not seen "Speed" Holman loop the loop in a Ford TriMotor and then fly the airliner inverted.

Pancho Barnes and the Mystery Ship.

She found that the rumor of Walter Beech's Mystery Ship had become fact. The Travel Air Model R designed by Herb Rawdon and Walter Burnham was as beautiful as it was fast. Actually, the airplane didn't incorporate startling new technology, but its low-wing monoplane design, high-powered engine, and the secrecy during its gestation explained the sensation surrounding its birth. The ship was nearly one hundred miles per hour faster than her J-5 Travel Air, and Barnes had to have one. So, she did. Only four of the magnificent racers had been built to date, and, as Barnes had plenty of money then, she immediately bought one. She soon challenged Earhart's speed record at 196.19 miles per hour; then, in 1931, Barnes installed a 300-horsepower Wright J-6 nine-cylinder engine in her racer. She eventually owned one of the last two Mystery Ships, through attrition, as the glamorous Model R's siblings perished in accidents through the years.

Pete Hill Jr.—who accompanied his father, the Travel Air test pilot, to modify the Travel Airs during the race and who worked for Beech later himself—offered the interesting observation that the Travel Air Model R Mystery Ship was a failure. From a market perspective it was true, with only five airplanes ever built and sold. But from a glamour and excitement perspective, the Mystery Ship was a huge success. Aviator Frank Hawks set more than two hundred records in the airplane. Shell Oil Company bought one that Jimmy Haizlip (husband of derby racer Mary Haizlip) and Jimmy Doolittle raced. Doolittle bailed out of the airplane due to aileron flutter and was thought to have made the lowest, successful jump at that time, stepping out into space under five hundred feet and surviving.

Barnes's life became centered around aviation in as many venues as imaginable. It suited her. The often-perilous challenges she embraced, well beyond the tenacity of other daring pilots, defined her brazen disregard for personal danger. The recognition of her peers meant everything. She flew for Union Oil, opened up a new route to Mexico City for an airline, and flew stunts for the movies, most notably the larger-than-life Howard Hughes film *Hell's Angels*. The silent movie was remade when "talkies" came in, and many of the engine sounds in the new version were Barnes's Mystery Ship. Barnes helped start a movie pilots' union and conceived the Women's Air Reserve to aid in disasters.

Barnes's flagrant lifestyle took its toll, though never in her lifetime did she comprehend the concept of managing money. Her generosity and fast lifestyle, combined with her disinterest in keeping any tabs on her money, came up against the Depression in the thirties. Barnes lost much of her income and her Laguna Beach house. She saw opportunity in the desert east of Los Angeles and bought a Mojave Desert alfalfa ranch. Her abandoned husband, Reverend Barnes, agreed that their teenage son Billy would benefit from ranch life. It was time the boy became acquainted with his mother.

Barnes didn't even pause. She scraped off a landing strip and almost immediately her Hollywood friends found their way out to the ranch. Just east of Muroc Dry Lake was a military bombing and gunnery practice detachment. The nearby soldiers lived in a tent city, and desert duty was grim.

This proximity equaled opportunity in Barnes's ever-fertile

mind. She bought more property, built a club including an outdoor swimming pool, and imported horses—no nags, of course. Barnes insisted on only the best (most expensive) horseflesh. She imported Mexican alcohol to stock her always-open bar.

As the desert military presence grew, so did Barnes's club (everything mortgaged, of course), and by the late forties, her parties were legendary. The place became so popular that she decreed it a private club, with the first official member high-profile aviator Jimmy Doolittle. Barnes brought in beautiful showgirl hostesses for her guests and put on a huge rodeo, including an incredible Lady Godiva performance. Ever evocative, she named her place The Happy Bottom Riding Club. After World War II, the military made the decision to turn the dry lake beds into Edwards Air Force Base. Test pilots made the Happy Bottom their second home. Barnes's outrageous vocabulary, airplane stories of the early years, free booze, and her uninhibited ways were a natural magnet for the free spirits of the early years of experimental rocket ship flying. In fact, in 1952, when Barnes made her fourth and last trip to the altar, marrying her ranch foreman, the base commander Al Boyd gave the bride away, and the famous test pilot Chuck Yeager was best man at the splashy event.

However, Barnes's relationship with the air force had peaked, and the wedding spectacle closed a chapter of her life. Barnes had always lived beyond her means, so when the air force started buying out her neighbors, she didn't have overabundant resources to resist. Taking the United States government to court in her quest to hang on was no small investment. It didn't matter. Barnes taught herself the law and sued the government over and over again for a "fair" return for her property. Barnes lost her fortune to live in a small stone shack with a dirt floor and no indoor plumbing even farther out in the desert. Nevertheless, she never gave up plans to create a new business and a runway there.

Sadly, Pancho Barnes, the pampered heiress of preposterous wealth, the most colorful character in aviation, died alone in her desert shanty—alone, save for her starving dogs who turned on the body she no longer needed. Barnes's son Billy dropped his mother's ashes over the old ranch house; then, within four years, he crashed and was killed while flying a warbird. The aircraft registry today shows that Billy's widow still owns Pancho's 1929 Beech Mystery Ship.

Marvel Crosson's tragic and mysterious death in the 1929 Women's Air Derby generated much speculation, just as Amelia Earhart's death would later. The news media reported that due to the rough air, Crosson had been obliged to jump from her aircraft, and her parachute didn't open. Since her broken body was found in the mesquite a distance from her demolished aircraft, encased in her parachute, this theory seemed to have merit. The searchers who found Crosson and her crumpled Travel Air found evidence that she'd vomited over the side. They deduced that since her parachute pack was opened and she had "broken every bone in her body," she must have jumped.

Louise Thaden conceived a different theory based on her own

experience with the Travel Air. Perhaps Crosson, like her, had been affected by carbon monoxide and had unfastened her safety belt to get her head over the side to vomit. In her dizziness, she accidentally flew the airplane into the ground. (The Travel Air seat was low in the cockpit, and it would be impossible for a woman to lean her head all the way out seated and strapped down.)

After Crosson's accident, a much-chagrined Walter Beech sent a crew to meet the racers at the next stop to modify the Travel Airs. Pete Hill Sr., his factory test pilot; Johnny Burke, a mechanic; and Pete Hill's teenage son, Pete Hill Jr., were the modification crew. As fate would have it, Pete Hill Jr. was able to give a first-hand verbal account of what transpired to this author. Witnesses had seen and heard the airplane impact with no parachute sighting. Crosson's body was tangled up in her parachute because the parachute pack, strapped onto her person, had ruptured upon impact. Pete Hill Jr. said they were convinced that Marvel Crosson had succumbed to carbon monoxide poisoning, just as Louise Thaden had en route to the race start. Based on their findings, Beech had the remaining Travel Airs in the race modified so each pilot could inhale fresh air rather than the killer exhaust fumes. There was no further trouble.

Though devastated by his sister's death, Crosson's brother Joe kept flying just as he was born to do. He became a famous Alaskan bush pilot, and, in 1935, he flew the bodies of Will Rogers and Wiley Post out from their disastrous crash in Barrow. Talk of a Congressional Medal of Honor for this flight was quashed by the modest Joe, who said, "It was not at all in keeping with what I did."

Marvel Crosson

Amelia Earhart continued seeking and achieving records. It was suggested that Earhart was caught up in the "hero racket," going for bigger and braver feats befitting her position as the foremost woman pilot in the world. On the other hand, all who knew Amelia Earhart testified that her motivation, indeed her obsession, was to promote and support women, not her own self-aggrandizement. Yet, it is Amelia Earhart's name, not that of the first female astronaut or airline pilot or military test pilot, but the woman lost at sea so long ago, that is known by every schoolchild even today as history's most famous woman pilot.

The concept of an advocacy group for women pilots was a subject of conversation before the 1929 Women's Air Derby and was more eagerly discussed during the race. Along with the other women in Cleveland, Phoebe Omlie and Neva Paris initiated an international organization of licensed women pilots called the Ninety-Nines. The group's formal election of President Amelia Earhart occurred two years later, after Louise Thaden had chaired the group on an informal basis. Thaden deferred leadership, generously acknowledging that Earhart's prominence would help the organization and its members.

Earhart's other lifetime affiliation with a women's group was Zonta International, a service organization of professional women. Even today, both groups offer generous scholarship programs in Amelia Earhart's name.

Following Charles Lindbergh's transatlantic trip, attention centered on finding a female pilot/passenger for a 1928 trip across the Atlantic. Amelia Earhart's name had been suggested to publisher George Palmer Putnam, Mrs. Amy Phipps Guest's agent in the task to sponsor a willing participant. After the flight, Earhart's fame led to a second-level career as a lecturer and author, particularly supporting women's issues and writing regularly for *Cosmopolitan* magazine. Her burgeoning career was soon managed by George Putnam, romance blossomed, and they married in 1931. Earhart let it be known that they had forged a prenuptial contract, agreeing to part within a year if the marriage didn't work. That didn't become necessary. Both Earhart and Putnam called each other by their initials, A. E. and G. P.

Earhart felt she didn't yet deserve the acclaim she had garnered for flying the Atlantic as a passenger. She longed to fly the Atlantic solo, which she did in 1932 through the support and promotion of her husband. She flew her Lockheed Vega from Harbor Grace, Newfoundland, to Londonderry, Ireland, inevitably earning and receiving the handle "Lady Lindy." The slender pilot with her boyish haircut, flying pants, and breathtaking adventures seemed to define the feminism of the era. She later wrote, "I, for one, hope for the day when women will know no restrictions because of sex but will be individuals free to live their lives as men are free. Women must try to do things as men have tried. When they fail, their failure must be but a challenge to others."

In 1935, Earhart flew the first solo flight ever from Hawaii to the mainland, then the first nonstop flight from Mexico City to Newark, New Jersey. She pursued and accomplished numerous other record flights. On land, she continued to write and lecture, raising funds for her flying. Although G. P. Putnam's public relations expertise set up her speaking engagements and writing, fund-raising was a constant and necessary burden for Earhart.

Earhart's outspoken support for women's equality did not take place in a vacuum. Progressive Purdue University in Indiana indulged their female students by hiring Amelia Earhart to be an aviation advisor, which included living in the dormitory with the girls. The students had daily access to the most famous, accomplished, supportive mentor of the day. A grateful Purdue Research Foundation settled accounts with the gift of a Lockheed Electra; they called it a "flying laboratory." Earhart could now fulfill her longing to circumnavigate the globe at the equator.

Amelia Earhart

Earhart's 'round-the-world flight early in 1937 started westward, ending in Hawaii with a ground-loop on the departure of the second-leg takeoff. The flat circle on the ground during the takeoff run could have been caused by a problem with the new and still experimental constant speed propellers, simply pilot error, or any number of other circumstances. Her accident fueled the gossip among some aviators that Earhart "wasn't really a very good pilot."

Critics easily overlooked her regular exposure to aircraft often a step or two beyond her current skill level. She was always game to try something new, and sometimes the newly designed experimental aircraft caused unexpected problems. She was a pioneer tackling what could only be called temperamental air machines. As Earhart wrote, "Courage was the price" she paid for flight, fame, challenge, and fulfillment.

After the Lockheed was returned to the mainland by ship and repaired at the Lockheed factory, Earhart and her navigator Fred Noonan restarted their record flight, this time flying eastward, since later in the year the prevailing winds had changed. This time, instead of crossing the Pacific Ocean first, they would depart from Florida to cross the Atlantic and continue on around the globe as close as possible to the equator. Though Earhart expressed her desire to wait until the next year and do the flight westward, funding constraints caused her to go ahead with the flight. Their hope was to be back on the U.S. mainland by the Fourth of July.

The pair was challenged all along their route with mechanical repairs, waiting for parts, and dealing with the situations that took them off schedule. However, their delay in Lae, New Guinea, had to do with communication problems preventing a precise time hack, vital to accurate celestial navigation for their longest overwater leg to an infinitesimally small island. The lack of absolutely accurate time had always imperiled long-distance flights, just as it had for the early sea captains, causing inaccurate navigational computations compounded by distance. Earhart and Noonan had no choice but to wait for an accurate time hack by long-distance radio telephone. Finally, on July 2, they took off substantially overloaded, carrying all the fuel they could squeeze in. Their refueling destination: a tiny speck in the Pacific Ocean, Howland Island. Witnesses at Lae said they and the crew together willed that airplane to fly as it dipped below the end of the runway and struggled out across the water, laboring under the extreme weight for flying speed and clawing for altitude.

**Amelia Earhart conducts maintenance on her airplane
during her 1937 attempted trip around the world.**

Earhart's radio equipment was far less effective than any ordinary training airplane today, rudimentary at best, though state of the art in 1937. Though the Coast Guard cutter *Itaska* heard her call approaching Howland Island, they were unable to make two-way radio contact with the famous aviator and her navigator—one of the most experienced ocean navigators of the era. Her calls were loud and obviously close, but she said she could not see the island. Soon there was silence. A huge search ensued, but Amelia Earhart and Fred Noonan were not found. Some of the search area was off limits to Americans due to Japanese control of thousands of miles of ocean. That loaded aircraft at Lae was the last sighting of the acclaimed and beloved Amelia Earhart.

Myriad imaginative theories about Amelia Earhart's disappearance have developed into a bottomless reservoir of books and movies over the years. Some say she detoured north over Japanese-held territory (just prior to World War II) and was spying for her friend Franklin Roosevelt. But where did she put all the fuel to go that distance? Another theory had her seen by eyewitnesses all over the Marshall Islands, shown off by her Japanese captors who picked the two up off Mili atoll. Others suggested Earhart and Noonan died of dysentery in prison. In another version, they were beheaded. And then the "secret Navy files" have the whole story, but they have never been released.

Amelia and a Pitcairn autogyro.

Amelia Earhart's name is still news. A little newspaper story recently read: "When Oceanside, Calif., police stopped the couple wandering along a roadway one recent evening, they possibly overlooked the story of the century. The woman claimed she was aviatrix Amelia Earhart. The man, carrying only a Holy Bible, was stark naked. They were searching, the couple said, for the woman's lost airplane. Officer Bob George says police gave them a lift to county mental health for seventy-two hours of observation. And the entry in the watch commander's log closed the case: 'Searched area but found no airplane.'"

I lunched one day with two old friends of Earhart's who were among the cofounders of the Ninety-Nines, Fay Wells and Nancy Tier. I asked Wells and Tier if Earhart had been spying for her friend President Roosevelt or had she just missed the island. Their response was fascinating, each certain of her viewpoint. Wells argued that there was no possible way Earhart would spy for the country, with which Earhart's friend Louise Thaden agreed. Tier was equally certain that Earhart would do it in a minute. In fact, their voices raised to the point where other restaurant patrons put down their forks to observe the senior citizens, seemingly refined ladies, shouting at each other. Had they only known these two were Amelia Earhart's contemporaries.

Earhart's saddened mother felt that her daughter was probably a prisoner of the Japanese. Louise Thaden, along with Earhart's sister, Murial Earhart Morrissey, believed that she simply missed Howland Island, ran out of fuel, and went down at sea. Morrissey named the Marianas Trench as her resting place. Earhart had said to Thaden before her risky last flight, "If I should bop off, it'll be doing the thing that I've always most wanted to do."

AMELIA

Somewhere a fin on a lazy sea
And a broken prop on a coral key,
Somewhere a dawn whose morning star
Must etch dim light on a broken spar,
Somewhere a twilight that cannot go
Till it kisses the surf with afterglow;
But here, only silence and weary eyes
And an empty hangar and empty skies.

Somewhere the toss of a tousled head
In the street of the angels overhead,
Somewhere a smile that would never fade
As the score reversed in the game she played,
Somewhere a spirit whose course held true
To do the thing that it wished to do;
But here, only silence and weary eyes
And an empty hangar and empty skies.

—GILL ROBB WILSON, 1938

Ruth Elder was called "Miss America of Aviation." Among all the derby contestants, she continued to be the darling of the national press, who sensationalized her glamour, always equating it with aviation. Elder's habits became a trend. Her brightly colored hair band was soon worn by stylish young women everywhere.

Following the transatlantic attempt, the New York ticker tape parade, and 1929 Women's Air Derby success, Elder turned her fame and adulation into a screen career. Her brave adventure in an airplane named *The American Girl* led naturally to Flo Ziegfield's movie *Glorifying the American Girl*, based on her aborted Atlantic crossing. She starred in two silent movies with Richard Dix and Hoot Gibson. Ironically, the popular beauty launched a $100,000 speaking tour about the same time her flying career was coming to an end and the Depression deepened.

The flamboyant aviatrix had lunched with President Calvin Coolidge and hobnobbed with European royalty. But even a good thing could be too much. At one point, Ruth Elder, determined to withdraw from the spotlight, went so far as to take the name Susan to diminish fame's glare. "A quarter of a million dollars slipped through my fingers, and soon there was nothing," she said.

Elder was married six times, twice to Hollywood cameraman Ralph King. He said she called him one day to ask, "'Daddy, are you married again?' I says no, and she says, 'Can I come home?' I says yeah, and there it was. We got married again. A real love story."

Ruth Elder

Ruth Elder died at age seventy-three on October 10, 1977, one day short of the fiftieth anniversary of her famous attempt to conquer the Atlantic. In tribute to her passion, her ashes were scattered over the Golden Gate Bridge from an airplane.

Claire Fahy, too, dreamed of setting records and making a name in aviation, but she was killed the year following the derby. When the engine failed on Fahy's taperwing Waco while taking off from Tonopah, Nevada, the terrain and altitude gave her few choices or chances to recover from calamity at the most critical point of flight. Her test-pilot husband Herb, who had taught Claire to fly, was killed the same year while demonstrating the first low-wing Lockheed

Sirius. It had been designed for Charles Lindbergh, who lowered the west to east nonstop transcontinental record in it.

~

Edith Magalis Foltz (Stearns) was another pilot who could lay some claim to that slippery word "first." She barnstormed her own airplane before and after the 1929 Women's Air Derby and, at the same time, sporadically maintained what could have been the first female airline copilot "job." Smitten by a longing to fly, women would take any opportunity they could get. Foltz became an unpaid copilot in a trimotor Bach on the West Coast Air Transport line between Seattle and San Francisco. Apparently, it was one of those go-along-when-invited situations, usually on charter trips. Nevertheless, Foltz logged nearly one hundred hours right seat in the Bachs, Fokkers, and Fords with West Coast Air. Western Air Express bought the line, and eventually sold out to United Airlines.

The accomplished early transport pilot continued racing, flying a Kinner Bird, placing third in the Women's Air Derby of 1931, and, in the 1932 Transcontinental Derby for both men and women, placing fifteenth overall. She was the second-place woman behind Gladys O'Donnell.

Prior to World War II, Foltz became operations manager for a new feeder airline in Portland, Oregon, Oregon Airways, where her husband Joe served as president. She taught primary civilian pilot training (CPT), and she remained active in the Ninety-Nines as the first Northwest Section Governor.

When war broke out, anyone who could fly was in demand—so long as he was male. The United Kingdom's need was so great that even female pilots were considered indispensable. Foltz was soon one of the twenty-five elite women pilots selected by Jacqueline Cochran to serve in Great Britain with the Air Transport Auxiliary (ATA), ferrying RAF heavies—Halifaxes, Wellingtons, and Lancasters. The ATA women flew anything, anywhere, anytime, in any weather. Their astonishing story is told in the Ninety-Nines Museum of Women Pilots. Edith Foltz's son Richard followed his mother's example and joined the U.S. Army Air Corps.

Edith Foltz

After the war, Foltz taught instrument flying to naval cadets in Corpus Christi, Texas, but she never lost her fascination with air racing. She flew the modern Powder Puff Derby twice in the fifties before she died at age fifty-one in 1956.

Mary Hays Haizlip caught the racing fever in 1929. She said her favorite races were the closed-circuit pylon races. In Chicago's National Air Races of 1930, she won a first, second, and third rounding the pylons. In Cleveland in 1931, she entered seven races, winning first or second in each. In 1932, she climbed into her husband's Wedell-Williams Racer in which he'd just won the Bendix and set a speed record of 300 miles per hour, which stood for seven years, eventually broken by Jacqueline Cochran. The year 1932 in Cleveland saw her winning the women's free-for-all in a Howard, then, the next year, pylon events in Los Angeles and Chicago. It was no surprise that Mary became the second-highest money-winner in air races, male or female. She later established an astonishing thirty-five-thousand-foot altitude record in a Buhl Pup airplane.

An interesting and tragic aside to the 1933 Chicago pylon races concerned Florence Klingensmith, who finished second to Mary Haizlip. Klingensmith was an experienced pilot. She had set a 1931 record of 1,078 consecutive inside loops. She finished second to Mary Haizlip in the 1933 Chicago pylon races, flying a Gee Bee built by the Granville Brothers. The airplane was a strange-looking ship, quite fast, seemingly all engine. Jimmy Doolittle had won the 1931 Thompson in a Gee Bee and would never fly one again. Every Gee Bee ever built eventually crashed, probably due to the airplane's instability; it was no longer built after 1934. Crashes were not uncommon at the air races, and the pilots, who loved the challenge of competition, glumly wondered if the public came out specifically to cheer a particular pilot or airplane design, or if they attended simply for the excitement of seeing someone die.

Mary Haizlip

The day after Florence Klingensmith's good showing around the pylons, she flew the Gee Bee in the mixed-feature race. The fabric peeled off one of the wings, the wing failed, and she was killed. However, the interpretation of her accident by race officials was that her problems were caused by her "time of the month." Not until women flew thousands of hours during World War II was the old precept that women were not safe to fly during menstruation dampened. Even then, it did not end entirely.

~

To make money, Mary Haizlip flew as a test pilot for three aircraft companies, Spartan Aircraft, American Eagle, and Buhl Aircraft. This dangerous type of flying took its toll when the entire tail assembly disintegrated on an experimental Monocoupe that she was testing. The intrepid aviator survived the crash with a broken back, crediting her husband Jimmy with saving her life. He had strapped her into the airplane so securely, she said, it was like "falling three stories strapped to a chair." Haizlip described a funny encounter with the inscrutable Howard Hughes, a story that is still repeated in aviation circles. She had a special Ritchie aperiodic compass for which she'd paid $125 that Hughes wanted to use for a flight. She offered to simply lend it to him, but he insisted on a five-dollar rental fee. For years, Haizlip said Hughes still owed her the five dollars. "Even then, Howard proved he was a clever man with a dollar. He returned my compass air freight collect."

Haizlip related another encounter with a famous aviator. When the famous General H. A. P. Arnold was a guest in their home, he and Jimmy Haizlip reflected on the Women's Airforce Service Pilots of World War II. "Hap" Arnold had worked with the mercurial Jacqueline Cochran, implementing her plan to train female ferry pilots to release male pilots for combat during the war. As the war's end was in sight, Cochran challenged the general, he said, telling him to either make her a general officer or she'd shut down the WASP. Mary Haizlip heard Arnold tell her husband, "I told her to go ahead. And she did."

Haizlip and her husband, Jim, later took a vacation trip to Europe, not on an ocean ship but rather an airship. They enjoyed passage on the airship *Hindenberg*'s second commercial crossing of the North Atlantic, with their Beech Staggerwing airplane stowed as baggage. With war approaching, the Haizlips returned and settled in the Los Angeles area where Mary became a realtor, Jimmy joining her later, in one of the most successful real estate companies in Malibu. Mary said that when all the fine young men came back from war, "they wouldn't need any little old lady test pilots." Both of the talented pioneer pilots ended the flying phase of their lives, living a full, contributing life in their community. Sadly, their house on a cliff above the beach burned in a Malibu fire, and all their flying memorabilia was lost. Characteristically positive, Mary's comment about the lost treasure was that "when they are in your memory, you don't have to dust them."

Both Haizlips were inducted in the Oklahoma Aviation Hall of Fame and were honored at "the gathering of Eagles." Mary was the only woman in both cases. Mary Haizlip died at eighty-seven in 1997, the second to the last survivor of the 1929 Women's Air Derby.

~

Jessie Maude Beveridge Keith-Miller (Pugh), nicknamed "Chubbie," had been a bit bored in marriage. Just like Pancho Barnes, Chubbie stumbled into the adventure of flight. What could be more fun and frightening than a first-ever flight in a ninety-horsepower, eighty-mile-per-hour cruise speed, unproven airplane from London to her home in Australia—with the bonus of fame and romance!

While vacationing in London, Keith-Miller responded to the intriguing plan of a Captain Bill Lancaster of the Royal Air Force who was looking for a copilot and a fund-raiser for his proposed record flight to Australia. Though not a pilot, Keith-Miller filled the fund-raising role and became Lancaster's business partner and passenger. The pair left England in October 1927 in an Avro Avian two-seat biplane. The trip required forty intermediate stops, including one crash and a broken nose for Keith-Miller along the way. A long delay for repair allowed another pilot to pass them by, though their March 19, 1928, arrival in Darwin gained them great publicity and instant fame. The scandal of Keith-Miller and Lancaster spending three months together on the flight, while each was married to another, diminished her regard at home in Australia. Nevertheless, Keith-Miller's fame and life's course were sealed.

Cashing in on the American public's interest in the colorful Aussie with the musical accent, the Bell Company entered Keith-Miller in the fifty-mile closed-circuit pylon race for women immediately following the 1929 Women's Air Derby. She was still flying her derby Fleet biplane. (Like Keith-Miller, airplane designer and manufacturer Reuben Fleet's young daughter Phyllis Fleet was also a charter Ninety-Nine, though she did not compete in 1929. In fact, the upstate New Yorker didn't attend the Ninety-Nine's charter meeting on Long Island, because her mother wouldn't allow her to wander the big city without a chaperone. Phyllis Fleet didn't meet the other women until some years later.)

Excited spectators of the pylon competition concentrated on well-known Phoebe Omlie, Amelia Earhart, and Ireland's Lady Mary Heath, who would undoubtedly place first, second, and third. The unknown Keith-Miller moved up because Earhart passed her on the inside of a turn and was disqualified. The crowd was astonished when Mrs. Keith-Miller, as the American press invariably called her, won the race and the headlines. Her fame in the United States was always greater than in her native country, possibly because the scandal of her association with Bill Lancaster was forgiven more easily in America.

Keith-Miller's first-place win encouraged her to compete further, and aircraft companies queued up to sponsor her. She flew the Ford Reliability tour for the Fairchild Aircraft Company, one of only three women among the thirty-eight starters. Unstoppable, she was the only woman to finish, and came in eighth overall. Her all-white jodhpurs, silk shirt, jacket, and flying helmet, along with her black boots, tie, and aircraft, added glamour to flying skill. Fairchild happily increased her prize money, and Keith-Miller moved into the big time.

When the stock market crashed just two months after the derby, it took aviation into its drowning embrace. The industry had been experiencing a stupendous period of growth, with commercial production increasing 193 percent over the previous year and flight hours tripling from 1928 to 1929. However, as some aircraft companies immediately struggled to stay afloat and their grandiose publicity events faded, others were able to continue in the business-as-usual mode for at least a short while.

The Wright Engine Company already had agreed to lend Keith-Miller an engine to attempt a transcontinental record, and she searched for an appropriate airframe for it from her narrowing sources. She settled on an Alexander Bullet with a 165-horsepower Wright Whirlwind engine. The airplane had a terrible reputation for haplessly spinning, but the optimistic pilot figured it was a straight-and-level race and she would "be careful." The daring Keith-Miller established a record both ways, between New York and Los Angeles, mastering the untrustworthy Bullet.

Keith-Miller was on a roll. When offered a Pittsburg-Havana round-trip record flight, again to be flown in the Alexander Bullet, she followed the S on her compass. Cuban crowds welcomed her at the end of the first leg, then she contracted a near-fatal case of "get-home-itis," a well-known aviation disease especially common to inexperienced pilots. It's a feeling of a great need to get home, with the good judgment and patience to wait out bad weather diminishing in direct proportion to mounting pressure to take off. An old saying in aviation points out that "the pilot took off in terrible weather and his funeral was held in bright sunshine." As Keith-Miller remained grounded in Havana by bad weather, her sponsor pushed her to complete her flight. She succumbed to the pressure and took off for Florida despite ominous weather, with plenty of fuel, but aided neither with instruments for flying in the clouds nor radio.

When she didn't arrive in Miami and her fuel was known to be exhausted, a search was initiated, then abandoned after two days. Actually, Keith-Miller had fought it out with a storm encompassing frightening winds, both horizontal and vertical, a lifeless compass, and a growing terror that she might spin the Bullet. When she eventually flew out of the storm, land was not in sight, and the fuel level was becoming critical. She finally saw land, even though it was jungle, and set down in a short clearing. The strong west wind had taken her to the Bahamas instead of to Florida. Only dumb luck kept her out of the ocean.

The Cuba fiasco was virtually the end of Chubbie Keith-Miller's aviation glory days, but a bizarre turn kept her in the news. As she worked with a ghost writer, Haydn Clarke, on her biography, she developed feelings for him, and her romantic entanglement with Bill Lancaster was jeopardized. Keith-Miller professed love for both men. Clarke was murdered, and Lancaster was arrested and charged with killing his rival in a fit of jealousy. Lancaster claimed that Clarke had committed suicide. There was a sensational trial. The *Miami Herald* said the "swashbuckler" Lancaster was lucky to have an outstanding defense attorney. Keith-Miller's pilot was acquitted, and the notorious couple left for England.

Not long after, Bill Lancaster attempted a record flight from England to Cape Town in an Avro Avian. His route took him across the great Sahara Desert with its endless uninhabited stretches of desolate sand dunes, and the adventurer never arrived at his destination. Twenty-nine years later, Lancaster's body was found by a camel corps, preserved by the dry desert heat. He had lived for a week after his crash, and his diary was said to have a message for Keith-Miller: "Chubbie, my darling, give up flying and settle down!"

Chubbie Keith-Miller did indeed marry again, this time to John Pugh, an airline pilot. They were in Singapore when the Japanese arrived in World War II. Chubbie Keith-Miller died at seventy-one in London in 1972.

~

Opal Logan Van Zandt Giberson Kunz, although only married once, came by her string of names as a result of the demise of her parents when she was twelve. Her mother gave Kunz her own name, Logan. Her father was William A. Van Zandt. When Kunz's aunt and uncle, Ed and Margaret Giberson, adopted her when her parents died, they added their family name. Kunz's marriage to world-renowned gem expert and Tiffany's vice president, Dr. G. F. Kunz, had been a major social event of 1923. The subsequent annulment drew much commentary. News reports never failed to mention the couple's forty-three-year age difference and Opal's prestigious address on Riverside Drive. She held her head high, saying that the annulment had been achieved in complete amity, that they would continue living together, and that Opal would run Dr. Kunz's household. Dr. Kunz died in 1932, leaving Opal half his estate, estimated at $1 million.

Opal Kunz

Kunz bought a 300-horsepower Travel Air for the 1929 Women's Air Derby, but she was not allowed to compete in it, since race officials said it was "too fast for a woman to fly." So, she rented a 200-horsepower Travel Air. Following the race, Kunz became prominent in the organization of the Ninety-Nines. The Tiffany's connection came into play with the prestigious jewelers designing the interlocking square nines, which became the badge worn by all members, even today.

Tiffany & Co. designed the Ninety-Nines official badge.

Kunz stunned a crowd of thirty thousand at the American Legion air meet in Philadelphia in September 1930, winning a spectacular and dangerous pylon race in open competition with men.

Opal Kunz's unequivocal patriotism led her to found the Betsy Ross Corps for women supporting national defense. (Like Pancho Barnes's Women's Air Reserve, this was another offshoot, though only the Ninety-Nines survived long term.) The Corps's purpose was to serve on noncombatant duty in time of national emergency. Opal Kunz's greatest pride was in teaching four hundred students to fly in the civilian pilot training program during World War II.

Her patriotism never waned. When Yuri Gagarin hurtled into space in 1961, sixty-five-year-old Opal Kunz wrote President Kennedy volunteering to go for the United States. She died at age seventy-one in 1967.

~

Ruth Nichols always believed that had her papers been processed expeditiously, she, rather than Phoebe Omlie, would have been the country's first female transport pilot. A law passed making tracking and numbering pilots' credentials a regional obligation. Unfortunately, it ensured that dates would always be questioned and challenged. Be that as it may, Ruth Nichols had soloed a seaplane in 1923, then she was licensed as the second female transport pilot. Ruth Nichols and Phoebe Omlie would continue to be nemeses.

Their mechanic licenses were a different matter. The two women took the mechanic's test on the same day, and they obviously should have numbered one and two. An official Department of Commerce investigation determined that even though Phoebe Omlie held mechanic license number 422 and Ruth Nichols number 401, Phoebe was actually licensed first, purely by chance.

With licensing, it became easier for pilots to locate other pilots. In 1927, Nichols had received a letter from Amelia Earhart suggesting a formal organization of the country's twenty-one women aviators. Earhart said, "Personally, I am a social worker, but fly for sport. I cannot claim to be a feminist but do rather enjoy seeing women tackling all kinds of new problems." Nichols responded in the affirmative.

Earhart's letter suggested several categories of membership: "[Fédération Aéronautique Internationale] for inactive flyers such as Katharine Stinson, active transport or private operators, and those in administrative capacities in recognized aeronautical concerns. They would also establish an associate membership category for any women who would like to boost aviation." As it turned out, membership in the Ninety-Nines two years later was restricted to licensed female pilots only.

After Nichol's encounter with the steamroller during the 1929 Women's Air Derby, her luck took a turn for the better. Obtaining sponsorship from Powell Crosley Jr., president of Crosley Radio Corporation, Nichols flew record flights in the big Lockheed Vega with its nine-cylinder 400-horsepower engine and CROSLEY painted in big gold letters along the fuselage. She set a transcontinental speed record for women in 1930—Roosevelt Field, Long Island to Los Angeles in sixteen hours and fifty-nine minutes, then back in thirteen hours and twenty minutes. Headlines the next morning read: "Ruth Nichols spans nation, beats Lindbergh."

Ruth Nichols

Early in 1931, Nichols's mentor and advisor Clarence Chamberlin stripped all the extraneous weight such as extra seats and door handles from the Vega to facilitate her climb for an altitude record. The already-powerful engine was supercharged, and a special climb propeller was installed. Nichols dressed in multiple layers of clothing and fur boots, preparing for the cold, and she quickly climbed to altitude. Chamberlin had rigged up a primitive oxygen system to keep Nichols's brain alive when she climbed above twenty thousand feet. The oxygen cleared her head, but with an outside air temperature of forty-five degrees below zero, the oxygen froze her tongue. As the airplane's rate of climb started to deteriorate around twenty-eight thousand feet, Nichols implemented Chamberlin's ace in the hole, an oxygen line feeding directly to the engine air intake for a last burst of power. Her altimeter read 30,350 feet before the airplane gave up and started down. When the sealed barograph was read on the ground, her official record altitude was 28,743 feet.

Unable to leave well enough alone, and with Nichols's push, of course, Chamberlin next uprated the Wasp engine to 600 horsepower and further streamlined the Vega's airframe for a speed record attempt. Sure enough, 210.685 miles per hour set a new women's speed record, thirty miles per hour above Amelia Earhart's previous record. To become the first woman pilot to fly solo across the Atlantic was her next goal. Crossing the big pond was a still-unfulfilled record ready for a taker.

Nichols flew her borrowed Lockheed Vega named Akita, an Indian word meaning *explore* or *discover*, to St. John's, Newfoundland, in June 1931, an intermediate stop prior to her starting point for Europe. Upon arrival in St. John's, she realized the landing strip was too short, and at the last moment on her approach, added power for a go-around for a second try. But her attempt at recovery came too late. Nichols left her landing gear in the treetops, and the big Lockheed crashed through the trees and boulders, shedding airplane parts along the way. Though badly injured, Nichols was desperately afraid of fire, and dragged herself out of the airplane. The accident and severe injury ended her challenge to Amelia Earhart. Nevertheless, the Fédération Aéronautique Internationale named Ruth Nichols the outstanding U.S. pilot for 1931. In 1932, Ruth Nichols joined the long line of women purported to be the first female airline pilot in America when she flew the inaugural flight for Clarence Chamberlin's new airline, New York and New England Airways. Years later, that claim generated an appearance on the television program *To Tell the Truth* as the first woman airline pilot in the United States. Ultimately, the Federal Aviation Administration denied the claim.

Nichols endured six major accidents in her aviation career, including numerous aborted record-flight attempts. The trusty Vega was finally destroyed, after multiple rebuilds, on a grossly overloaded takeoff with enough fuel for a nonstop transcontinental flight. As another world war approached and her record flights ended, Nichols turned to humanitarian causes, just as other early women pilots had and her Quaker ancestry demanded. In 1940, she founded Relief Wings to support civilian disasters. When World War II did come and civilian flying was curtailed, Nichols's Relief Wings was melded into the Civil Air Patrol, and she continued her service through that organization.

Ruth Nichols

Appointed as a special volunteer correspondent for UNICEF, Nichols served as a "courtesy extra pilot" on a 'round-the-world UNICEF fact-gathering flight in a DC-4. They made stops across Asia as Nichols carefully reported progress in the feeding and care of needy children. Completing her surveys, she left that flight for alternative transportation out of Rome, headed for home. Unbelievably, her airplane crossing the north Atlantic was forced to ditch in the ocean, and exiting the sinking airplane, she spent the night in a life raft. After rescue and return home by air via Ireland, and in absolute disbelief in how she accomplished it, Nichols was recognized as the first woman to complete a globe-circling flight.

When Nichols's friend and rival Amelia Earhart was lost in 1937, Nichols's omniscient comments were: "If it must come, this was a fitting end to a flyer's career—to disappear at the peak of fame, on a final glorious attempt to conquer new frontiers of the sky; never to know the erosions and disappointments of age; to live on in memory as young, golden, and unafraid." Ruth Nichols continued to fly all her life and died at age fifty-nine in 1960.

Blanche Wilcox Noyes commented at the end of the race on the public's lavish interest in the Women's Air Derby. "I think I've autographed everything but flypaper," she exclaimed. She described her en route rough landing as "one of the most inexcusable and foolish things a person can do. I had my eyes open and my brain tight shut." The Cleveland crowds loved their hometown girl.

An actress, Noyes learned to fly from her dashing airmail pilot husband, Dewey, shortly before the race. She jumped into aviation with both feet and stayed there for life. In 1930, Blanche and Dewey took ninety-year-old John D. Rockefeller for his first and only airplane ride.

In 1932, Noyes flew the Pitcairn autogyro for Standard Oil Company. This machine combined conventional fixed-wing with vertical takeoff, rotary-wing concepts. The autogyro involved a free-turning rotor for lift and a conventional tractor engine and propeller for forward thrust. Spanish designer Juan de la Cierva had worked out the principle that was then further developed and expanded by Harold Pitcairn in the United States. Pitcairn's concept was that the autogyro would become an affordable, easy-to-fly, mass-market aircraft, and he envisioned them as common as automobiles. Although Pitcairn won the Collier Trophy in 1930 for his achievement and furthered the later development of the practical helicopter, the autogyro suffered excessive accidents and never sold well in the marketplace. Nevertheless, it was pretty impressive to see this tiny woman, big grin on her face, climb out of the large, unwieldy ship.

In 1936, Noyes was Louise Thaden's copilot, winning the Bendix Air Race from New York to Los Angeles against both men and women. In the same year, and for thirty-five years thereafter, Noyes worked in the government's air-marking program, supervising the construction of seventy-five thousand air markers across the country. Before the era of the modern navigational radio, pilots depended upon identification markers on the ground to supplement their navigation skills. Her employer called Noyes a "champion of safety."

As soon as the program got up and running, World War II broke out. The markers along the coasts were removed for fear they would be helpful to enemy planes. After the war, they were reinstalled.

Blanche Noyes

Noyes was the recipient of many awards and honors. One colorful writer wrote that Blanche Noyes's experiences "increased the stature of her soul."

Having known Noyes during her FAA years, I can testify that she never failed to fulfill her fun quotient. She particularly enjoyed her Watergate address during its notorious Nixon years. Charter Ninety-Nine Blanche Noyes died at age eighty-one in 1981.

Gladys Berry O'Donnell's second-place win in the 1929 Women's Air Derby whetted her racing appetite. Although she had flown only forty-six hours prior to the derby, she was the winner of the 1930 event. O'Donnell was a ferocious competitor in the pylon races and was awarded the Aerol Trophy by the National Aeronautic Association (NAA) in 1930. She was considered the outstanding woman flyer of the year. She was a natural, winning $8,800 in prize money that Depression year and twenty-nine subsequent competitive events, usually flying her Taperwing Waco (which was streamlined to the limit), all while rearing two children.

Gladys O'Donnell

O'Donnell started a club of the 1929 Women's Air Derby pilots called the Skylarks. But as the Ninety-Nines developed, those members became charter Ninety-Nines and the Skylarks were absorbed. O'Donnell, who was from Southern California, acted as the first governor of the Ninety-Nines' Southwest Section.

Gladys and her husband, Lloyd, operated a flying school in Long Beach, California, for which Gladys instructed. Gladys became an early movie pilot. She was a champion of women's rights, and her later years were devoted to Republican politics, beating Phyllis Schlafly for President of the National Federation of Republican Women in 1968. Gladys O'Donnell died at age sixty-nine in 1973.

~~~~

Phoebe Fairgrave Omlie topped her victory in the Women's' Air Derby by winning the Dixie Derby in 1930. She won the $3,000 purse, and a glamorous Cord automobile, by flying her Monocoupe, Miss Memphis, in the 1931 National Sweepstakes Race. With this leg up, Phoebe and her husband, Vernon, left barnstorming and racing behind, and settled into "serious" flying in Memphis. The glamorous couple was the toast of Memphis. They loved to dance in the Peabody Hotel ballroom where the spotlight would pick out the tall, handsome Vernon and his tiny wife, Phoebe, as they entered.

The Depression forced the Omlies to sell the majority interest in their business, and Phoebe became more involved in politics. Flying the campaign trail in 1932 for President Roosevelt led to an unprecedented governmental appointment for Phoebe, the first woman appointee in aviation, with the title Special Assistant for Air Intelligence on the National Advisory Committee for Aeronautics. In her position, Omlie was responsible for air marking. Louise Thaden and Blanche Noyes worked with her, Noyes staying on for over thirty years.

Omlie introduced another first: Vocational education in the

Memphis public schools. Eleanor Roosevelt called Phoebe Omlie one of the "eleven women whose achievements make it safe to say the world is progressing."

Vernon Omlie taught author William Faulkner and his brother Dean to fly. The Faulkners became so enamored of barnstorming that they flew themselves, and wrote of it. Faulkner's novel *Pylon* included the thinly disguised Omlies.

Phoebe Omlie

Tragically, Vernon died in 1936 as a passenger on an airline's botched instrument approach in fog. Phoebe lived another nearly forty years, reduced by illness to poverty and self-imposed isolation. William Faulkner understood her not wanting to be remembered as she was at the end of her life. She was part of a bygone era. He said sadly, "There was really no place for (barnstormers) in the culture... everybody knew that they wouldn't last, which they didn't." Phoebe died at age seventy-two in 1975.

Neva Finlay Paris took action after the gathering under the grandstands at the end of the derby. The women were determined to organize, and Paris was the detail person who pulled it all together. She declared they would "promote good fellowship among licensed women pilots, encourage flying among women, and create opportunities for women in commercial aviation."

Neva Paris

Paris signed a joint letter along with Frances Harrel, Margery Brown, and Fay Gillis Wells, to all the then 117 U.S. female pilots, of which ninety-nine eventually chartered the group. Consensus was to name the organization after the number of charter members at the postmark deadline date. Newspaper accounts of the women pilots' group, as it was in process, referred to it variously as the 86s, the 97s, and finally the 99s, or the Ninety-Nines. And so, it was.

Paris's enthusiasm permeated the group, and plans were made for regional structure and gatherings, communication about jobs, and service to the aviation community. Two planning meetings were held and officer selection was underway. Then tragedy struck.

Opal Kunz was to write on January 13, 1930, "It should be remembered by all of us that this club was really founded by Neva." Paris had just been killed in a spin at Woodbine, Georgia, en route to Miami.

~

Margaret Gilbert Perry recovered from the typhoid-fever attack suffered during the race, and she migrated to California to operate an airport in Culver City; she was probably one of the first women in the country to manage an airport. Some thirty women pilots wearing their white flying outfits flew in for the dedication of the airport. There, in California, she married Larry Cooper, a movie-stunt pilot who also flew for Texaco Oil Company.

Margaret Perry

Perry was always active in the Ninety-Nines, with membership in the southwest growing from seventeen to ninety-six while she was governor of the section. Margaret helped found the popular magazine *Airwoman*.

Later, bringing tales of women's adventures, employment, and competition opportunities to a broader audience, she returned to her home state of New York and married Harold Manser. Perhaps her most fulfilling Ninety-Nines project was involvement with a fitting tribute to Amelia Earhart as trustee of the Amelia Earhart Memorial Scholarship program. Perry's life was one of constant service until her death in 1951.

Thea Rasche, known as Germany's "Flying Fraulein," returned home to Europe following the derby to qualify in seaplanes (a first) and gliders. Rasche was forced to sell her airplane upon the Nazi rise to power, and she became editor of an aviation magazine. She crewed with two Dutch pilots on a DC-2 flying the eleven-thousand-mile Mac Robertson Air Race from England to Australia, took first place, and was the only woman to finish the race. Unfortunately, the event cost Rasche her editing job, and her three books were banned after charges of "too much sympathy for the Anglo-American enemies."

Thea Rasche

Rasche joined the Nazi party hoping to continue flying, spending the war years in Berlin. She was later tried in 1947 in the United States for her Nazi activities. It was ironic that she was penalized both for her American sympathies and also for Nazi loyalties. She was cleared in the German court, due to a lack of evidence that her pilot skills had affected the war effort. Interestingly, Rasche was one of only three female honorary members of the low-profile men's aviation group, the Quiet Birdmen. Quotable Rasche said that "sex bombs are as dangerous as atom bombs," and flying was "more thrilling than love for a man and far less dangerous." She died at age seventy-two in 1971.

Louise Thaden was among the women who gathered under the grandstands post-derby. Like the others, she was determined to develop a formal advocacy group composed of women pilots. At that time, it was all but impossible for the women to secure jobs in their chosen field, and the power of an association made sense to all. Neva Paris became the temporary chairman of the group, but her death en route to the air races in Florida sent the new club into turmoil. Louise Thaden took over as secretary and ran things informally for the first several years. Though asked to serve as president, Thaden stepped aside, insisting that Amelia Earhart was better known and would be a better spokesman for the group. She served as Earhart's vice president after the Ninety-Nines' first formal election in 1931.

Thaden flew her Travel Air 4000 in the pylon races in Cleveland at the terminus of the Women's Air Derby. It was a dangerous business. The racers lined up for a racehorse start, all headed for the scatter pylon straight ahead at which time they would turn left for a rectangular course with pylons at the four corners. The scatter pylon did just that—scattered the racers. All the racers would jockey for position at the first pylon, staying just outside the pylon—cutting inside meant the pilot would be disqualified. Everyone would stay low, about fifty feet, to be able to see that they were outside the pylon, which was also about fifty feet tall. If they climbed, the pylon was hard to see, and they could be disqualified for cutting it too close. If they did stack up, they would dive for the finish line trying to pass those ahead. Of course, this was all at full throttle, and there were collisions and deaths in pylon racing.

Louise Thaden

The Travel Air Model R Mystery Ship was completed only a week prior to the start of the Cleveland Air Races. The test pilot flew it at 225 miles per hour flat out, and he knew he had a winner. Doug Davis was the first to race the speed demon in an event. While zooming around the pylon course at Cleveland, Davis was afraid he'd missed the last pylon. Not wanting to be disqualified, he circled the pylon a second time and still a third. Despite all that delay, Davis won the race at an average speed of 194.96 miles per hour, the fastest speed yet recorded for a commercial airplane. Walter Beech's goal was to beat out the army competitors—which his pilot did.

Louise Thaden had opportunity to sit in the stands among the bloodthirsty fans interacting with the racers. She was stunned at what she heard and wrote it down—the reaction of a spiritual and normally demure woman whose children never heard her utter an obscenity. She responded to the ferocity of the crowd:

> *I go to the national races*
> *I sit with the crowd who roars*
> *"Get goin' you goddamn pilots,*
> *Get goin' and make a score."*
> *"What the hell your personal safety,*
> *What the hell your wife and kids—*
> *Just make a record and keep it,*
> *So take off the goddamm lid!"*
> *"Get goin' you goddamn pilots,*
> *Get goin' to make a score!"*
> *"What the hell do we care for pilots?*

There always are plenty more!"
Maybe you'll win some money—
Maybe you'll get a large prize,
But what profit, fame or glory
If in a grave you lie?
Soon you'll be forgotten—
Soon there'll be others more
Who'll far surpass your record
To the same crowd's lusty roar.

—LOUISE THADEN

The Mystery Ship had problems, and Thaden never got to fly it. Walter Beech quietly withdrew the airplane and shipped it back to Wichita via train. He replaced the Chevrolet engine, which was not working out with a Wright engine. Both Jimmy Doolittle and Jimmy Haizlip later raced a Mystery Ship, though Doolittle bailed out of his when the wings failed and it burned. Although it was a racing fool, only five were ever built.

Louise Thaden and her husband, Herb, moved to Pittsburgh to operate his Thaden Metal Airplane Company, and Louise got a job as director of the Women's Division of the Penn School of Aviation. Between the birth of her son Bill and her daughter Pat, Louise and fellow aviator Frances Marsalis achieved a new record in a refueling endurance flight. They kept a Curtiss Thrush aloft for over eight days over Long Island, including seventy-eight air-to-air refueling contacts. The lissome couple pumped two hundred gallons by hand every twenty-four hours.

In 1936, Louise Thaden and Blanche Noyes stunned the aviation world by winning the Bendix Trophy race from New York City to Los Angeles, which had chivalrously been opened to women. Once again under Walter Beech's sponsorship, they flew a stock Beech Staggerwing. When Thaden came through Wichita and Beech found out they'd been flying at cruise power, he told Thaden in no uncertain terms to open it up to full power. She said okay, but continued to fly it the way she wanted, at cruise. At the finish line, her mentor grinned. "Nice work, fella. The Old Man knows what he's talking about, doesn't he?" Thaden and Noyes beat all the men, as well as Amelia Earhart and Helen Richey who were flying Amelia's Lockheed. Thaden received the nation's top aviation award, the Harmon Trophy, and she was named the outstanding woman pilot in the United States for 1936.

Throughout her lifetime, Louise Thaden flew airplanes and urged others to apply their talents to aviation. She continually supported various Ninety-Nines projects and inspired Civil Air Patrol Cadets. Her son Bill learned to fly and made a career as an airline pilot, and both Louise Thaden's daughter, Pat Thaden Webb, and granddaughter, Terry von Thaden (Bill's daughter), became pilots and members of the Ninety-Nines.

Louise Thaden's perspective was certainly affected by flying airplanes. She said, "Flying does something to one spiritually; it makes all life a bit more worthwhile; it gives one a sense of values. When big estates dwindle to less-than-doll-house proportions when viewed from the air, why be concerned over petty troubles—or if one's own castle happens to be a combination living-bedroom-kitchenette?

And the immensity of the universe—it takes a flight high up in the air to bring its giganticness really home."

Thaden wrote in her book *High, Wide and Frightened*: "To us, the successful completion of the derby was of more importance than life or death. We women of the derby were out to prove that flying was safe." Her book emphasized the pilot's competitive nature, but also evoked her self-effacing temperament and the reasons why she is not as widely known today as other pioneer pilots.

Thaden is the heroine of the modern Staggerwing Club, a group of owners of one of Walter Beech's most popular designs, and the airplane that draws pilots to stop and stare even today. A good part of her aviation memorabilia is enshrined in the Staggerwing Museum in Tullahoma, Tennessee, including her original pilot's license number 6850 signed by Orville Wright.

Staggerwing Club enthusiast Dub Yarbrough undertook a years-long quest to find Thaden's original Travel Air, and he eventually located remnants of the old airplane. After a multiyear restoration project, Susan Louise Dusenbury, a DC-9 captain for Airborne Express, flew the sixty-year-old NC671H on a sentimental journey along the original route of the 1929 Women's Air Derby. Dusenbury was the first female in the United States to hold an FAA Inspection Authorization (she's a licensed aircraft and power plant mechanic). Since Dusenbury restores airplanes herself, she could not be more appreciative of the restored aircraft or its historical significance.

It was my privilege to fly formation as a passenger in a Beech Staggerwing with Dusenbury alongside, leading in the Travel Air, into Beech Airport in Wichita on that recreated historical flight. For a period of time, Beech Field served as my own home field. It was also the home of both airplanes. Photos of Louise Thaden always held a prominent place in Mrs. Beech's office.

The actual airplane in which Thaden flew to fame in 1929 is now owned and treasured by the Ninety-Nines Museum of Women Pilots located on Will Rogers World Airport in Oklahoma City. Ninety-Nines also hold Thaden in their hearts, and her cloth flying helmet was carried into space by astronaut and Ninety-Nines member Linda Godwin, then it was returned for display in the Ninety-Nines Museum.

Asked to compare the first Women's Air Derby run in 1929 and the modern Powder Puff Derby, Thaden had declared them to be "not of slightest kin. They are as totally different as a horse to a rabbit. It [the 1929 derby] not only was the first of its kind but has since proved to be the last of its kind as well. It was an exciting, thrilling, sometimes chilling pioneering adventure, replete with unknowns, an inevitability of all firsts."

Nobody summed up flying better than Thaden: "There is really nothing nicer than flying in a good airplane over pretty country on a beautiful day—you just feel so good, so exuberant, so, oh, I don't know, but there is a feeling that you would like to beat yourself on the chest and emit several howls à la Tarzan, pure joy of being alive."

Evelyn "Bobbi" Trout apparently hadn't had enough adventures in the air derby, so she proceeded to have another en route home. A new distributor for the Golden Eagle Chief asked if he could ride along with Trout from Cleveland back to California. Trout was glad to have the company. She flew the first leg to St. Louis herself, then turned the controls over to the other pilot west of St. Louis. Encountering a storm, the two found a likely looking field in which to land, but they discovered too late that it was what Trout described as "gumbo." "The minute our wheels touched down, the small wheels were grabbed as if we flew into a pool of glue, and our nose and left wing went up and down and around like scrambled eggs," she described. They weren't hurt, but the airplane was indeed, and the frustrated pilots were obliged to catch a train home.

Bobbi Trout celebrates the completion of her endurance flight.

Bobbi was eager to attempt a refueling endurance flight. Her derby sponsor, Golden Eagle, wished her well, but the company was sinking in the throes of the Depression and was no longer a source for Trout. A new sponsor and flying partner appeared at exactly the propitious moment. Trout and Eleanor Smith were offered Commercial Aircraft Corporation's Sunbeam biplane with a Wright Whirlwind 300-horsepower engine for a record-breaking effort.

The refueling airplane, a Curtiss Carrier Pigeon, could deliver 185 gallons in 4 minutes during each refueling contact. While practicing the refueling operation, the rigging was adjusted and readjusted until the Sunbeam could stay positioned under the Pigeon comfortably for their twice-a-day refueling operation.

They were given an enormous radio for contact with the ground and the other airplane, but they left it behind since its position in the baggage area made the tail heavy and the airplane unstable. Hand signals would have to do. The two were finally ready to practice receiving a bag of food, oil, and mail by a rope from the airplane above, and to position the gasoline nozzle from one airplane to the other. On the first try, when the contact broke, Trout was sickened, swallowing a mouthful of gasoline. On November 27, 1929, Trout and Smith and their refueling pilots were ready for the record try.

The women decided on four-hour shifts of flying the airplane and alternately sleeping on top of the gasoline tanks. The engine oil had to be changed twice each day, and the thirty-six Alemite connectors to the rocker arms on the nine-cylinder engine had to have grease applied with a grease gun. On the fourth refueling, the formation-flying Pigeon began producing black exhaust smoke, and the women broke away. Though dragging the fuel hose through a fence on landing, the Pigeon landed safely with no fire, but it was unable to fuel the Sunbeam again. Trout and Smith continued to fly until almost 4:00 a.m., when they had to land at Los Angeles's Metropolitan Airport because they were out of fuel. The two stayed aloft over forty-two hours, successfully completing the first refueling endurance flight ever made by women.

Eager to top her interrupted record endurance flight, Trout was invited by young movie starlet Edna May Cooper and her sponsor to undertake another flight, an invitation she immediately accepted. This time, they flew a Challenger Curtiss Robin with engine rocker oiling lines and a filler pipe for adding oil to the crankcase from the pilot's seat. After a rough start, the flight smoothed out, and on January 7, 1931, Trout's twenty-fifth birthday, a large chocolate birthday cake was lowered to the two women. At 172 hours and spewing oil, their flight was cut short due to a cracked piston. Yet, another record was in place.

Bobbi Trout was a cohort of Pancho Barnes in their patriotic Women's Air Reserve. They pledged to serve their country in time of national emergency. In 1934, the Gilmore Oil Company sponsored a round-trip transcontinental flight for the Women's Air Reserve to publicize their cause. General Pancho was the leader of the three J-5 Stearman airplanes painted "Gilmore yellow" with the red Gilmore lion painted on the side. They relished untold adventures, but came home broke.

Trout was always an inventor and innovator. During World War II, her Aero Reclaiming Company salvaged discarded rivets from various aircraft manufacturers and recycled them. She also had a deburring company for airplane parts and a printing business, and she was a prospector, realtor, and investor. Trout's uplifting personality, unending enthusiasm, and tales of the early years made her an enduring popular after-dinner speaker. Trout passed away in 2003, and her biography, *Just Plane Crazy*, is a fascinating pioneer story.

Mary Von Mach was the first woman admitted to Parks Air College in southern Illinois, where the racers landed en route. Though reluctant Oliver Parks admitted her only on three-month's probation hoping she would wash out, she graduated in 1931 with her transport license and flight instructor's rating. During World War II, Von Mach renounced her dream of operating a flight school. Instead, she did final inspections on the Pratt & Whitney engines for B-24 bombers for the war effort—a contribution for which she was honored by the War Congress of American Industry.

Mary Von Mach

She also was awarded the OX5 Bronze Star for "using an OX5-powered aircraft, distinguished himself (sic) by a successful

'FIRST' which contributed to our progress in aviation." As she had been the first woman in Michigan to become a transport pilot and to own and operate an airplane, Von Mach was installed in the Michigan Aviation Hall of Fame. She died at age eighty-four in 1980.

Vera Dawn Walker, who had been a stand-in for Tom Mix in the movies, achieved her transport license after the 1929 Women's Air Derby. At ninety-four pounds, she became known as the "pint-size test pilot." She flew a forty-eight-state sales tour demonstrating the Panther McClatchie experimental Rocker Armless Engine. Its claim to fame was having less moving parts than more conventional engines. The tour's ordeals led her to declare herself the unofficial forced-landing champion of the world. Carl Lienesch, an early race director, said of the tiny racer: "Vera Dawn always struck me as a sweet, little, trusting girl who could get herself into the dangest tangles (with an airplane, I mean) but could always extricate herself before the bomb went off!"

Amelia Earhart and Vera Dawn Walker

Walker flew an Inland Sport in the Dixie Derby, dropping out with engine trouble the second day. After a repair, she proceeded on to the National Air Races to try her hand at pylon racing. She did well, taking a first place and then a second, only three seconds behind Mary Haizlip.

In 1931, Walker delivered a Pratt & Whitney–powered Stinson to Guatemala. The exhilarating flight over dense forest and an active volcano was highlighted by a forced landing at the edge of a lake, resulting in a week-long aircraft retrieval. Walker soon returned home to recover from tuberculosis and never flew again. She died at age eighty-one in 1978.

AFTERWORD

The twenty pilots of the 1929 transcontinental air race wasted no time in formalizing their support group, then they opened their already international Ninety-Nines club to additional pilots. The accomplishments of the women who followed, resting on the foundation established by the Powder Puffers, are significant. Their flights, persistence, and bravery have enriched aviation and widened the world to women. Early pilot Margery Brown ran her own survey in 1928 at Curtiss Field in Long Island, New York, asking women what flying meant to them. What was it that made the fragile, noisy, dirty, dangerous, undependable airplanes so irresistible to women?

Their responses were as varied as they would be at Curtiss Field today, had it not been turned into a shopping center. One woman said it represented a conflict with fear and risk, then overcoming it. Another admitted to a romantic pull—it was handsome Lindbergh who drew her to flying. A third wanted to make flying a career, and she took it very seriously.

Margery Brown announced that dozens of women were flocking

to the airport for instruction. Today, thousands are doing so. Flying airplanes is still a male bastion, but a long line of impatient, innovative, courageous women have demonstrated their love of flight and refused to be left out or shunted aside.

The current pilot population shows that around 6 percent of pilots are female. But the breakdown of that number is enlightening. About 25 percent of male U.S. pilots are some of the highest paid pilots in the world, and only about 4.5 percent of women pilots hold the same level of expertise. Interestingly enough there's a rather new statistic that 2.5 percent of female pilots are now Aircraft and Powerplant Mechanics. The early female pilots often handled their own repairs; however, A&P is now a legal certificate.

We've been rich in pathfinders, with nary a Miss Milquetoast to be found. Laura Ingalls, like Amelia Earhart and so many others, dealt with the disapproving parents syndrome. (And what loving parent would want their child to risk her life in "one of those things"?) Laura Ingalls learned to fly on the sly, but keeping her bizarre record flights quiet was impossible with such dizzying feats as 980 consecutive loops and 714 barrel rolls, which did not go unnoticed by the press.

Ingalls soon settled into the serious distance flights, since in the early thirties, fame seemed the only route to fortune for females in aviation. She made a seventeen-thousand-mile tour of Central and South America crossing the Andes in a Lockheed Air Express monoplane. Such a feat in the single-engine airplane at high altitude in predictably unpredictable weather is astounding. In 1934, Laura Ingalls won the Harmon Trophy as the world's outstanding woman flyer. (Clifford Harmon had been an aviator/philanthropist who established three international trophies in the early twenties, to be awarded annually to the most outstanding aviator, aviatrix, and aeronaut [balloonist], in the world. A fourth category, astronaut, was added later.)

Ingalls's exploits and daring made her one of the most admired and famous women pilots in the country. War clouds were billowing, and possible U.S. involvement was argued passionately on both sides of the issue. The darling of aviation dropped antiwar pamphlets over the White House and was subsequently accused of being a spy. She admitted guilt, and she was convicted and imprisoned for "acting as a paid agent of the German Reich without registering with the State Department."

WORLD WAR II

During the thirties, aviation sponsored by governments was growing all over the world. Sixty-five thousand German men were being trained as pilots and mechanics, and nearly two hundred thousand were training in gliders. Japan had fifty-one thousand pilots, Russia was training six hundred thousand in aeronautics. The United States had a mere twenty-three thousand civilian pilots, the majority ranked amateurs.

At the end of 1938, President Roosevelt authorized the Civil Aeronautics Authority (CAA) to train twenty thousand private pilots a year in the nation's colleges. The program was called the Civilian Pilot Training (CPT) Program, and its purpose was twofold: to stimulate aviation's growth and to build up a reserve of pilots to whom the military might turn. The CPT program was a huge success, and, despite adverse quotas, many women pilots learned to fly under the auspices of CPT or they taught in the program.

The idea of women flying in the military was not on anyone's radar in the United States in the late thirties. Charles Lindbergh, touring the Soviet Union in 1938, was dismayed to find women flying in the Russian Air Force. He grumbled, "I do not see how it can work very well. After all, there is a God-made difference between men and women that even the Soviet Union can't eradicate."

In fact, Russian women made a disproportionate contribution to their country's war effort. One of the bravest fighting groups of World War II consisted of Russian women. They flew old, World War I surplus, slow, open-cockpit airplanes in air battles, particularly in the defense of Leningrad. Since they couldn't possibly outfly modern airplanes flown by the Germans, the women flew at night with no navigation or position lights so the Germans couldn't see to shoot them down. When elite German pilots were downed and survived, they were mortified to learn that the deed was accomplished by a woman. The humiliated Luftwaffe pilots swore that the women who flew in the dark were witches, and they became known as the Night Witches.

Upon their entry into World War II, the British immediately recognized that airplanes don't know the difference between male and female pilots. Though the Brits weren't ready to send women into combat, they readily acknowledged the need for more pilots of every kind. To join the British Air Transport Auxiliary (ATA), 275 "Yanks" had crossed the Atlantic to ferry new combat airplanes from the factory to bases and to maintenance, freeing combat pilots for their primary assignment. Although civilians, the pilots were outfitted in uniforms and held rank. The ATA eventually numbered thirty-five hundred personnel from twenty-four countries, of which six hundred and fifty were pilots. One hundred and seventy-four were killed.

Twenty-five highly qualified American women were recruited by Jacqueline Cochran for the ATA even prior to U.S. entry into the war. The women flew one hundred and twenty different aircraft—small, large, and huge. Hazards were very real even without flying combat missions. Since all aircraft observed radio silence and updated en route weather was not available, the sarcastic aviation "must go" adage was firmly in place: "The weather doesn't matter since we're going anyway!" Flying in crummy weather was the norm. Barrage balloons surrounded major cities and airports, and they were held aloft by cable to deter low-flying German airplanes bombing and strafing.

If ATA pilots took off during an attack, the barrage balloons were lowered for them along a specific path. Getting a green light invariably meant taking off in low visibility and holding a compass heading with assurance that the obstructions had been pulled down along their narrow route. That kind of flying took not only skill but faith. Britain's own famed pilot, Amy Johnson Mollison, was killed flying for the ATA. She was seen parachuting through layers of clouds, landed in water, and her body was never recovered. Her husband was convinced that she had been shot down.

When the United States entered the war, unprecedented numbers of pilots were needed, and the need could not be met. The Army Air Force Ferry Command was allowed to utilize women on a noncombatant status, recruiting twenty-three pilots, each with at least five hundred flying hours. This small group became the Women's Auxiliary

Ferrying Squadron (WAFS) under the command of Nancy Harkness Love. These women were already experienced pilots, easily able to move into the assorted airplanes, releasing male pilots for combat.

Tiny Betty Gillies, who used wooden block rudder extensions so that she could reach the rudder pedals, became the first WAFS member. The pilot described her need for rudder blocks for the Lockheed P-38: "If I had put enough cushions behind me to reach the rudder, my nose would smash right into the gun panel."

Cornelia Fort was the second WAFS member. Fort had been a flight instructor in Honolulu, teaching a student in a Piper Cub on December 7, 1941. During the training flight, Fort noticed a military airplane coming right at her. She grabbed the controls away from her student to make a steep turn away. Looking back at the airplane that had come so close, she saw red balls on the tops of the wings. She actually heard bullets all around her.

Fort suddenly realized that an entire formation with the emblem of the Rising Sun was over Pearl Harbor. There were bombs exploding in the water and on ships, and parked airplanes were blowing up in neat lines at the airport. She made it home safely, simply because she was not a worthy target for more than one pass. However, others of the school's little yellow Cubs washed up on shore within days, casualties of war. When Fort joined the WAFS, she said, "I, for one, am profoundly grateful that my one talent, my only knowledge, flying, happens to be of use to my country when it is needed. That's all the luck I ever hope to have."

While ferrying a BT-13, Cornelia Fort was reported to have been struck by a show-off army pilot; however, the army denied any military involvement despite witness reports. What is known is that Cornelia Fort gave her life for her country.

Director of the Women's' Training Program, Jacqueline Cochran was instrumental in bringing lower-time female pilots into the Ferry Command, ferrying aircraft and towing targets pulled behind the airplanes for gunnery practice. Yes, some target-tow airplanes were hit. It was a dangerous business.

The Women's Airforce Service Pilots (WASP) evolved and absorbed the WAFS. Walt Disney created a symbol for the WASP, a lady gremlin with wings named Fifinella. The pilots later, with good humor, called themselves the "Order of Fifinella." Dependence upon the WASP grew as the women flew everything built in the United States.

In a training demonstration, WASP Dorothea Moorman and Dora Dougherty were checked out in the B-29 Superfortress by Lieutenant Colonel Paul Tibbets Jr., later-famed pilot of the A-bomb airplane *Enola Gay*. Their mission was to demonstrate the behemoth with its crew-killer reputation to reluctant transitioning male pilots. They flew the maligned "beast" to Alamogordo, New Mexico, to demonstrate the airplane to flight crews there. Dougherty reported, "Flight crews, their male egos challenged, approached the aircraft with renewed enthusiasm."

Was the WASP program successful? It was. Safety and reliability were outstanding, and the purpose of freeing male pilots for other flying surely was accomplished. Civilians Barbara Erickson (London) and Nancy Love received the Air Medal, and Jacqueline Cochran received the Distinguished Service Medal.

Jacqueline Cochran went on to fly a Northrop T-38 jet and break every speed, altitude, and distance record for women. In 1962, she established more than thirty speed records in a Lockheed Jetstar, then flew 1,429 miles per hour in a Lockheed F-104G Starfighter. These airplanes were not readily available to other women, but Cochran's connections with the military opened the door for her.

Jackie Cochran's achievements belied her origins. Orphaned at an early age, the little girl's schooling ended at the third grade. She had worked in a beauty parlor, which led to a successful cosmetics business of her own. The always hard-charging Cochran had learned to fly at age twenty in three-weeks' time at Roosevelt Field, Long Island, simply to run her business more efficiently by not being dependent upon airline schedules. Competition fever was a natural for Cochran. She won the Bendix Race and became a multiple Harmon Trophy winner. She served the Ninety-Nines as president.

Cochran's one failure was not being able to have the WASP become part of the armed forces. Though under the control of the military, wearing uniforms, and carrying weapons, members of the WASP were never attached to the military. As a result, if a pilot was killed in training or in service—and thirty-eight were—the women had to take up a collection to send the body home. There were never any benefits until 1979, when Congress finally passed legislation for veteran's benefits for the surviving members of the WASP.

Hanna Reitsch was probably the most astounding woman pilot to come out of the war, and she can still be named one of the greatest test pilots of all time. Reitsch was a German-Austrian who started flying at age eighteen in gliders. Her first world record came early in her training when, totally unplanned, she stayed aloft for over five hours in a glider, establishing a world record for women.

Reitsch abandoned plans for a career in medicine and dedicated herself to aviation. She was the first woman to fly jet airplanes, rocket planes, and helicopters, the first pilot to fly a glider over the Alps, and the only woman to fly a robot V-1, commonly known as a buzz bomb, modified for pilot control. During World War II, Reitsch tested all types of military airplanes for the Luftwaffe.

An intriguing chapter of her life concerns the final days of World War II. It has been reported that Hanna Reitsch flew Hitler to safety in a helicopter and that he fled to South America in a submarine, but she said that was not true. She has described her last flight into Berlin, landing on the street, and meeting the demented Fuerher in his bunker. On the last day of Hitler's life, Reitsch escaped the bunker in a tank amid falling buildings and gunfire. Into the 1970s, this remarkable woman was still setting glider and helicopter records.

INTERNATIONAL PILOTS

A Korean woman, Kyung O. Kim, whose name translated to "Beautiful Golden Tree Castle," startled her traditional father with her wish to fly. She learned to fly in the Republic of Korea (ROK) Air Force, which during the Korean War was composed of 34,999 males and one female. Beautiful Golden Tree Castle became a captain in the ROK and carried classified documents to and from military airports in L-19s. The lone Korean female civilian pilot came to the United States in 1957 for college, and she met a host of sister pilots who became intrigued with her dream of flight for other Korean women in a country with no civilian airplanes.

The New York/New Jersey Ninety-Nines began a project called

a "Colt for Kim," which spread nationally and internationally. They started collecting S&H green stamps to purchase a Piper Colt trainer for teaching Korean women to fly. In 1962, Kyung O. Kim was presented with the keys to her Colt. The woman who had arrived in the U.S. with neither English nor any path to her dream returned home with a college degree and an airplane, plus the solid support of the American aviation community.

Australia's "First Lady of Aviation," Nancy Bird Walton, was a barnstormer in New South Wales. She described early flight planning done by telephone: "Follow the river to the fork, look for the sheep shed, then look for a gate with fresh droppings around it, the strip is just a bit further." Having learned to fly in 1933, Nancy Bird (her name was an interesting coincidence) became involved with the Far West Children's Health Scheme. Children of the station hands, shearers, and boundary-riders in Australia's distant western regions suffered from various crippling illnesses caused by dust and flies, their illnesses amplified by the absence of fruits and vegetables. Nancy Bird used her airplane to carry children out for medical attention and to respond to all manner of emergencies.

Flying conditions included desolate country with no navigational aids, three-digit temperatures, and dust storms that howled for days. Bird had to be prepared to handle breakdowns and emergency landings herself. Though the people of the outback had seen airplanes come in before, their experience did not include the startling sight of a slip of a girl climbing out of the cockpit. One station laborer exclaimed in astonishment, "My God! It's a woman!" and Nancy Bird adopted that exclamation as the title for her book. She laughed,

"Many of the stock-buyers needed a couple of whiskies before they had enough Dutch courage to fly with me." Always an optimist, Nancy Bird observed that "above the clouds the sun is always shining."

When in Australia, I commented to Nancy Bird how friendly Australians were when they heard my American accent. "Of course," she said, "the British had their own troubles in the war and were unable to come to our aid in our time of great peril. You Americans helped us, and we've never forgotten it."

Britain produced daring and colorful women pilots in the early years, particularly Amy Johnson Mollison, who flew solo from Britain to Australia in 1930 in an open-cockpit biplane, taking nineteen days for the task. Take out a world globe and trace your finger along that route, imagining nineteen days in that frangible airplane over jungle, desert, and ocean. Upon the brave pioneer's arrival in Sydney, all six of Australia's women pilots joined into a formation flight to meet and escort her. Amy, the U.K.'s Amelia Earhart, died while serving her country in the ATA during World War II.

The colorful Irish lass, Lady Mary Heath, withdrew from the 1929 Women's Air Derby, but competed in the pylon races in Cleveland that year. She had soloed her Avro Avian on the Cape Town to London route, a treacherous flight in 1928. Later, she flew seventy thousand miles with KLM as second pilot in Fokker Tri-Motors.

Lady Heath fought the bureaucratic battle in Britain for women who followed, with the English Air Ministry skeptical about entrusting passengers' lives to a woman. Finally, a committee resolved the issue of physical tests for women pilots, and the athletic Lady Heath accomplished the breakthrough. Nancy Bird Walton loved to point out a condition of employment in English aviation in the late twenties: "Must be of the male sex."

Strikingly beautiful Sheila Scott had been an actress and fashion model before her addiction to flight. She became Britain's first pilot to fly around the world solo, doing so in a single-engine Piper Comanche 260 in 1966, just the first of three global journeys. Achieving over one hundred world records was no small task. However, her 1971 polar flight was the most remarkable and difficult.

Scott undertook a thirty-four-thousand–mile flight from equator to equator via the north pole. NASA tracked her Piper Aztec via satellite to prove that she did actually fly right over the true north pole, which is hard to find exactly since the magnetic compass doesn't work there. Scott carried instrumentation for three experiments in the environmental, biomedical, and position-ing fields. The data was transmitted via the satellite Nimbus to the Goddard Space Center in Maryland. Her major awards included the Harmon Trophy and the Britannia Trophy, then Her Majesty Queen Elizabeth decorated Scott with the Order of the British Empire (as she did Nancy Bird Walton). Scott authored three books describing her spectacular flights. Only cancer could shoot her down.

WORLD FLIGHTS OF THE SIXTIES

Was it prosperity? The women's movement? More women flying? I don't know, but the sixties seemed to be the time for world flights—the completion of Amelia Earhart's disrupted 1937 circling of the globe.

When Jerrie Mock complained of momentary boredom in 1963, her husband suggested, "Why don't you fly around the world?" This led Mock to resume Earhart's attempted around-the-world flight. The mystery of Earhart's disappearance had generated a light industry for historians, researchers, promoters of wild theories (and the sale of their books), snake oil salesmen, and charismatic authors of dumb conjecture.

Jerrie Mock wasn't really interested in solving the mystery or disproving that Amelia Earhart was living with Elvis in Wisconsin. She saw an incomplete project. Unfinished. In default. She committed to fulfilling Amelia Earhart's dream, which had been laying fallow for some twenty-seven years.

Along with a partner, Jerrie and Russ Mock owned an eleven-year-old single-engine Cessna 180. She chose to make the flight in this small airplane because that's what they had. I met Jerrie when she was a 700-hour private, instrument-rated pilot. She was getting fuel tanks installed in Wichita, Kansas, for ocean-crossing range, which left room for only one five-foot-two-inch pilot. Of course, the skeptics were certain there was no way she could pull this off.

Though she was barely edging into her fortieth year, the press patronizingly dubbed Mock "the flying grandmother." True, the grandmother owned a mighty slim logbook for such an ambitious flight, but she knew her airplane, and she was a quick study of the volumes of information necessary to marshal that little airplane around the world. Complication intervened in the person of Joan Merriam Smith, a twenty-seven-year-old likewise diminutive dynamo, who had fallen under the same spell. Neither woman knew the plans of the other. When the media discovered that two record flights were underway, they, of course, turned it into a race.

Smith was planning a longer flight than Mock, sticking more to Earhart's route along the equator. Of the two, Joan Smith's scenario made more sense, since her Piper Apache had two engines and she was the more experienced, professional pilot. On the other hand, the airplane was old, and Murphy's Law was firmly in place. For Mock, everything that could go wrong, did.

Smith got off first on March 17, 1964, with Mock following two days later. Both suffered mechanical problems on the shakedown leg.

Mock's radio problems were eclipsed by Smith's leaking fuel tanks, and though on widely separated routes, both encountered abysmal weather. Amazingly, with unparalleled self-confidence, Mock made the first actual instrument approach of her life to the Azores after crossing the Atlantic Ocean.

Both pilots surmounted enormous challenges along the route. But Mock's mechanical problems continued. Jerrie Mock completed her flight around the world, Columbus to Columbus, in 158 flying hours over 22,858 miles in 29 days. She entered history as the first woman to make such a flight, and she did so alone, twenty-seven years after Amelia Earhart had tried it with a navigator. A congratulatory telegram from Joan Merriam Smith awaited her return, and President Lyndon Johnson presented Jerrie with the FAA's Decoration for Exceptional Service.

Meanwhile, Joan Merriam Smith plowed onward on her longer course, finishing in twenty-three actual days of flying, but fifty-nine elapsed days from takeoff. The next year, early in 1965, Smith's beloved Apache burned after an emergency landing. Five weeks later, at the age of twenty-eight, Joan Smith died while testing Rayjay blowers on a Cessna 180 (ironically, Jerrie Mock's airplane of choice). She was awarded the 1965 Harmon Trophy posthumously.

Anniversaries seem to attract significant commemoratives, and so did the thirtieth anniversary of Earhart's 1937 flight. Ann Pellegreno's airplane mechanic Lee Loepke mentioned in 1962 that he'd acquired a "basket case" Lockheed 10, a sister ship to Earhart's, and he was rebuilding it. He suggested that Pellegreno might like to fly it around the world on the thirtieth anniversary of Earhart's flight. Pellegreno was then a one-hundred-hour Aeronca Champ (trainer) pilot, and Loepke idea seemed pretty silly at her experience level, but he'd planted the seed.

As it happened, in 1967 the airplane was finished, and Pellegreno—by then a commercial pilot with multi-engine and instrument ratings—flew the airplane around the world on the Earhart route with a crew of three.

They dropped a wreath over Howland Island where Earhart's voice had last been heard. Ann's Lockheed had originally been of Canadian registry, and afterward it went home to Ottawa to be displayed by Air Canada.

OCEAN FLYING

A "first" can only happen once. Interestingly enough though, "first" women have had a pretty realistic perspective of their accomplishments. Amelia Earhart was quite embarrassed by the hoopla when she became the first female pilot to fly across the Atlantic—as a passenger. She hastened to fly it herself solo, becoming a real first, and often pointed out that men had already done what she was doing. Jerrie Mock said, "This is something men do all the time. It was about time a woman did it."

The first woman to fly solo across the Pacific was Betty Miller. She delivered a Piper Apache to Australia, which brought her the 1964 Harmon Trophy for the outstanding accomplishment by a female pilot. (She got the 1964 Harmon Trophy instead of Jerrie Mock.) Miller didn't have a burning desire to participate in the Earhart mystique. Rather, she simply completed a business trip, putting fifty-four hours in her logbook. If sitting behind one lone engine with a propeller out front and flying across hundreds of miles of water could ever be called routine, perhaps another woman of the sixties, Louise Sacchi, made it seem so. During World War II, Sacchi had taught celestial navigation to British pilots. She longed to fly the ocean, but complained to her friend Marion Rice Hart that she couldn't get a job ferrying airplanes because she'd never flown the ocean herself. Rice Hart said, "We can fix that." The two women climbed into Rice Hart's single-engine Beech Bonanza and flew across the Atlantic.

Sacchi got a job ferrying airplanes, mostly Beeches, then formed her own company, Sacchi Air Ferry Enterprises (SAFE). She made over three hundred crossings of the both the Atlantic and Pacific Oceans, the majority of which were in single-engine airplanes. She ferried eighty-five airplanes to Spain, for which she was awarded the country's highest medal. She passed her expertise along when she wrote a book describing how to fly across the great waters.

And what of the woman, Marion Rice Hart, who gave Louise

Sacchi her first trans-Atlantic ride? She was one of aviation's great characters who can only be described as a little old lady from Pasadena in tennis shoes. Fashion was at the very bottom of Rice Hart's priority list. Her father was a financier, musician, lawyer, inventor, chess expert, and president of a score of companies, including the Holland Submarine Torpedo Boat Company, which supplied the U.S. Navy with its first submarine. Her mother also was an overachiever: a musician and a physician.

Rice Hart took a degree in chemical engineering from MIT, the school's first female graduate, then a master's in geology from Columbia. She started sailing in 1936. She bought a seventy-two-foot ketch that she sailed around the world for three years. When the United States entered the war, Rice Hart tried to enlist in the Coast Guard and was declined. However, the navigation book she wrote was accepted by the Coast Guard, and fifty years and several editions later was still one of their primary celestial navigation texts.

Marion Rice Hart started flying in 1946 at the age of fifty-four, and thirty years later, she was awarded the Harmon Trophy. Her flight instructor said that to hear her give a spontaneous, off-the-cuff lecture on the properties of gasoline to students hanging around the flight school was awesome. A newspaper reporter quoted Rice Hart at the time of her seventh single-engine ocean crossing: "It's not so remarkable," the eighty-one-year-old flier said.

Marion Rice Hart's no-nonsense take on the feminist movement and Equal Rights Amendment is not really a surprise. She said, "If I can do these things, so can any woman; why do you need legislation and all that demonstration fuss? Just do it!"

THE AIRLINES

So, who was America's first female airline pilot? There are so many candidates. How do you define airline or employment? Do a couple of weeks or number of passengers factor in? Aircraft weight? Number of engines? Do "regional" or "major" matter? What other countries had females flying the big birds? You can make an argument for a dozen women, but my vote goes to Emily Howell Warner, and since the Smithsonian's Air and Space Museum displays her uniform labeled the "First U.S. Female Airline Pilot," I'm in good company.

Emily Howell Warner was flying light Cessna twins around the Colorado Rockies for a charter company in the sixties, paying the hardest kind of dues while learning her trade. Winter flying in non-ice-carrying airplanes, and summer flying at hot, high-altitude airports taught Howell Warner a lot about flying. However, she was quick to notice that men well below her experience level were moving into airline jobs and flying more sophisticated equipment at much higher pay. And she also noticed that there were no women in that little room facing forward in the front of the transport airplanes.

Howell Warner started making a nuisance of herself at the head offices of Frontier Airline in Denver. She presented her application for employment. She did it again. And again, and again, and again. Finally, in 1973, Chief Pilot Johnny Myers, whose own wife Donna had been a wing walker and international president of the Ninety-Nines, couldn't think of any reason not to hire Howell Warner since she was so overqualified compared to the male pilots they were already hiring. Not having a separate female restroom didn't seem as important an issue as it once had.

Howell Warner described her first days as a copilot, or first officer, in the employ of Frontier Airline. Her first day on the job was filled with friendly greetings from controllers and bouquets of roses at each stop. But soon a crusty old captain with whom she flew had three words for her on the entire flight, and those words were "don't touch anything."

Emily Howell Warner's efforts opened the door for thousands of women who followed her, running their own gauntlets.

Though Howell Warner's inroads captured the historical benchmark, a case can be made that Helen Richey became the United States' first female airline pilot the last day of 1934. She was holding down the right seat of a Ford Tri-Motor for Central Airlines and had made a scheduled run on a commercial airliner from Washington to Detroit. Despite strike threats in opposition from the pilot's association, Richey stuck it out until October 1935, at which time she resigned. Since the Bureau of Air Commerce wasn't allowing the airline to use her in bad weather, it was time to move on. Disappointedly, she had flown less than a dozen trips in ten months' time.

Helen Richey proceeded to work for the government with the air marking team, flew distance and altitude records, and raced the Bendix with Amelia Earhart the same year Louise Thaden won. When war came to the UK, Richey was among the elite group of American women recruited to fly for the ATA. Sadly, when Richey was unable to obtain a flying job after the war, the frustration level took its toll, and she took her own life.

My own experience in the early sixties, when the airlines were hiring young men anywhere they could find them, was enlightening. I was interviewing the owner of a large flight school in southern California. He had an enormous roster of students and flight instructors (and I noticed that his wife carried the heaviest load of students). I asked how he hung onto flight instructors against the predatory airline recruiters. He said, "I try to hire only two kinds of flight instructors— cripples and women, because they can't go to the airlines."

The International Society Affiliation of Women Airline Pilots (ISA+21) was formed in 1978 by twenty-one female pilots who met to form a support group (shades of the Ninety-Nines nearly fifty years before). The group assists women entering the profession through their information bank, networking, and service projects. The organization keeps a master seniority list that shows Emily Howell Warner as the first female U.S. airline pilot dated January 10, 1973, with Bonnie Tiburzi two months behind her at American Airlines, and Rosella Bjornson in Canada one month later.

Quiet and reserved, Rosella Bjornson grew up flying on her father's knee off the family farm in southern Alberta. And she still has her father's same Cessna airplane today. Bjornson's playhouse was an old Anson Mark V from World War II, which she "flew" minus wings with her dolls and sisters as passengers. She joined the majors with impeccable flying credentials, flying for Transair Limited in a Fokker F28 twin jet.

ISA+21 also shows Durba Bannerjee flying for Indian Airlines in 1966, a good seven years before Emily Howell Warner made the breakthrough in the United States. Italy's Fiorenza de Bernardi also predates Howell Warner. The United States was not first to open the fraternity to women.

A fascinating and seemingly impossible combination is Tagareed Akasheh of Middle Eastern Muslim roots. She joined the Royal Jordanian Airlines in 1975, graduated from the Royal Jordanian Air Academy on the Boeing 707, and made captain two years later. Jordan's aviation-immersed king may well have been responsible for Jordan's forward-thinking attitude.

Mimi Tompkins was hired by Aloha Airlines in 1979, one of the smarter moves that airline made. Tompkins was an eight-thousand-hour pilot flying the leg from Hilo to Honolulu on April 28, 1988. Without warning, a twenty-foot section of the upper fuselage separated from the aircraft at twenty-four thousand feet, leaving the two pilots flying a top-down convertible. There was no logical way the crippled airplane could continue to fly, but the strong Boeing did.

As the wounded airplane approached the airport, witnesses couldn't believe what they were seeing—passengers sitting out in the open, some seats hanging out in space, the wind buffeting suspended debris. Somehow, the pilots maintained their professional cool and brought the airplane to a safe landing with sixty-one injured passengers and the loss of one life—the flight attendant who was blown out of the plane as the structure failed. Tompkins was honored for "exemplary conduct under extreme duress" in the never-before-encountered emergency.

A true airline pilot who was never "official" was Doris Langher. Hired by United Airlines in Chicago, Langher trained pilots in the early Link trainers, the forerunner of today's flight simulator. When World War II came along, she had to choose either to join the WASP or to stay with United on the chance that she could be their first female pilot. United won the toss. After the airline moved their training to Denver, Doris Langher participated in the training of every pilot who flew for United. Her timing was wrong, though, and by the time her employer opened up the pilot ranks to women, Langher was too old to fly the line.

She always kept her skills sharp in real airplanes, not just the simulators, and became type-rated in the exciting new Lear jet. When riding along in the back end while another pilot received dual instruction in the Lear, something went terribly wrong, and Langher died in a Lear jet crash as a passenger.

MILITARY

Shortly after the airlines unlocked the cockpit doors to women, the United States military decided women could fly their airplanes, though actually, the buck stopped at Congress. Way back during World War II, more than three hundred fifty thousand women had joined the armed forces. Clerical fields were their first stop, but soon there were female truck drivers, airplane mechanics, parachute riggers, and lab technicians. Although not allowed in combat, women were, in reality, in every theater of the war and were shot at, wounded, killed, and taken prisoner. At war's end, Congress passed the Women's Armed Services Integration Act, restricting the number of women to 2 percent of the total force and their rank to colonel. One colonel per service.

The 2 percent ceiling and grade limitations were finally lifted in 1967. Colonel Jeanne Holm was selected as the first air force female general officer in 1971, and five years later, the service academies began admitting women. In the eighties, women flew "noncombat" in KC-10s, KC-135s, and F-111s in Granada, Libya, and Panama, and finally, Congress saw fit to repeal the combat exclusion law for women in 1991. During Operation Desert Storm, women served in tanker, transport, and medical evacuation aircraft.

Naval aviator Lieutenant Kara Hultgreen had her eye on space. She thought the best path to her goal would be through naval aviation, specifically as a test pilot. The daughter of parents who encouraged their daughters to take on any career they chose, Hultgreen wrote her mother, "Mom, thanks for telling me I could do anything." She liked to quip, "Someone forgot to tell me when I was young that being born a girl was a birth defect."

Another (male) member of her squadron described Hultgreen: "She had that aggressive attitude towards success that it takes to be a good fighter pilot. But I don't think people should keep referring to her or any other woman as a 'female pilot.' Kara was a good pilot, and a good person that happened to be a woman, not the other way around."

On October 25, 1994, Hultgreen was approaching the U.S.S. *Abraham Lincoln* in her F-14 at 145 knots preparing to "trap" (catch the wire on landing)—what Hultgreen called the "sport of kings." Witnesses saw a puff of smoke from the engine, and as the jet lost altitude, collision with the ship appeared inevitable and the crew scrambled for safety. She turned away from the ship as her back seater ejected safely. Seconds later, as the airplane rolled, Hultgreen punched out also, but too late, and she went straight into the water. She was the first female fighter pilot to perish while in the service of her country.

Witnesses aboard the carrier considered Kara Hultgreen a hero. "Who knows how many lives she saved? As far as I'm concerned, she sacrificed herself to save the ship," said flight director Brian Kipp. Airman Stephen Snow, an aircraft handler on the flight deck, echoed those sentiments. "I saw the back seater eject just as the jet rolled away from the ship. The pilot was ejected into the water, head-first. But she saved a lot of people first. A ramp-crash could have started one helluva fire. Who knows what could have happened? That lady had some guts."

Lieutenant Kara Hultgreen was buried with full military honors at Arlington National Cemetery.

BUSINESS

Women's role in the business of aviation has grown. Evelyn "Pinky" Brier came home from flying in the WASP during the war, and she settled into the flying business with her husband Joe. They owned the private Tri-Cities Airport in San Bernardino, California. Pinky flew charter (which is like saying Mother Teresa was a nun), and Joe kept the airplanes under repair—a man with a magical ear for a sick engine. Pinky advertised that she would fly anywhere at any time, and she did. She knew every grain of sand between the Los Angeles basin and Las Vegas, often flying gamblers over, then sleeping in her airplane awaiting their readiness to return. If she slept in a real bed, Pinky's home was in the back of the hangar.

Pinky Brier was one of the few who flew an honest-to-goodness one thousand plus hours per year in her string of twenty-seven Bonanzas and one Twin Bonanza, retiring with over forty-five thousand logged pilot hours. How she also squeezed in teaching students is a mystery, but Pinky taught hundreds of safe pilots, having been issued the first U.S. flight instructor certificate by the CAA in 1938. Pinky and Joe Brier's private airport contained a prominent sign showing an annual tax bill of $60,000 on the airport property. Their busy, grass-strip airport at the east end of the Los Angeles basin exemplified the heart and soul of aviation's post-war development in the United States.

One of the more colorful of the early women pilots was Edna Gardner Whyte, who learned to fly in 1926. Somehow, she missed being a charter Ninety-Nine, but she missed little else in aviation. Gardner Whyte taught thousands of people to fly, and her greatest pleasure was greeting airline pilots who came back to see their first instructor. She told the story of the student who said she had taught his instructor's instructor and asked what relation that made them. Gardner Whyte told him he was her great-grand pilot.

Her passion was always competition, and she had to add a room onto her house to hold her more than one hundred trophies. After passing her seventieth year, Gardner Whyte bought property between Dallas and Forth Worth, and built Aero-Valley Airport. The airport was a resounding success, as it quickly filled with airplanes and hangars. She continued to teach until the end of her life. She loved aerobatics and always said that flying upside down kept the blood flowing to her brain and kept her young.

At the other end of the country, in a different kind of flying and a different time, Ellen Paneok, of Eskimo heritage, flew charter flights out of Barrow, Alaska. She contended with engines so cold they didn't want to run, even if they consented to start. She conducted her preflight of the airplane with an eye out for curious polar bears. Her reward was giving the gift of transportation to those old and ill, unable to travel the old, roadless way. Paneok described wavering northern lights that applauded her landings with "crackling curtains" in the far north country's minus thirty-five degree temperatures. Ellen Paneok was a charter pilot, writer, and artist, and she passed away in 2008.

Page Shamburger was another aviation writer, the author of seven aviation history books and fifteen hundred freelance articles. As a youngster flying her first airplane, a little Cessna 140, legendary aviation newspaperwoman Tony Page hired the aspiring aviator to land at every airport in the countryside and write about it. The little southern girl with her slow drawl and big grin soon got a helicopter rating, bought a Bonanza, rode with the Hurricane Hunters, rode in an F-1 Phantom Jet, and, whenever on the ground, the woman of the South rode to the foxes.

Beryl Markham was horsewoman, pilot, adventurer, and a writer. Ernest Hemingway, who did not throw compliments around carelessly, said in a letter to a friend, "Did you read Beryl Markham's book, *West with the Night*? I knew her fairly well in Africa and never would have suspected that she could and would put pen to paper except to write in her flyer's log book. As it is, she has written so well, and marvelously well, that I was completely ashamed of myself as a writer. I felt that I was simply a carpenter with words, picking up whatever was furnished on the job and nailing them together and sometimes making an okay pigpen. But she can write rings around all of us who consider ourselves as writers. I wish you would get it and

read it because it is really a bloody wonderful book." The memoir
was rediscovered in 1983 to worldwide literary acclaim, called by
some "the most inspiring aviation literature ever written."

Markham was raised by her father with the same kind of freedom
and male influence as Pancho Barnes. However, in a different time
and a different place—in Kenya. She grew up alongside the sons of
Nandi warriors, tracking game and competing, and she was a totally
free spirit. She excelled at training thoroughbreds, the first woman to
do so professionally in East Africa. About the time of the American
Women's Air Derby, Beryl Markham was bush-flying out of Nairobi,
spotting game for hunters. Always daring, she could not be dissuaded
from making a solo flight across the Atlantic—the wrong way, into
the wind, east to west. It had not been done before from England,
which, of course, challenged the courageous Markham. She flew a
new Percival Vega Gull in 1936 from England to New York, into the
prevailing wind. She did experience engine trouble, but fortunately,
it came as she arrived over land, putting the airplane on its nose in a
Nova Scotia bog.

Martha King writes too, in every medium, but can't be catego-
rized. She's been responsible for the flight training of thousands of
student pilots of every level via books, videos, and every other kind
of training material. She is also a businesswoman—the co-owner of
King Schools—and became the only woman to hold not only every
pilot category and class rating (including gyroplanes and airships)
but also every flight and ground instructor rating the FAA offers. She
was the lone woman among eighty men so qualified.

The earliest heroines in aircraft manufacturing were Olive Ann

Beech and Katherine Stinson. Mrs. Beech's daughter Suzanne said that it always bothered her when people gave her mother a backhanded compliment for "taking over the business" when her father, Walter Beech, died. She said, "Mother always ran the business. Dad was a promoter, a pilot, and an engineer. Mother was a businesswoman."

There is another Katharine Stinson who came along after Katherine of the Stinson Aircraft Company. This Katharine Stinson grew up in North Carolina and, in a life-changing chance meeting with her heroine, was inspired by Amelia Earhart to become not only a pilot, but also an engineer. Easier said than done. What self-respecting engineering school would take on a girl in the late thirties? But Katharine Stinson persevered and, with perfect timing, became the first female engineer hired by the FAA when the men all went off to war. Stinson worked on the supersonic transport, saying, "Our country made a terrible mistake not making that airplane." She worked with Howard Hughes on his extraordinary Spruce Goose. Her department was responsible for certificating every new aircraft design, striving for total safety for the flying public. Today, the university once reluctant to train a "girl engineer" proudly honors their successful alumna.

HELICOPTERS

Ruby Sheldon flew for the government doing some mapping. A remote sensing specialist for the U.S. Geological Survey, she flew throughout North America using the Grumman OV-1B (Mohawk), Sikorsky H-19, and Bell Huey helicopters as instrument platforms collecting data for hydrologic studies. In 1975, she operated the

Huey on a drifting ice island four hundred miles north of the Alaska coast for the U.S.–Canadian Arctic Ice Dynamics Joint Experiment. Navigating in whiteouts without terrain checkmarks and little help from the compass is right down Ruby Sheldon's alley.

Watching tiny, white-haired Sheldon stroll across the ramp—well actually, she doesn't stroll, she usually jogs—is a lesson in false perceptions. Most folks would suppose this lady is somebody's little grandmother come to visit. Or if they see her get out of a DC-3 along with a strapping young man, they don't comprehend that *she's* the flight instructor.

A lady named Jean Ross Howard also learned to fly a helicopter and then, to her great good fortune, gained employment in the helicopter industry. She said, "They paid me too." Ross Howard, being the organizer type, decided all the women flying those crazy machines should rally 'round to fend off their detractors, and put together a fun organization, the Whirly Girls. Of course, the members don't have meetings, they have hoverings. Any woman who has achieved any government's blessing to fly rotor is a Whirly Girl, her membership number in the order of her rating. Jean Ross Howard is, naturally, the Mother Superior. The Whirly Girls sponsor scholarships and support the establishment of hospital heliports.

Whirly Girl number one was Germany's famous test pilot Hanna Reitsch. In 1938, she demonstrated the world's first helicopter, up and over the unbelieving audience *inside* Berlin's convention center. Whirly Girl number two, Ann Shaw Carter of Fairfield, Connecticut, became the United States's first female helicopter pilot and flew tourist rides. A spectacular French woman made a name in helicopters. Jacqueline

Auriol, called the fastest woman in the world, flew both rotor and jets. She had survived an accident as a passenger in a seaplane and required fifteen operations to rebuild her face. Not deterred from flying, Jacqueline Auriol, who was also the daughter-in-law of the French president Vincent Auriol, was determined to break the speed record of the American Jacqueline Cochran. She did so by over thirty miles per hour in 1952 and was awarded the French Cross of the Legion of Honour and the American Harmon Trophy, aviator of the year.

The U.S. Whirly Girl number four was Nancy Livingston. After serving as an ATA pilot in England in World War II, Nancy and her husband, Arlo, operated Livingston Helicopters in Juneau, Alaska, to transport skiers, survey snow and water levels, fly rescue missions, give sight-seeing tours, and even count bears.

Loretta Foy was a Warner Brothers "Busby Berkeley Girl," dancing in movie musicals in the late thirties. Foy learned to fly and became a WASP in World War II. She made a career in helicopters after the war, setting up the helicopter traffic routes in the Los Angeles basin and gaining a reputation as a top rotor instructor. She also set up a police helicopter pilot training program which spread across the United States and to twenty-one foreign countries. Ironically, Loretta Foy was rescued out of her own swimming pool by helicopter during a devastating Los Angeles fire that surrounded her home and neighborhood.

New York State's first Whirly Girl was Doris Renninger Brell. Renninger Brell held down a highly prestigious job as the general manager of the Wings Club in New York City, the stomping grounds of virtually every giant of aviation industry, history, and achievement.

Another kind of businesswoman flies helicopters in her

occupation, putting meat on our tables. Pat Jenkins and her husband own a large cattle ranch in the desert country of southeastern Oregon. Distances are so great that moving cattle and mending fence are especially time-consuming, whether in pickup trucks or on horseback. Pat flies the fencelines and moves recalcitrant steers with her cowpony, "Woodstock," a yellow Hughes 300 helicopter, never flying much more than fence height.

Jenkins says, "Initially I knew nothing about how to move cattle, either on horseback or with a helicopter. To learn, I watched how the cowboys do it and tried to do the same thing. They don't barge into a bunch with whoops and hollers, so neither do I. I begin pushing one cow at a time from the perimeter in the direction they need to go. I fly just above the sagebrush and as far away from the cows as I can, and still get them moving. I don't want my cows to run wildly. I just want them to walk at their own speed. I fly low and slowly behind them in a hot, dusty hover."

AIR SHOWS

Displayed at the Smithsonian Air and Space Museum is a tiny airplane designed by Curtis Pitts and built in 1946, called a Pitts Special. The airplane weighs about 550 pounds, is open cockpit and biwing, and is a single-seat sport and exhibition aircraft with a wingspan of only fifteen feet. The ultimate competitor, aerobatic champ Betty Skelton saw it and had to have one for competition. On her first flight home after purchasing the airplane, it showed her its most famous quality, a propensity for turning about its own axis upon landing—a ground loop. When Skelton muttered, "You little stinker!" the airplane got its name and went on to become one of the most famous aerobatic airplanes ever built. *The Little Stinker's* registration number is N22E, two, two easy. Betty Skelton excelled not only in flying, but also as a race car driver, and even drove jump boats in Cypress Gardens, Florida.

Another woman whose signature airplane is owned and displayed by the Smithsonian Air and Space Museum is Patty Wagstaff, whose historic Extra 260 is displayed in the Pioneers of Flight Gallery. She pinned down the U.S. women's aerobatic championships in 1991 and 1992, and was particularly proud to win the Betty Skelton First Lady of Aerobatics Trophy. However, she was not satisfied until she was named the U.S. aerobatic champ, without the "woman" modifier. Sure enough, in both 1992 and 1993, Patty Wagstaff was the U.S. champ, period. She continues as a major draw on the air show circuit today.

Racing fever emanates from diverse motivations—fun, camaraderie, experience, challenge. Marion Jayne raced to win, and her results fill a large display case in the Ninety-Nines Museum of Women Pilots.

In thirty-one years, Marion Jayne won more than twenty cross-country airplane races and twice flew races around the world. Fellow competitors knew that Jayne was not afraid to push the edge to win. Flying across Siberia and contending with thunderstorms, ice, negligible navigational aids, and air traffic controllers minimally acquainted with the language of aviation (English) should have been more than enough of a challenge on one flight. However, Jayne had a propeller spinner fly into her windscreen in that same race creating a hole, and took second place. On another similar around-the-world race, she and her daughter won.

PHILANTHROPY

Some women who fly airplanes are compelled to share their good fortune. When Pat Blum learned to fly, she noticed how many corporate airplanes at her home airport in Westchester County, New York, departed with several empty seats. Blum and her friend Jay Weinberg were both cancer survivors and knew how difficult it was sometimes for ordinary people to locate comfortable transportation to where their cancer treatments were. Blum and Weinberg formed Corporate Angel Network in 1981, a nonprofit organization that matches those empty seats with patients who need rides to far-off treatment centers.

Ida Van Smith fulfilled her dream of flight well into her career as a teacher, which inevitably led her to aviation education. She produced a coloring book designed to give children a piece of aviation history, hosted a weekly TV program for children, and taught an introduction to aviation college course. As a black woman who understood children of poverty and their sometimes limited career motivation, Van Smith founded the Ida Van Smith Flight Clubs in 1967, exposing youngsters to careers in aviation and space. She delighted in giving the children their first airplane ride and watching their enlightened awareness of life and careers outside their own, limited arena.

FLIGHT INSTRUCTION

The base for all of aviation, without whom there is no need for aircraft manufacturers, agricultural aviation, Air Force One, fighter jets, commercial transportation system, or the exploration of space, is the flight instructor. The person who met that youngster with dreams of flight at the airport fence and taught her to fly. Women have excelled in the flight instructor ranks. They're patient. They're loyal. They see their students through tough times. They're willing to work for less pay. They love the satisfaction of teaching.

Evelyn Bryan Johnson became the highest fly time pilot in the United States. In her fifty-five years of flying, she logged nearly fifty-seven thousand flight hours. She achieved this by flying students all day, every day—even at ninety years of age. She received countless recognitions from her peers: Flight Instructor of the Year, Elder Statesman Award, induction into various halls of fame, and the Carnegie Award (for saving a pilot from a burning helicopter). But her true legacy is the army of more than two thousand students populating every aspect of aviation today.

Gerda Ruhnke was born to German parents, though she never lived in that country. She grew up in Montevideo, Uruguay. When she married and moved to the United States, Ruhnke started a flight training operation in a small trainer at the Washington Dulles Airport, of all places. Knowing her unmistakable accent, the tower often called her by name instead of her aircraft number.

She died in the most bizarre of circumstances on an instruction flight. She was a small woman and had been booked to give a first flight to quite a large man. As the details evolved, it turned out that the man was intent upon suicide in an airplane, and took this stranger with him, overpowering her and her ability to control the airplane.

Ruhnke's Washington, DC, Ninety-Nines chapter honored her with
a perpetual Amelia Earhart scholarship in her name.

THAT SLIPPERY WORD "FIRST"

Aeronaut Connie Wolf flew for more than sixty years and, at one
point, was pronounced by the FAA the oldest active female pilot
in the country. Age aside, Wolf's love of ballooning expressed her
deepest feelings of patriotism. To commemorate Philadelphia's
tricentennial, she designed a balloon bearing the likeness of William
Penn and flew it from Penn's Landing, Philadelphia, to New Jersey.
Wolf donated the $20,000 balloon to the Franklin Institute. The
institute's namesake surely would have approved. Legend has it that
Ben Franklin had witnessed a balloon flight in Paris in 1783 and was
asked, "Of what use is it?" To that, Dr. Franklin replied, "Of what use,
sir, is a newborn baby?"

Connie Wolf once piloted a balloon over Paris and London to
promote Mike Todd's movie *Around the World in 80 Days*. In 1962,
Wolf became the first woman to pilot a hydrogen balloon over the Alps
from Switzerland to Italy. She received the Montogolfier Diploma, the
first American woman to hold this highest of ballooning honors.

Loftia El-Nadi was the first Arab woman to throw off the veil
and learn to fly. She soloed in a Gypsy Moth in Cairo and received
Egyptian pilot license number thirty-four in 1933. It was considered a dishonor for Egyptian women of a certain class to work, but
El-Nadi decided that she would not tolerate the subjugation and
would try to make something of her life. Working as a secretary for a
flight school, she slowly paid for her lessons. Though she flew only

five years before medical problems ended her flying, Loftia El-Nadi competed in air races, learned aerobatics, and served as an icon to other women of her heritage and era.

Jeana Yeager was the copilot of the experimental aircraft *Voyager* during record-breaking distance flights. In July of 1986, Yeager and pilot Dick Rutan established a closed-course endurance record for unrefueled flight. However, the flight covering 11,857 miles in more than 111 hours was only a warm-up for the "main event," which came later that year.

In the last week of 1986, Yeager and Rutan landed at Edwards Air Force Base in California after completing a nine-day, twenty-six thousand mile, nonstop flight around the world in the *Voyager* airplane, truly a flying fuel tank with long, glider wings. The flight was accomplished without refueling en route, thus becoming the first plane to circumnavigate the world without refueling. Conditions during the flight were changing constantly, as the crew dealt with inclement weather en route, various mechanical problems, and the discomfort of two people confined for nine days in a noisy cockpit described as the size of a telephone booth.

Yeager, Rutan, and the *Voyager* team received numerous recognitions for their astonishing flight, but perhaps the most prestigious was the 1986 Collier Trophy, one of the most coveted aeronautical honors in America. Yeager was the first woman ever listed on the Collier. The *Voyager* airplane is now the first thing a visitor sees upon entering the lobby of the Smithsonian's Air and Space Museum.

SPACE

Back in the late fifties, an Oklahoma pilot, Jerrie Cobb, was flying for the Aero Commander Company. The Russian and American astronaut programs were just gathering steam when an aerospace medicine specialist, Dr. Randolph Lovelace, became curious about the possibility of including a woman astronaut in the U.S. program. As the fifties drew to a close, he asked Jerrie Cobb to take the astronaut tests, which she agreed to in a heartbeat. Cobb did so well that Dr. Lovelace invited a whole group to test, and thirteen women pilots passed his physical exams. Coincidently, when NASA and the Mercury astronauts got wind of Dr. Lovelace's program, it was instantly terminated. Jerrie Cobb took her special flying talent to the Amazon jungle and flew medicines and doctors to the indigenous peoples of the Amazon for nearly forty years. For this, she was nominated for the Nobel Peace Prize.

It was twenty years before a group of women joined the space program as astronauts, and they were highly qualified scientists, engineers, and physicians. Though they learned to fly airplanes, they were not selected primarily as pilots.

Sally Ride made the breakthrough as the first American woman in space, though Valentina Terashkova, a Russian sport parachutist, had flown in space first. Finally, Lieutenant Colonel Eileen Collins, an air force test pilot, was assigned to be a shuttle pilot, and other female astronaut shuttle pilots followed. As she became shuttle commander, Collins was quick to point out that she didn't just one day appear in the left seat of the most sophisticated air machine ever built. She said, "Everything I ever learned—every flight instructor I ever flew

with, every airplane I ever flew, and every airport I ever flew into—
has come together in my job today. The ultimate test pilot job is to
be an astronaut."

Donna Shirley, who grew up in Wynnewood, Oklahoma, entered
the university at seventeen and quickly gathered a string of pilot
ratings. Her primary interest in aviation turned to engineering,
though in her college days in the late fifties she had been counseled
that girls couldn't be engineers. She did anyway. Later, as a thirty-year
veteran at the Jet Propulsion Laboratory in Pasadena, Shirley worked
on varied space projects, one of the most exciting being the design
of the miniature rover to explore Mars, the Mars Sojourner Rover.
Soon, Shirley headed up the entire Mars exploration program, and
hers was the happy face we all saw on television signaling the successful probe of a neighboring planet.

After many successes and honors in her chosen field, Shirley
came full circle and returned to her home state and the University
of Oklahoma. After awarding her an honorary doctorate and then
recruiting her as associate dean of the engineering school, it seemed
apparent that Shirley's college had grown in enlightenment.

POWDER PUFF DERBY

The 1929 Women's Air Derby, nicknamed by Will Rogers the Powder
Puff Derby, continued for a few years into the Great Depression. The
war years were coming, and the women's race fell by the wayside. By
1947, postwar aviation was booming, and general aviation airplanes
were rolling off the assembly lines. A Florida group of Ninety-Nines
was holding an air show and contacted the Los Angeles group,

inviting them to fly down for it. Dianna Bixby said, "Let's make it a race!"

Weather prevented a Santa Monica start, so the two entrants, Carolyn West in an eighty-five-horsepower Ercoupe and Dianna Bixby in her Douglas A-26 Invader, started from Palm Springs. Timing was on the honor system. Carolyn West and her copilot spent the first night at El Paso, stopping early because of sandstorms—shades of the 1929 derby! The second night was at Monroeville, Alabama, then they arrived at the finish in Tampa, Florida, having flown nearly 22 hours at an average 102 miles per hour. Only upon their arrival did the winning pilots learn that their competition had never taken off due to engine trouble. Their cash prize was enough for their fuel.

The Florida women wanted to try it again in 1948, and this time, the race drew six entries. Jacqueline Cochran sponsored the race, which finished at Amelia Earhart Field in Miami, Florida. Mother Earhart, as the women called Amelia's mother, greeted the winners and congratulated Fran Nolde, who won in her Navion.

Gathering steam, the 1949 race from San Diego to Tallahassee was now called the All-Woman Transcontinental Air Race (AWTAR) though invariably, through the years, it was always the Powder Puff Derby to the public. A dozen airplanes were entered. Rules tightened up with airplanes impounded and inspected and Simplex time stamps employed. Again Jackie Cochran donating the $1,500 purse. They were off and running.

For an added element of humor and camaraderie, costumes and themes appeared. For the fourth derby, in 1950, Dottie Sanders obtained sponsorship from Chicken of the Sea tuna. The two tuna pilots wore matching capeskin jackets and hats shaped like a tuna, with colored tassel tails and ping-pong balls for eyes. Their sponsor was so taken with their costumes and good showing in the race that the two women spent three weeks after the finish making costumed tuna appearances. Costumes and themes proliferated thereafter. Another successful sponsor promotion was for Armstrong Wax. Everybody noticed, and photographed, the airplane that said in big letters across the fuselage, "These women have more exciting things to do than scrub floors!"

Racers habitually stripped anything extraneous off themselves and their airplanes to lighten the load and gain speed any way they legally could. They paid great attention to upper winds, and polished their airplanes until they gleamed. Some thought the obsession with speed might be a little excessive. The 1966 race was the longest ever, from Seattle to Clearwater, Florida—2,876 statute miles—and was to prove that an additional knot or two here and there meant everything. Bernice "B" Steadman and Fran Bera were flying the same model airplane, a Piper Comanche 260, with slightly different equipment, making their individual handicaps ever so slightly different. At the end of 2,876 miles, Steadman's average speed was 208.71 miles per hour (22.71 above her handicap), and Bera scored 208.54 (22.54 above handicap). After flying clear across the United States, they were that close!

One of the famous tales of the Powder Puff Derby was when Joan Steinberger answered a distress call from a racer who was lost and low on fuel. Steinberger turned around to help, which, needless to say, ruined her good score. Milton Caniff's Steve Canyon comic strip included a girl pilot named Bitsy Beeckman. Caniff picked up Steinberger's generous act, and she joined Bitsy in the comic strips.

Over the years, Fran Bera became the supreme derbier. Bera won the Powder Puff Derby seven times and placed in many more. Though a fierce and successful competitor, Bera generously helped novice racers and was equally accomplished in the business world of aviation, selling airplanes.

Many of the women who flew the Powder Puff Derby and the more recent Air Race Classic save their money all year for their annual vacation—racing their airplanes. The Air Race Classic includes everyone from ninety-year-olds to college girls. In one Powder Puff Derby, there were actually fifty-five grandmothers racing.

There are other races with not quite the longevity of the Powder Puff Derby and Air Race Classic but offering women pilots the same challenges: to get the most they can out of the airplane, learn from more experienced racers while enjoying their company, experience the beauty of our magnificent country, and understand the ever-changing weather. Possibly the only thing better would be to view it all from a little higher—say, out in space.

The glue forming the bond among women pilots comes from an unknown source. However, its enduring adhesion is obvious. Louise Thaden would call it a spiritual bond. Amelia Earhart would perhaps say it's "us against the elements." For Cornelia Fort it would be patriotism. No matter how serious a woman pilot's purpose might be for flying airplanes, the words Amelia Earhart chose for the title of her book probably say the best reason of all: *For the Fun of It.*

AUTHOR'S NOTE

As a female pilot myself, I was quite taken with the histories of our pioneers. I'm a fanatic for historical accuracy, so I gave myself nearly ten years to research the story thoroughly. It was my great good fortune that some of the 1929 air racers were still living as I researched, and they generously shared their stories, particularly Louise Thaden, Bobbi Trout, and Mary Haizlip. In fact, when I was flying for the Beech Aircraft factory, walking by Mrs. Beech's office revealed a photo of Louise Thaden, who happened to be an early, dear friend of Walter and Olive Ann Beech.

Since Mrs. Beech was quite sentimental about Walter's first airplane, the 1929 Travel Air, she also named a much later model the Travel Air. I flew all dozen Beech models in production in the sixties, including the more modern Travel Air, thirty plus years after the 1929 Travel Air flown by the racers.

Another fantastic resource for the book was Oklahoman Will Rogers, a great admirer of women pilots who, in fact, named their race the "Powder Puff Derby" and carried their luggage to Cleveland. The women pilots mourned along with crowds of admirers who ran into the streets crying upon the news of Will's death flying with Wiley Post in Alaska.

Sky Girls talks about the Ninety-Nines organization the racers developed under the grandstands at the finish of the 1929 Women's Air Derby. The Ninety-Nines purchased the 1929 Air Race–winning Travel Air in the late eighties, and it's displayed near their headquarters building in Oklahoma City. The organization remains to this day a thriving organization for female pilots, and it provides professional opportunities to women in aviation.

The Ninety-Nines treasures our ninety-nine original founders and their stories. We are now worldwide. Today women pilots fly everything, even into space exploration. The 1929 Women's Air Derby story documents our heritage.

Gene Nora Jessen, 2018

ACKNOWLEDGMENTS

Page Shamburger

Bob Jessen

The Ninety-Nines Museum of Women Pilots

Bonnie Robinson

Judy Hambley

Loretta Gragg

Tony Hulse

Pat Thaden Webb

Bill Thaden

Glenn Buffington

Willis M. Allen Jr. of Allen Airways Flying Museum

Bobbi Trout

Mary Haizlip

Pete Hill Jr.

Verna West

Julie Castiglia

Prof. Richard W. Kamm, St. Louis University

Kansas City Public Library

Ted Nott

Tershia d'Elgin

Star Photo Service of Boise

Jim Cross

Will Rogers Memorial and Birthplace

The Howard Hughes Corporation

Purdue University Library

Lisa Cotham

PHOTO CREDITS

BIBLIOGRAPHY

Adams, Jean and Margaret Kimball. "Heroines of the Sky." Books for Libraries Press, 1942.

Aeronautical Chamber of Commerce. *Aircraft Year Book*. New York, 1929–1930.

Bierman, Brad (publisher and president). Aviation Quarterly 1, no. 3 (1974).

Bird, Nancy. *My God, It's a Woman*. Air Facts Press, 1973.

Carter, Joseph H. *Never Met a Man I Didn't Like : The Life and Writings of Will Rogers*. Avon Books, 1991.

Douglas, Deborah G. *United States Women in Aviation* 1940–1985. Smithsonian Institution Press, 1978.

Faherty, William Barnaby. "Parks College, Legacy of an Aviation Pioneer," S. J. Harris and Friedrich, 1990.

"Flying—Aviation: Past, Present and Future," *Flying Magazine* 50th Anniversary Issue (September 1977).

Grun, Bernard. *The Timetables of History*. New York: Simon and Schuster, 1991.

Hart, Marion Rice. *I Fly As I Please*. The Vanguard Press, 1953.

Hoehling, Mary. "Thaddeus Lowe America's One-Man Air Corp." Julian Messner, Inc., 1958.

Josephy, Alvin M. Jr. *The American Heritage History of Flight.* American Heritage Publishing Company, 1962.

Kessler, Lauren. *The Happy Bottom Riding Club.* New York: Random House, 2000.

Ketchum, Richard M. *Will Rogers: His Life and Times.* American Heritage Publishing Company, 1973.

Lauwicke, Herve. "Heroines of the Sky." Frederick Muller Ltd., 1960.

Markham, Beryl. *West with the Night.* New York: Farrar, Straus and Giroux, Inc., 1994.

Moolman, Valerie. *Women Aloft.* Time-Life Books, Inc., 1981.

Noggle, Anne. *A Dance with Death.* Texas A&M University Press, 1994.

Oakes, Claudia M. *United States Women in Aviation 1930–1939.* Smithsonian Institution Press, 1991.

———. *United States Women in Aviation through World War I.* Smithsonian Institution Press, 1978.

Phillips, Edward H. *Travel Air: Wings over the Prairie.* Flying Books International, 1994.

Sacchi, Louise. *Ocean Flying.* McGraw-Hill Book Company, 1979.

Schultz, Barbara Hunter. *Pancho.* Little Buttes Publishing Company, 1996.

Shamburger, Page and Joe Christy. *Command the Horizon.* A. S. Barnes and Company, Inc., 1968.

Thaden, Louise. *High, Wide and Frightened.* Air Facts Inc., 1973.

"Time Capsule/1929," Time Inc., 1967.

Veca, Donna and Skip Mazzio. *Just Plane Crazy*. Osborne Publisher, 1987.

NEWSPAPERS CONSULTED

The Abilene Reporter-News

The Arizona Republican

The Cincinnati Enquirer

The Cleveland Plain Dealer

The Columbus Dispatch

The El Paso Herald-Post

The Fort Worth Star Telegram

The Kansas City Star

The Kansas City Times

The Los Angeles Times

The Midland Reporter-Telegram

The Pecos Enterprise and Gusher

The Phoenix Gazette

The St. Louis Post-Dispatch

The San Bernardino Daily Sun

The Tulsa Tribune

The Wichita Beacon

The Wichita Eagle

INDEX

READING GROUP GUIDE

1. *Sky Girls* is about only a short event in history, but its implications are immense. Which part of the story affected you the most and why?

2. Is there a pilot in *Sky Girls* who resonates more strongly with you than the others? If so, what part of her story or character stood out to you?

3. The women's flight across America carried the shadow of possible sabotage, and although Louise Thaden denied its existence, it was never proven to be completely above board. Do you believe someone tampered with the planes, and if so, what reasons would he or she have had to do so?

4. The Women's Air Derby followed closely behind the stock market crash and was at the beginning of America's Great Depression. The period surrounding the derby was filled with experimentation and glamour, but also fierce sexism. What

do you think it must have been like to live in a time filled with such success and triumph and also such darkness?

5. The women pilots were constantly reminded of their feminine place: Powder Puffs, Ladybirds, Sweethearts of the Air, etc. Where else do you see women being taken down a notch in their profession, in history or modern day?

6. At the end of the 1929 air race, the women gathered to form an organization to support each other for jobs flying airplanes. Women pilots today fly everywhere, including in the military, space, and airlines. Nevertheless, of all the pilots flying commercially, less than 6 percent are female. How would you suggest introducing more girls to career opportunities in aviation?

7. How were you inspired by the women of the 1929 Women's Air Derby, and how can you carry that onward to incite change in your own life?

A CONVERSATION
WITH THE AUTHOR

What inspired you to write the fascinating story of the first Women's Air Derby in *Sky Girls*?

I'm interested in history, and as an aspiring pilot I was curious about the women who went before. What kind of women would undertake the adventure of climbing into those fragile, undependable airplanes and race across the country?

It was surprising to see a story featuring Amelia Earhart where she's not the only pilot! The other women had just as many, if not more, accomplishments. Why do you think they aren't written down in the history books as frequently?

Amelia Earhart had a very wealthy husband, a publisher and public relations expert. He was able to provide her with the airplanes she wanted (and attendant costs), and he was married to a popular and famous woman—each benefitted. Then the mystery of her disappearance perpetuated interest in her. There are continuing Earhart "search" excursions—annually visiting the areas where she had been "sighted." Of the unending theories, my favorite is that she's living in New Jersey under an assumed name. Her sister thought she's in the trench, the deepest part of the ocean. I'd go with that one.

While researching the book, you became friends with some of the original racers; additionally, as a woman pilot yourself you must have felt a special connection to their passion. Did this relationship to the subject matter make it easier or harder to write the book?

Easier, of course. They were an inspiration!

When and why did you get involved in flying, and does it remain an important part of your life?

My older brother heard about the Civil Air Patrol and told me about it. They had a youth program so I joined in 1954. My family didn't have a car, so on Saturdays I'd catch a ride to PalWaukee Airport in Chicago and get an airplane ride with a senior member who gave me "stick time." One day he told me, "You're a natural." As a flight instructor, I know that you say things to encourage a student, but I believed that and he planted the seed that perhaps one day I could be a pilot. Some ten years later, while I was flying for the Beech factory and on a trip, I stopped in Chicago and gave that man an airplane ride. We both got a kick out of that. Over sixty years later, I still fly.

Who are the Ninety-Nines (never Ninety-Niners), and why was this club started?

At the end of the 1929 Women's Air Derby, the racers gathered to talk about forming an organization for women pilots to assist each other in obtaining flying jobs. A letter went out to all the licensed (more correctly, certificated) women pilots in the United States—slightly over one hundred. Ninety-nine women responded by the deadline. Cutesy names were considered, but the number of charter members was decided upon. The Ninety-Nines organization is now worldwide and members fly everything—including airlines, military and space vehicles. Their headquarters and museum are in Oklahoma City and among numerous projects their Amelia Earhart Scholarship program has helped thousands of women along in their aviation careers. I was international president 1988–1990.

There's an interesting connection between you and outer space. At one time, you might have been an astronaut! What is the story behind the Mercury 13?

Dr. Randy Lovelace had a large clinic in Albuquerque with a NASA contract to provide extensive physical examinations in the astronaut selection process. At the time of the original Mercury 7 astronauts, their vehicle into space was very small and Dr. Lovelace decided to test women pilots who were smaller. Without the knowledge of NASA, he selected and tested twenty-five women for the quite thorough weeklong testing at his clinic. Thirteen women passed the tests, and a Hollywood producer later named the group "The Mercury 13," which caught on. (An inappropriate name since we really had nothing to do with either NASA or the Mercury program.) Dr. Lovelace arranged for the group to go to Pensacola for the continuing selection process and two weeks of testing there. I was teaching flying at the University of Oklahoma then and had to quit my job to take two weeks off at the beginning of a new semester. NASA got wind of Dr. Lovelace's plan and shut it down. So, I became an unemployed astro-not. As a result, I searched for an aviation job and became employed by the Beech Aircraft factory with the dream job of all time, flying their entire line in all forty-eight contiguous states.

What do you do when you're not writing books or flying planes?

I met Bob Jessen while we both flew for Beech Aircraft and we married in 1964. We left Beech in 1967 to start a dealership in Boise, Idaho, where I operated the flight school and Bob sold airplanes. I also went into the airplane insurance business, and we raised two perfect children—I taught our daughter to fly (who has provided us with three grandchildren), and our son works for Disney. I've always been quite active in the Ninety-Nines, and I served on the Boise Airport Commission, have flown the Air Race Classic transcontinental air race ten times, and do speaking engagements, etc. We're now retired, and at eighty I continue to own an airplane and fly.

Sky Girls was originally published as *The Powderpuff Derby of 1929* and was released in 2002. How would you hope this new release will engage and inspire this new generation of readers picking up your book?

A nontraditional aviation career selection for young girls has moved over to the somewhat more common side of the ledger. And, yes, I've taught women over age sixty to fly. I believe an introduction to the pioneers will light the fire so women readers will think, *I can do that!*

ABOUT THE AUTHOR

Illinois native **Gene Nora Jessen** was introduced to flying as a cadet in the Chicago Civil Air Patrol. She was drawn to the University of Oklahoma's flight training program, became a flight instructor on the flight school faculty, and finished working her way through college teaching flying. Along with twenty-five female pilots, she was invited to participate in an astronaut research program about the time of the original Mercury astronauts in 1961. Along with twelve other candidates, she passed the physical exams and they became called the Mercury 13, although further testing was canceled.

Beech Aircraft Corp. (1962)

The stars were aligned in Jessen's favor, and she was hired by Beech Aircraft Corp in Wichita for what she considered the dream job of all time. She became one of the "Three Musketeers," flying one of three airplanes in formation for three months across forty-eight states introducing the new Beech model. Continuing on at the Beech factory, she obtained further ratings and flew the entire Beech line.

Boise Air Service (about 1982)

Gene Nora met her husband Bob at Beech, and they soon migrated to Boise, Idaho, to found a Beech dealership.

Jessen has remained active in aviation, serving on the Boise Airport Commission; being installed in the Idaho Aviation Hall of Fame; receiving the Mercury 13 NASA Award, Master Pilot Award, and an honorary PhD; and becoming an international president of the Ninety-Nines. She is the author of three books— on aviation, of course.

Gene Nora and Bob Jessen, who was a World War II B-29 pilot, are the parents of two children and are now retired. Gene Nora Jessen flew a dozen air races through the years and is still flying.